Picky

Picky

From fussy child to professional gourmet

Jimi Famurewa

HODDER &
STOUGHTON

First published in Great Britain in 2025 by Hodder & Stoughton Limited
An Hachette UK company

The authorised representative in the EEA is Hachette Ireland, 8 Castlecourt
Centre, Dublin 15, D15 XTP3, Ireland (email: info@hbgi.ie)

1

A CIP catalogue record for this title is available from the British Library

Hardback ISBN 9781399739542
ebook ISBN 9781399739559

Typeset in Electra LT by Hewer Text UK Ltd, Edinburgh
Printed and bound in Great Britain by Clays Ltd, Elcograf S.p.A.

Hodder & Stoughton policy is to use papers that are natural, renewable
and recyclable products and made from wood grown in sustainable
forests. The logging and manufacturing processes are expected to
conform to the environmental regulations of the country of origin.

Hodder & Stoughton Limited
Carmelite House
50 Victoria Embankment
London EC4Y 0DZ

www.hodder.co.uk

For Mum. And for my much-missed Uncle Gori – thank you for the love, the lessons, and the pancakes.

Contents

INTRODUCTION

A Proustian Mush

You may not have been in this specific south-east London cafe but there's a good chance you'll be familiar with its particular aesthetic. Sunlight gushes in through vast windows on to raw plaster walls and gatherings of drooping succulents and cacti. Noodly experimental jazz drifts from Sonos speakers at a volume that is deliberately just a little too high. There are septum-pierced staff wiggling foamed milk out of metal jugs and into matcha lattes, shell-shocked new mothers hemmed in by a wagon train of expensive prams and, most of the time, at least one fretful dachshund trembling beneath a table.

For all that my life as a restaurant critic is somewhat predicated on boundless variety, this is the sort of pacifying, predictable environment that I tend to gravitate towards when I am off-duty. There is stasis, routine and a screensaver-mode familiarity. I may mutter quiet curses at the parody of millennial entitlement that I'm implicitly partaking in – the braying, public Teams calls, the fussy little coffees – but there is comfort, drift and a pleasing lack of surprises. Or, at least, there has been. Today, for the first time ever, one of the staff has brought over my usual morning security blanket, a bowl of creamy porridge and seasonal fruit, with an unbilled side order: the ghost of my former self.

It is the fruit that is the issue. What is normally a handful of blackberries, a roughly quartered plum or, sometimes, thin sliced wisps of pear is, on this occasion, thick coins of chopped banana, fanned out in a neat, ornamental crescent. To be clear, I do actually eat and enjoy bananas. Whether that means smooshing them into pancakes, turning them into banana bread or just downing a perfectly ripe one with the fervour of a glowering peak-period Pete Sampras topping up electrolytes between sets.

No, it is more that bananas presented in a specific, outwardly innocuous way – cut into the embellishment for toast or cereal, or into those faintly brown, softened rounds that fill out low-grade fruit salads – snap me back to the irrational revulsion of my youth. Never mind that I have fashioned a career out of a willingness to essentially eat anything that is put in front of me. Never mind that, these days, I am exactly the sort of person to pile excitedly into curried snail flatbreads, springy lobes of honeycomb tripe, guffing, lavatorial lengths of andouillette sausage and, on one occasion, guacamole garnished with a crushed handful of dead grasshoppers.

To be faced by banana, in a form and context outside my usual precise specifications, is to feel this enthusiasm and openness temporarily slip away. All at once, I am my younger self. The kid who had a squirming dislike of basically all fresh fruit and vegetables. The kid who, in my mother's telling, would wail and gag theatrically if anyone had the temerity to peel a banana or messily devour an overripe mango in his immediate vicinity. If eating well is exploration, the excitement of questing out to unfamiliar territories, then I was a committed recluse, hermetically shut away from a universe of potential culinary hazards – grimly thick cucumber slices, cherry tomatoes, any fish not neatly entombed in bright-orange breadcrumbs – and safe in my refuge of fearful, nose-wrinkling avoidance.

This was the apparition from my past that wafted up from that steaming bowl of porridge: the truth about my inner nature that I could somewhat outgrow and carefully obscure but never truly escape. Everyone who has ever been a fussy eater will know that it manifests most as different forms of panic. The fear of forcing down something unpalatable; the fear of judgement if you decide not to. And the shadowed fear, also, of the hunger that you know could be the end result of such stubborn avoidance. Being picky can feel like an arm wrestle between selves. Between the version of you that wants to fit in and the version of you that unapologetically knows its own mind and palate. To be reacquainted with these feelings by some inoffensive slices of banana was to re-encounter the boy I was.

*   *   *

Why am I telling you this? Why, in an exciting and varied eating life that has taken in mind-expanding Californian tacos, transcendent rotisserie chicken from a grimy Tangier storefront, and hushed, three-Michelin-starred temples to high French gastronomy, am I choosing instead to begin this book by alighting on a decidedly ordinary cafe breakfast eaten on a nothing Monday? I think my reasoning, insomuch as it exists, is twofold. First is the firm belief that it is the small, seemingly inconsequential and oft-repeated meals that truly define us. There is a tendency, particularly in the scrupulously photogenic, like-chasing world of modern food media, to focus on food experiences that project rarity, specialness and importance. To edit entire lives of eating into a selective highlight reel of all those big, universally recognised signifiers of culinary importance: the long-haul pilgrimage to a supposed bucket-list spot, the starred, special occasion lunch, the whirling locus of hype and attention, ornamented by a snaking queue, where the entire point is to decide whether the reality is worth the fuss.

Don't get me wrong. These blockbusting, generally fancy instances of consumption have a justified status as the nucleus of the food landscape. And yet I am aware, as someone who writes about not just my own eating habits but those of the wider culture, that the undue prominence of these sorts of gastronomic experiences can lead to a skewed picture. Yes, meals that present as particularly meaningful or important are often just that. But what about the steadying handrail of a Pret breakfast baguette, all soft crunch and tumbling flecks of peppery egg mayonnaise, that you've eaten more times than you could accurately count? What about the puffy, brutish, jalapeño and pepperoni personal pizza that feels like the absolute quintessence of your grubby, snakebite-burping university existence? Or the musty hospital vending machine coffee that reminds you of heartbreak, but also of hope?

Succour. Sustenance. Joy. Life's meaningful memories, connections and lessons coalesce around these little, decidedly unglamorous instances of nibbling, crunching, slurping and inhaling. Food writing tends to valorise the buzzed-about and aesthetically immaculate, the complicatedly wrought and multiple Michelin-starred. It is wholly understandable, but it does rather subject you to the tyranny of momentousness, where the eating life you project doesn't really tally with the one that you live and value. To the feeling that, as a restaurant critic, you are living an inadvertent lie of omission. This book, then, is my attempt to set the record straight. To show how I really eat and have eaten – how we all truly eat – and untangle why it's so important to how we see the world and our place in it.

That issue of identity is the other reason the chopped banana incident – and its attendant reflux of childhood emotion – feels like the ideal portal to the world you're about to enter. To be snapped back into youth is to be confronted with all manner of instincts, habits and impulses that you have likely spent most of a lifetime trying to unlearn. Fussiness around food is something a person grows out of, an amusing, unexpected piece of personal trivia to break out while spooning mignonette on to a plump Carlingford oyster.

But the truthful edges smoothed by time are still truthful. Decades after the fact, I can look back at my intensely finicky childhood relationship with food and see the bigger picture. Food is identity and agency; likes and dislikes are how we try to impose our will on an often confusing, adult-initiated world. What we think of as childhood fussiness around food is, at root, often just a strong set of gastronomic opinions without the means to properly articulate them. More generally, our eating proclivities betray the historical and social context that we have grown up in. That which we unanimously regard as delicious – the fried starches, piquant, ketchuppy sauces and sugared puddings that can generally counteract fussiness – is usually the product of human ingenuity, circumstance, corporate will or some combination of all three. That widening of the frame, the 'why' of tastes that even a picky child like me found irresistible, is part of the stories you are about to read.

There is more to it. To spurn a dish is to semaphore a message. And so, if we follow this line of thinking, what was it that the younger me was trying to communicate about his unglimpsed essence, through those strong aversions at the dinner table? What can we divine about the persona and perspective I was trying to cultivate for myself from the squeamish rejection of all things perishable, pungent and messy, the unhealthy obsession with cartoonishly proportioned American convenience foods, the youthful conviction that 'curry wasn't for me' despite never having actually gone to the trouble of trying it? Well, the truth is, my eating identity, like my actual identity, is knottily complex. There is Nigerianness. There is Britishness. There is the reverberative impact of parental abandonment, bursting suitcases of cultural baggage, and the kind of class incongruence that tends to go hand in hand with an immigrant background.

All of this and more plays out in the disputed territory of my palate, an ever-shifting mass of likes and dislikes that offer a broader insight into the varied cultural forces that have shaped and continue to shape me. To the vexed tussle between how I define myself and how the world seeks to define me as a black man. This is the nub of it. In exploring my journey from maddening fusspot to professional taster – and how that youthful pickiness is inextricably linked to the exacting, analytical nature that I've been able to turn into a career – I will also unravel how food relates to identity. Not just for me, but for all of us. Because there is normally more to our culinary passions than meets the eye; more that we can learn from a resurfaced banana phobia and a reacquaintance with our former selves. Sometimes, when you are chased by a ghost from the past, the best thing you can do is allow yourself to be caught.

I should make a point, as we set the table, about those ghosts, memories and ownership. These stories are based on my own recollections and perspective. As attempts to corroborate details have proven, other people who were there either remember things starkly differently or don't remember them at all. Throw in the conspiracy of silence that is traditionally part of Nigerian family histories, a code of secrecy that would shame most organised crime syndicates, and you can hopefully see why I have chosen to tread carefully. Where others are involved – and my disclosure naturally strays towards revelations that are not mine to make – I have tried to be circumspect. Names have frequently been changed to add what is hopefully a freeing veil of anonymity, but this is very much the truth as I saw, tasted and felt it.

That, again, is part of why I have begun things at this particular point. The past is to be questioned but, also, very much listened to. And so, amid the contented burble of that cafe, I pushed the chopped banana to one side. Not quite ready to fully let go of the picky eater I used to be. But eager to understand how I had got from there to here.

1

LAGOS I

Lagos, London and
Doomed Cow Stew

Working as a food writer can have a warping effect on childhood memories. This is a lesson that I have learned over and over again, given that, at this point, I have been involved in this broad, occasionally perplexing field for almost a decade. What once were the soft-edged, wholly random recollections of early consciousness inevitably become a resource to be carefully mined for content. Formative food experiences exert a gravitational pull; the past becomes an editable shared document. And before you know it, you are so adept at embroidering your backstory for the purposes of written work, so accustomed to seeing a varied life solely through the prism of food, that it can become difficult to distinguish between what is real and what is a retconned piece of narrative convenience affirmed by repetition.

Through either a giant fluke or something like fate, I can say with wholehearted conviction that the very first things I can remember relate to both food and Nigeria. The genesis of my appetite and my identity is rooted in Africa's most populous city. It is a place where I was not born; somewhere I have visited barely a handful of times in the last three decades. Nonetheless, in the beginning there was only the intermittent darkness of another power cut. In the beginning, there was only Lagos.

The memories are hazy, as nascent ones inevitably are, but there is something about their essence that has always exerted a mysterious magnetism. The first – memorialised, after the fact, in a primary-school-era homework project of sellotaped baby photographs and scrawled Berol pen recollections – is of a crab-apple tree in the yard of Ebun Street: the sprawled, labyrinthine complex that was my maternal grandfather's custom-built bequeathal, his wife, my grandmother's eternal home, and is the closest thing we have on that side of the family to an ancestral seat. Though I would have been four at the oldest when this memory was formed, I have such a clear and piercing picture of it, and the feeling it engendered. Splayed branches stretching out beneath an overcast, muggy sky; fragrant, overripe fruit tumbled down on to higgledy-piggledy paving slabs. If that homework project is to be believed, these shrunken little things were something that 'we would grab and eat as long as . . . Grandma didn't catch us'. And, well, not to quibble with my nine-year-old self, but this was either a bit of artistic licence from a budding memoirist or an aberrant period of my childhood when I didn't regard the eating of fresh fruit as a disgusting act of barbarism.

Anyway, I digress. The other memory is of my aunt and uncle's house (a place that my homework project notes, with braggy, prepubescent tactlessness, was 'much bigger and nicer than my grandma's'). This time, the searing image is of the blessedly cool darkness of a long corridor, the low, murmuring buzz of a chest freezer that seemed to dwarf me, and an almost violent, unshakeable desire to get inside it and grab one of the slender, multicoloured ice pops that I knew were encased inside. It is funny, now I am a harassed parent, to zoom out and imagine the sight of a probable toddler, pawing at a freezer and yelping indecipherably like a hungry labradoodle for something that would give them a blue tongue, a terrible sugar crash and faintly hellish nappies.

Zoom out in a more figurative sense and it's arguable, I suppose, that these two stories form the opposing poles of my eating identity: differing forms of forbidden fruit and proxies for the respective devil and angel I have long had perched on each shoulder when it comes to both cuisine and culture. On the one side, there is the imperfection, tradition and faintly virtuous natural bounty of my grand-mother's crab-apples. On the other, there is the mass-produced, synthetic hit of those luridly bright ice pops.

It is a driving, personally significant contrast. These memories illustrate the clamped psychic and emotional grip that Lagos – and, more broadly, Nigeria – has on my being and my appetite. It is a place of both nagging familiarity and bewildering disquiet. To be back in Nigeria is to feel like I am wandering the shadowed recesses of my mind. Never quite sure what I will find around each corner or, for that matter, what effect it will have on me.

Legend has it the armed robbers were opportunists. Having threatened household staff at my aunt's house, they realised it was part of a conjoined duplex with my own family's home, and so effectively sought to get a larcenous BOGOF deal. It was a Sunday morning in 1985. My mum had gone ahead to church and left other relatives and de facto nannies to get her children – me and my two primary-school-aged older brothers – ready before that morning's service. Stubby machine guns were brandished; threats were made to those who didn't 'face down'; goods, including drawers of gold jewellery that my mum had recently bought for her sister's wedding, were hurriedly stuffed into bags. And then, again as legend would have it, I emerged from the bathroom – a stark naked two-year-old with a tufted widow's peak of hair – brandishing a toy gun, thinking it was all a game and ready to return fire before, mercifully, someone picked me up and forced me into the same supplicant pose all the other people in the household had adopted. The robbers fled and James, the family's driver, ran all the way

to the church, a distance of about three miles, to breathlessly let my mum know what had happened.

Now, the cynic in me wants to say that this tale – a well-
thumbed chapter in the unabridged annals of Famurewa
family history – is almost certainly a piece of heavily apocry-
phal comic exaggeration. Truthfully, though, the point is
not whether you buy me as a kind of tiny, rusk-eating John
McClane. It is more to illustrate that this was very much the
kind of thing that would happen in cities like Lagos in the
1980s.

Violent robberies. Carjackings. Mown-down bodies left
in the street. These were the stories that were offhandedly
relayed to me about the brutal reality of the country during
this period – as the oil boom prosperity of the 1970s
contracted into an atmosphere of political unrest, punitive
taxation and everyday disorder that would ultimately
precipitate the corruption, governmental ineptitude and
subsequent brain drain of the 1980s and '90s. 'That was
Nigeria,' said my mum, resignedly, when I asked her to
verify the details of the armed robbery. My brother, Folarin,
similarly brushed it off when he recalled that he had
watched a fatal shoot-out from our balcony a week before
the armed robbery. This could be the national condition.
Bleak daily realities metabolised through world-weary
acceptance and protective black humour.

Naturally, social realities like this – alongside my middle
brother's urgent need for a childhood medical procedure,

the tractor-beam lure of the British education system, and my mum's traumatising loss of the infant twins she was pregnant with before me – would ultimately prompt my family to make a long-term move to the UK. Nigeria was home. Yet, because of the inescapable facts of life there – the crime, the chaos, the constant energy outages that characterised NEPA (officially the National Electric Power Authority but, colloquially, the far more accurate Never Expect Power Always) as a recalcitrant deity – the negative mood music about it could be deafening. Nigeria was also something that we were privileged to have been able to escape, a place both terminally damned and hopelessly romanticised.

Growing up, being 'sent back to Nigeria' was the decisive threat used to bring misbehaving children to heel; the fate that had befallen all those unsuspecting, London-raised Sholas and Kunles who thought they were going for a summer holiday in Lagos only to find, after a few days, that their passports had mysteriously disappeared and enrolment at some nightmarishly strict rural boarding school beckoned. At the same time, the essence of Nigeria – its culture and humour, its generosity and religious values, its mix of frank honesty and adaptive wiliness – was something that elders would constantly pine for amid the disorienting chill and impertinent racist hostility of Britain. We only badmouthed Nigeria because we saw its limitless potential and specialness. It was like the beloved, dysfunctional uncle that only those in the family were allowed to constantly disparage. A place that, as I was weaned on all this folklore in suburban south-east London, I came to view as both a paradise and a penal colony.

Understandably, this kind of mixed messaging gave me an interesting relationship with Nigerianness and Nigerian culture. In fact, that is probably putting it too coyly. The negativity and fear around Nigeria – the sense that it was a place of violent, mistrustful roughness and basic disadvantage, no matter how wealthy you were – got its hooks into me. British life and Britishness was something I felt I needed to cling to tightly, lest I end up back in this faintly bruising place that my elders would occasionally talk about as if it was a particularly brutal combat theatre that they had escaped.

What's more, beyond the sociopolitical and economic situation, the environment of Nigeria seemed to have a strange physiological effect on me. From the moment the family returned to Lagos, around six months after my birth in London, it became apparent that the change in geography was eliciting strange, physical symptoms. I would cough, splutter and wheeze; my lips would dry out and darken; proximity to stockfish – the dried-out loofahs of a preserved cod that form the pungent base of countless Nigerian soups and stews – would make my eyes stream and itch. On trips back to London or other parts of Europe, these issues would mysteriously dissipate, only to return mere hours after we had touched back down at the airport.

'He's allergic to Nigeria,' my brothers would say, with gleeful certainty, every time the cycle repeated itself. The real culprit was, in all likelihood, childhood allergies and symptoms from the nascent asthma that hadn't yet been formally diagnosed. Yet these things stick; these lessons are absorbed. And so I grew up not just wary of the atmosphere of Nigeria and its associative tendencies, but convinced, partly because I had been told as much, that something in my constitution was fundamentally incompatible with life there.

So how did this feeling relate specifically to food? Taste, after all, is a reliable access point to cultural identity, the way the world sees us, defines us and teases us. Not for nothing is *ajebota* – or 'butter eaters', in a hybrid form of Yoruba and pidgin English – the teasing name given to high-born Nigerians or diasporans who have shamefully adopted the posh cosmopolitan ways of places like Britain in the kitchen and beyond.

The standard assumption, in the case of how I experienced Nigerian culture through appetite, would be that any apprehensiveness I felt would have attached itself to the cuisine. That's how it normally goes for second-generation children, steeped in one heritage but brought up in the alluring glow of another. It is not uncommon for diaspora kids to take a palate-first approach to assimilation, to absorb small-minded attitudes about the supposedly 'smelly' foreign dishes that are their birthright or to somehow project a paradoxical romance and exoticism on to things like fish fingers, Potato Smiles and turkey dinosaurs.

Blessedly, that wasn't me. Or at least not completely. Whatever my love of the lurid processed foods that I saw being expertly hawked on television, and that love really was mighty, it never completely subsumed my affection for lots of the Nigerian culinary repertoire that I was mostly raised on. I cannot remember a time when I didn't have a border-line obsessive fondness for salt-flecked oven chips, baked beans with an unnecessary additional Zorro stripe of ketchup, Herta frankfurters nuked in the microwave until they popped and split; in my family's telling, the only way to buy my compliance as a gurgling toddler was with the dangled offer of a malted milk biscuit.

Even so, my proclivity for these heavily processed western foods, and the social acceptance they represented, always ran parallel to an unshakeable love of certain Yoruba dishes. Would shame, self-stigmatising or cultural fearfulness ever stop me from bowing contentedly before an oil-glistened mound of fried rice and a piquant dollop of brick-red beef stew? Would it cause me to turn my nose up at a ragged blob of *ewa riro*, or stewed honey beans, thrumming with spice and nuzzled beside burnished coins of sweet fried plantain? Or inhibit my enjoyment of the thick planks of yam, served with soft scrambled egg and a slurried, better-than-it-sounds, spicy corned-beef sauce, that were our traditional post-church lunch and, therefore, the precise taste of hard-won freedom?

Of course it wouldn't. Even from a very early age, nothing could quell any private misgivings I may have had about Nigeria like the indulgent, unusual joy of some of its most famous dishes. I remember once hearing that our culinary tastes are first formed in the womb; that we share in the antenatal smorgasbord of whatever our mothers happen to be eating. This chimes with the cellular-level affection I have for many Nigerian dishes – their penetrative layers of spice, their unexpected jolts of sweetness, their hits of pacifying starch. It is an unbroken link and connection that feels almost umbilical.

But it is also nothing if not highly selective. Throughout most of my youth, my taste in traditional flavours tended towards the approachable and decidedly Fisher Price. If it was fried, doused in a faintly ketchuppy tomato sauce or obligingly bland (in Nigerian terms, I would stress), then I was interested. Similarly, if it was one of the many, many West African dishes that fell outside those parameters, I was vehemently opposed to it. *Amala*, the vigorously whipped, fermented yam flour 'swallow' (from a broad category of doughs which operate almost as a cross between a giant, soft dumpling and an edible utensil) that came together as an intense, taupe-coloured heap of mashed starch. *Moin-moin*, the banana leaf parcels of tamale-ish, steamed bean cake that would always prompt a sharp-elbowed scrum at family parties. Stewed okra, the notorious 'draw' soup – that name describes the signature viscosity – with a stretchy, mucilaginous consistency that plants it somewhere between tapioca pudding and ectoplasm.

To even describe these dishes in implicitly negative terms feels almost dangerous and self-hating; the kind of shameful, *ajebota* behaviour that my ancestors would greet with a dismayed shake of the head at how far the bloodline had fallen. But it cannot be denied. As a child, so much of the broad span of Nigeria's wider culinary canon triggered my pickiness. I was, in essence, someone who only wanted to engage with the crowd-pleasing hits; an avowed 'Now That's What I Call Approachable West African Cuisine' fan with no desire to crate-dig in the more challenging depths of the gastronomic library.

This is not especially unusual – practically every global cuisine can be divided into the rudimentary, nursery slope dishes beloved by children, and the hardcore, black run preparations (chitlins, durian, jellied eels) that elude some, but not all, juvenile palates. Yet it is revealing, I think, that, beyond a kind of undeniable, crossover deliciousness, the Nigerian dishes I gravitated towards were the ones that weren't inextricably linked to my elders. To be a second-generation Nigerian kid is to be constantly told all the ways you are drifting away from the source code of your ancestry. *Ah-ah do you not understand Yoruba? Ah-ah, do you not know how to properly greet your uncle? Ah-ah, have you forgotten that this is not our country?*

Much of this is delivered with a needling fondness. Still, it can't help but make aspects of Nigerian culture – food, customs, communicative cues – feel like the impenetrable possessions of your elders. To never seem to quite get it right is to slowly lose the desire to try. For me, beyond the simple, youthful apprehension that can shape notions of disgust, this meant that, for better or worse, I came to strongly associate certain dishes with first-generation, Lagos-born family members.

Pounded yam was a kettle-bellied uncle on the sofa, nudging me with a bare foot when it was time to grab him another bottle of stout. *Egusi* soup, clogged with indeterminate animal parts, was my grandmother noisily sucking the marrow from crunched chicken bones. Kola nuts, which I knew to be as bitter as paracetamol, were my mum nursing a late-night Harveys Bristol Cream after a day on her feet. As an eight-year-old, I'd have been just as likely to develop a taste for these dishes as I would to take a sudden interest in watching the news or arguing loudly about Nigerian politics. Again, pickiness here was a way to try to define myself in opposition to my cultural surroundings. Albeit one that split the culinary world – beyond things like jollof rice, which got a special pass – into a naive binary where everything Nigerian was fusty, old-fashioned and challenging, while everything western was glamorous, forward-thinking and impossibly desirable.

Of course, a lot of this was related to a broader issue. Namely, being overly reliant on relatives and parents as an access point to heritage; to feeling, as I always feel in Lagos, that I'm never able to explore or make my own mistakes without a more knowledgeable chaperone.

Related to this, also, was a youthful aversion to the 'how' as well as the 'what' of Nigerian dining as the older generation saw it. As in a lot of non-white communities, one of the central tenets of Nigerian culture is respect and servile deference to your elders. You bow and prostrate yourself before them when they enter the room. You give up your seat if they need it and, regardless of any actual shared DNA, you always append their name with an honorific 'uncle' or 'aunty'. And when it comes to food and drink, you're signed up for a sort of non-negotiable, unpaid butlering apprenticeship as soon as you're old enough to heft a tray or fetch a drink from the fridge. To be a Nigerian diaspora kid in a big, boisterous family is, yes, to be immensely loved and cherished. It is also, undeniably, to be the useful possession of a diffuse family unit, forever expected to make bumper rounds of tea, fix up buffet plates, and convey toothpicks to finger-snapping uncles.

Obviously, once you have ascended in age to the point that you can benefit from this system, once obedient young nephews and cousins start appearing at your shoulder with a steaming plate of food and a perspiring, ice-cold can of Sprite, your perception of the racket shifts. But I have such clear memories of the knackering misery of waiting hand and foot on some visiting relative; of all the comically huge buckets of tea (Nigerian matriarchs favoured XL, Sports Direct-style mugs long before they became a popularised thing) that I had to make for my grandma when she made a months-long visit to stay with us in London during the mid-90s.

Separately, my mother tells a story about a Nigerian friend who came to stay with certain service expectations. Firmly adhered to the sofa for the duration of her visit, she would send my siblings and me scurrying whenever she wanted a drink, a snack, the TV remote that was on the other side of the room. Bemused and frustrated, and with no access to an official HR department, I complained to my mum with words to the effect of 'does she think this is a hotel?' It was an impudent move by me. One that could have massively backfired. However, to my mum's immense credit – particularly given she was opening herself up to all sorts of pointed accusations about what sort of selfishly un-Nigerian *ajebota* children she was raising – she backed me and explained that there were different social rules and customs in Britain and that they were to be respected. 'When you're here,' she said, to her no doubt scandalised friend, 'it's DIY.'

This last memory perhaps says it all about the confusion of what it was to live and eat in the overlap between two cultures. Nigerian dining's perceived incursion on my liberty (and the severity of this is up for debate) was another thing that cast it in a negative light. Add in those inadvertent scare stories related to armed robberies and unrest, the

rhetoric of luck and privilege that characterised our presence in London, and a desire to be somewhat independent
from the appetite and attitude of my elders, and I think there
is a sense of how my negative fearfulness towards all things
Nigerian took hold. Or, perhaps, even got out of hand.

In addition to this, there was the specific way that I
absorbed my family's cultural pride. The conversational
drumbeat to my early years, for all the fatalism about our
motherland's prospects, was a kind of chest-beating Nigerian
exceptionalism. In England, we were constantly told by
Mum that we were Africans and Nigerians before we were
anything else. That we were held to a different standard and
that the privilege and freighted potential of life in London
came with a matching weight of responsibility. The distinct,
all caps vigour of our identity – the language, the food, the
arcane traditions – seemed so obvious and overbearing that
I would never be able to plausibly deny it.

This, in turn, bred a form of cultural complacency. Why
make any effort to strengthen my own bonds to the Nigerian
way of life, why take any independent interest, when all the
hectoring grown-ups around me were doing so much of the
work? Obviously, I'm inclined to cut the younger me some
slack (hard to see the value and significance in Yoruba
history when your animating passions are Saturday morning
television, Ghostbusters action figures and chain-eating
Breakaway bars). Yet, these days, I do regard my youthful
obliviousness to the colonial and political circumstances

that had brought my family to the UK as a telling bit of incu-
rious entitlement.

From early on, certain I was so steeped in the culture that
it wouldn't matter, I let my connection to it drift. I didn't
experiment with any Nigerian dishes beyond the half dozen
or so I loved. I loosened my grasp on understanding Yoruba
and wore the fact that I didn't speak it as a weird badge of
assimilatory honour. When my brothers and I were formally
awarded British citizenship and corresponding passports in
the late 1990s – a significant, years-in-the-making act of life-
altering immigrant deliverance that I can barely do justice
to here – I let my green-jacketed Nigerian passport expire
without even considering a renewal. The delicate balance
of identity, the code-switching between British and African
that had been modelled for me from an early age, had decisively tipped one way.

All of which is to say that, during my two decades of
committed Lagos-avoidance, whenever the question of
returning to Nigeria was posed by a relative or even just a
kindly, inquisitive cab driver with some shared heritage, the
answer seemed obvious. I would make excuses. I would
invoke flight costs, complicated visa acquisition procedures
and repentantly say that, yes, I knew I needed to go back
'home'. But the truth is that I never thought I really would.
That, simply, beyond a creeping, abstract sense of duty, I
really didn't want to. All those stories of Lagosian unrest and
dysfunction, punishment returns for misbehaving children,

Nigeria's strict, unbending culture, and the immense fortune of being in Britain had taken hold and inculcated not just a fear of the place, but a feeling that going there for even a short trip would somehow compromise my Britishness. That my claim on the cosseted life I loved in London was so conditional and tenuous that even the briefest interaction with my motherland could jeopardise it. Sure, our culture had its delicious benefits. But the western world, with its functioning infrastructure, soft-spoken civility and bound-less opportunity, was the horse my elders were implicitly urging me to back, wasn't it?

This was the unverbalised, shameful feeling that kept me away from Nigeria for the bulk of my adult life. It was also, ultimately, what shaped the ensuing outsider status that coloured my trip back there in 2019.

On the very few occasions that I actually did it, travelling around Lagos always seemed to involve one kinetic double take after another. Roadside sellers approach the car window hawking bagged plantain chips, bottled drinks and dart-boards. Four passengers are wedged like Tetris bricks on to one grumbling motorbike taxi. A man wearing what appears to be a 1998–9 season Middlesbrough away kit unzips and relieves himself beside the road. The sound is the constant, crazed hammering of vehicle horns; the vibe is of an encounter that is eternally pitched at some unknowable midpoint between a joke, a business transaction and a violent confrontation. It is a place with a constant back-ground hum of weirdness. But it is a weirdness that can feel strangely recognisable and soothing. And few moments encapsulate this pervading sense quite as deftly as what I have come to think of as The Day of the Doomed Cow.

It was the early summer of 2019, that febrile, unencum-bered twelve months when we were all obliviously perched on the edge of an epidemiological volcano and, perhaps, made long-haul trips that would be eternally suffused with retroactive significance. My uncle was turning seventy. A fact that meant, in the typically extravagant traditions of the Yoruba people – the supremely self-possessed Nigerian ethnic group that my family belongs to – there would be a week-long jamboree of parties and events. Having only been back to Nigeria once in the past thirty years (and for a funeral, at that), the chance for a celebratory homecoming was seized, flights were booked, and, as May bled into June, I was dumped once again into the megacity's volatile social cocktail of hustling bodies, cacophonous noise and close, pit-dampening heat.

One of the realities of visiting Lagos as a London-raised westerner, soft of both hand and spirit, is that it can be a strangely infantilising experience. Customs related to hospi-tality and a general nervousness around the unforgiving, tooth-and-claw nature of Nigeria's urban environments conspire to rob the visiting diaspora kid of all control, auton-omy and agency. If you know basically no one else in the city – and I absolutely did not – then you are suddenly reliant on local family members and their proxies for travel, shelter, safety and any semblance of an itinerary. I may have boarded the plane at Heathrow as a thirty-something restaurant critic, new-minted broadcaster and fairly streetwise, proudly self-sufficient father of two, but I touched down at Murtala Muhammed International Airport and found that, once again, I had been turned back into a watchful child – forever being ferried by family drivers to some engagement or errand, fussed over by cheek-tweaking old aunties and uncles, but not often burdened with the details of where the hell I was going or why. My view of the city, over the first day and a half of the trip, generally came from the air-conditioned back seat of an SUV piloted by one of my uncle's drivers; a blur of deliveries, drop-offs and transactions conducted in coarse, machine-gunned Yoruba that I only caught every third word of. Yes, an extremely privileged way to negotiate Lagos's hectic swarm. But also: an intensely impotent and perpetually bewildered one too.

Which, I think, just about sets the scene for what transpired, on the morning after my evening flight into the city, when we went to visit the surviving remnants of my wider family at Ebun Street. This, remember, was my late grandma's old house; site of that crab-apple tree, those fuzzy first memories and, now, home to various generations of aunties, uncles, cousins and all manner of wafting spectres of the past. The day before my uncle's main parties (the plural is both correct and instructively Yoruba), I made my way there, alongside Folarin, my eldest brother, to meet our mother – who had flown in a few days earlier – and an unknown quantity of other relatives. We had already stopped, in the midst of a bucketing tropical downpour, at a rudimentary garage to attend to some issue relating to the car; there had been another unplanned and unexplained detour to pick up decorations from a bar and hotel run by a cousin. I had already glazed over somewhat by the time we got to Ebun Street. We stepped from the chill of the vehicle into the rainy swelter of the morning, and pushed beyond heavy gates to find what I can only describe as a particularly chaotic pop-up abattoir. In the private yard that encircles the two floors of the house, there lay, in a glistening span of blood, viscera and partially hosed concrete, the fallen, headless body of a recently slaughtered cow; three unknown men in rain-soaked T-shirts and shorts worked around its carcass with the brutal efficiency of mob hitmen covering their tracks. Limbs were hacked and pulled away. Dripping buckets were hefted. There was the hydraulic hiss, whirr and rumble of some piece of machinery (a kind of reverse cattle vacuum, I later learned, that is used to puff up the body in order to ease the shaving off of hide). And there, slow-blinking and with its soulful gaze facing away from the bovine horror movie playing out over its shoulder, was another, very much alive cow, awaiting its fate.

Either my brother or our driver that day – a smiling-eyed, roguish character called William – must have acknowledged what we were witnessing. Someone surely made reference to the spectacle of a horrifically bloody meat-processing facility being established in the front garden of a family home, or even just explained to me that this was the culturally mean-ingful preparation of a traditional feasting gift bequeathed to my uncle ahead of his landmark birthday. But, truly, all I remember is Folarin snapping a couple of photos, a pervad-ing atmosphere of shrugging disinterest as the two of them made the one-storey climb up to the front door, and the word-less exchange I had with the terminally imperilled beast. Was it communicating fear? Resignation? The despairing shriek of some unknown, ruminant-specific swear word? All I knew was that another indelible Lagos food memory had sprung from the same patch of earth as that crab-apple tree. The doomed cow looked at me. I looked back. And with a disbe-lieving shudder, I made my way upstairs and into the house.

Inside, there was a familiar environment and a familiar sense of languid mid-morning drift. The Ebun Street house (eternally just 'Ebun' to those in our family) is a squat build-ing, huddled up shoulder to shoulder against similar corru-gated-roofed complexes and barbed-wire-fringed yards on a potholed road in a historic area of central Lagos called Surulere. This was the place where my maternal grand-mother – a statuesque, quietly formidable woman, who was

Henrietta Oyeyinka on her official documentation and Grandmama (emphasis on the very last syllable) to everyone else – lived until the grand old age of ninety-two.

In the intervening decade or so since her death, it had become accommodation and life raft to a rotating, multi-generational cast of blood relations and kindly women whose role seemed to sit in some undefined hinterland between family friend and employee. Visiting US-based uncles installed themselves there for the months they would be tending to mysterious business ventures; young, tween-age second cousins were billeted there with their parents as part of experimental, temporary forays into the Nigerian school system. Its spartanly decorated first-floor living area and puzzle-box of concealed anterooms may as well have had a revolving door. Though only half a dozen of our wider clan ever lived there at any one time, it always felt, by dint of either the familiar faces or the layered memories and plentiful ghosts, like our spiritual home.

And, today, mine and my brother's arrival had added a charge of excitement to Ebun's atmosphere. As we entered the cool darkness and faint chintz of that main living area, there were whoops of excitement, bodies emerging from bedrooms, and a ragged line-up of hug-seeking relatives, dimly recalled family acquaintances and outright strangers had started to form. A sturdy stand-up fan whirred and twirled in the corner, pushing air past the wall's inactive AC units. My mother, who had evidently slipped into the more

overtly Nigerian, Lagos-appropriate version of herself –
which is to say, she was the usual five-foot sprinkler system
of constant jokes, theories, anxieties and questions, with all
the dials cranked up to the highest possible setting – gripped
us both in an embrace and took charge of the introductions
and reintroductions.

You know those official engagements when a visiting
dignitary, politician or royal makes their way down a line of,
I don't know, eager leisure-centre employees, and they
always have an on-staff advisor muttering names and job
descriptions in their ear as they grip, grin and make small
talk? Well, imagine that, but with lots of people who met
you when you were a baby and are about to either say you
look like another relative or cheerily mention that you've
put on weight.

'This is Aunty Funmi, you remember?' Mum would say,
with an expectant tone, as my head swam with images of
disassembled cow carcasses. 'You know,' she would add,
persisting. 'Who came to see us and looked after you? When
we went to Brent Cross with Aunty Toyin Leicester?' This
was how it went for the next few minutes. Hugs, enquiries
about my children and sing-song renditions of my name
while I smiled and reciprocated, nodding and pantomiming
a eureka moment of belated recognition even when there
was no real recognition there. There appeared to be a young
hearing-impaired girl who, rather than being a family
member, was there because she was giving one of my uncles

quite a rigorous pedicure, right there on the living room's patterned rug. (Did I mention that Lagos is reliably weird?) Tennis highlights blared from the big, generator-powered TV. My cousin Femi was sent out, with great bustling urgency, to buy bottles of Nigerian Fanta: the lusciously tangeriney and only slightly gaseous version of the familiar soft drink that, like tea in Britain, often acts as a stand-in for declarations of love, sympathy and the rolling out of the red carpet for a guest.

Soon, things settled into the sort of tranquillised rhythm that I always forget is a big part of how my elders experience Lagos. Fanta flowed alongside deep-roasted groundnuts in repurposed glass bottles. Waves of pronouncedly Yoruba conversation and interaction – brutal teasing between my mother and her siblings, collective attempts to correctly remember some past story or incident, chatter about the following day's big party, flagrant cussing out of any number of people who weren't there – waxed and waned at an unhurried pace. At my uncle's urging, and after a prolonged round of haggling over price, my gnarled Hobbit feet were invited to be next in line for the services of the young girl that I still hadn't actually been introduced to.

Conspicuous by its absence among all this, and most rele-vant to me, was the lack of any meaningful reference to the ad-hoc slaughterhouse that had been established down-stairs. 'Meat,' my mum had said, simply, when I asked about the scene playing out underneath us and why it was being undertaken there. 'For tomorrow.' No one else seemed especially interested in the specifics of the butchering, and I think there was probably a degree of bemusement about why I was so curious. Even so, I couldn't let it go. Not just because it was such a comically violent reminder of the grisly reality of how food makes its way on to plates, and of the decidedly hands-on, unflinching culinary traditions that are a part of my DNA. But also because it seemed to speak to the particular crossroads I was at when it came to dining habits, culture, privilege, code-switching and more. Because, really, the doomed cow represented so many of the tangled contradictions of my food identity.

I had arrived in Lagos nine months into my gilded new life as a restaurant critic. There had already been a first, sweaty-palmed appearance on *MasterChef*, meals everywhere from the River Cafe to a mountain-set St Moritz ballroom with a live harpist, and righteous, high-handed takedowns of restaurants that had committed grievous crimes against under-seasoning. It felt like a different universe to what I had seen in the yard at Ebun. And yet, having grown accustomed to the scrutinising and analytical relationship I had with food, the closeness I felt to the process whether I was evaluating a dish or trying to recreate it in the kitchen at home, it felt more than a little strange to arrive in Nigeria and to be kept at arm's length from almost all aspects of food apart from the eating bit. There was never any suggestion of me popping downstairs to carry a steaming bucket of cow offal. Never a question that I would trifle myself with what was happening or why. This was the lot of the soft, western-coded outsider; another aspect of the reality of Lagos life that my elders had, perhaps correctly, deemed me too squeamish or vulnerable for.

This was not to disregard my own part in constructing this narrative. My reaction to the Doomed Cow; the daily feeling of bewilderment in Lagos; the fact that I only seemed able to experience the city and the culture from my climate-controlled, protective bubble. All of it could be traced back to the fact that I had consciously left Nigerianness behind, readily drinking the propagandist Kool-Aid of an era in which African culture was both demeaned and misunderstood. An unvisited home, after all, probably ceases to be one.

Later on, as promised, the young girl who had been snipping and filing my uncle's toenails – who I now saw was merely wearing a hands-free earpiece for her phone rather than a hearing aid – got to work on mine. While the work of butchering was happening on the ground floor, I was on the first floor literally having a pedicure. If you had suggested it in a Hollywood script meeting, you'd have been laughed out of the room for crimes against clanging dramaturgical symbolism.

This, ultimately, was the thing that the encounter with the doomed cow had shown me. Nigerian traditions related to food and culture were something I couldn't ever escape but, equally, I always felt I could never quite access them on my own terms. But if I felt fated to always be an outsider in what was, technically speaking, my ancestral homeland, then I couldn't really pass the buck. If anyone was to blame for a conflicted relationship with Nigeria then, well, it was probably me.

Narrative expedience would demand that the Doomed Cow and I had a poignant reunion. If this were neat fiction rather than messy, uncooperative fact, following its journey from livestock to sustenance, then there would have been a moment at my uncle's birthday party when I was presented with a piece of meat that I knew came from that particular condemned beast. There may even have been a significant moment of hesitation as I jabbed my fork in; a muttered, tearful apology to no one in particular as I chewed down on the piece of steak with which I had experienced a moment of guilty connection in the yard at my grandma's.

The truth is, I had absolutely no clue. Not just because this wasn't the sort of traceability-obsessed modern restaurant where a mulleted waiter brightly relays the star sign of the ex dairy cow on the menu, but also because it would have been basically impossible to look at the frenzied abundance of that event – the hustling regiments of cooks and serving staff, the hundreds of assembled guests, the horizonless platters of food and drink – and easily discern precisely where anything had come from. Even allowing for the context of a party-obsessed ethnic group in a party-obsessed nation, let me just say it: my Uncle Layi's seventieth birthday felt, by every conceivable metric, like the biggest family party I had ever been to.

That it practically started the night before only supports this instinct. In the evening after we had visited Ebun, my brother and I made our way to the function room of a ritzy country club (accessed via a red-carpet-style photo backdrop and ersatz gold columns rendered in cardboard) to a kind of primer event predominantly for business associates. It was various stews and sundries in gleaming warmer trays, bursting sprays of white roses, warm bottles of malt – the biscuity, brown-bottled sugar bomb that is another Nigerian soft drink obsession – and a brief, perfunctory appearance from the birthday boy himself. Mere hours later we were up early and in our suits for a marathon church service; after that, there was a mass wardrobe change into shimmering native-wear, or *aso ebi*, the matching ceremonial dress that puts women in sculptural headscarves and men in tailored smocks or billowy *agbada*. Then came another traffic-snarled motorcade to the final boss battle of the main event.

That temporal boundaries seemed to become permeable, that one lavish but gently chaotic event on the programme bled into another, spoke to this final party's sense of opulent, brain-scrambling hugeness. Here was a cavernous, stadium-sized hangar of a hall, dressed in drooping fabrics and twinkling festoon lights. Here was a stage dominated by ten-foot photographs of my uncle and a multi-tiered cake suggestive of marriage to oneself. Here was the aqueous, hip-swaying sound of live West African percussion, a jostling, excitable crowd of countless wider family members taking their places at circular tables flickering with battery-operated, LED candles. Here was ornate costume and, with it, politics, pageantry and carefully choreographed performance.

My Uncle Layi, as you can probably infer from the grand-ness of this scene, is an inspirationally successful business-man; a doctorate-holding geologist of sharp, formidable intellect, stolid, unsentimental generosity and unexpectedly mischievous humour, who has nonetheless softened with age. He is not, however, someone I would readily identify as a natural partier. Nonetheless, tonight, even he enthusiasti-cally observes the strict Yoruba tradition that dictates the so-called celebrant at any major event must not just walk up to the high table, but *dance* up to it, with all the unhurried razzle-dazzle of an oiled pro wrestler making their way to the ring. If you want to understand Yoruba culture's animat-ing paradox of extroverted misrule and strictly observed, almost Downtonian codes, rules and traditions then the place to do it is amid the heat, pageantry and ever-present subplots of a big party.

Naturally, this same air of largesse and specificity applied to the spread of food and drink. The offering at Nigerian parties is often an exercise in wish fulfilment. Dishes that are laborious, special occasion treats you may eat once or twice a year, dishes that involve days of hulled and soaked black-eyed peas, the boiling, frying and then simmering of stew meat, or slow-proved batters for *puff-puff*, are corralled into a single endless parade.

The unlikeliness of their easy availability is the precise point. Even so, the offering in that fabric-draped hall was like experiencing the manifested whims and desires of everyone in the multi-generational crowd. Did people want fried rice, mined with little, steamed commas of prawn, a gathered shoal of crisp-skinned whole croaker fish, or three different swallows, sandbagged into a huge pile, beside an intricately wrought rainbow of corresponding stews? Did they want beer and spirits and even palm wine, ceremonially brought out by female servers in matching outfits who, like Yoruba versions of the shot girls who roam provincial nightclubs with holstered bottles of flavoured schnapps, poured great sploshing measures into shallow drinking gourds? What about an all-you-can-eat candy floss machine in the corner?

The only problem with this feast, however, was that, early on, none of it was actually being served. Lagos life is a constant grapple with a culture working to its own mercurial schedule and rhythms. There is interminable traffic and there are snaking queues for petrol and, at the end of it all, there is a city that meets your impotent frustration with shrugging indifference. That 'African time' is a limiting cliché does not detract from its central, self-perpetuating truth. What's more, the hierarchal traditions and symbolism of celebration dining complicate things further. The elders and men at every family gathering I have ever been to are the ones who genuinely eat first; seated, unmoving figures honoured with a steaming tray of food, a perspiring bottle of stout and a neatly folded sheet of kitchen roll. In the traditions of Nigeria's Igbo ethnic group, each part of a shared chicken – the gizzard and liver to denote the eldest male's status, the scant meat of the head to signal the supplicant position of children – is parcelled out to a different family member. Nigerian parties are complex, courtly networks of favour, social manoeuvring and pointed excommunication related to age, proximity to the celebrant, and intangible notions of status. It is the politics of the serving pecking order at any wedding multiplied by about a hundred and enacted by people that are physically incapable of holding their tongues.

Though almost all the invited guests were in the venue, my uncle, my aunt and their children had danced their way to a top table that was showered in sparkling confetti, and everyone was happily availing themselves of the free drink, the lunch service seemed to be dangerously delayed. The beckoning scent of what was being prepared in the large hatch kitchen, the great wafting plumes of frying plantain and cooked meat, hung there like an unfulfilled promise.

As the live band conjured a rolling, effervescent wave of music and the MC exhorted the crowd to cheer and praise

Jesus in the name of my uncle, people grew restless; increasingly ratty uncles asked harried staff what the hold-up was. My mother, feeling the grievous insult of slack food service at such an important event, remonstrated first with my cousins and then directly with a sombre-looking young woman that I took to be some sort of catering manager. In this, my mother was being completely true to her nature. Not only is she a fierce keeper of the flame of tradition, but food is her primary communicative tool. To feed people exactly what they need is a form of love language but also of control. And so, to subcontract that control to another party was to cede a defining power.

Mum's frustration with the sluggish service grew as I wandered off to the bathroom, rearranging the stiff traditional hat, the *fila*, on my head and happily greeting relatives on the way. When I came back, she had apparently shoved her way into the hatch kitchen and started to ladle out food on to plates herself, perspiring at the exertion and emotion of it all as staff stood around her, frozen. Folarin, whose special bond with my mother stems from their matched temperaments as much as his status as firstborn, strode over to petition her to stop, an unlikely peacekeeper. Eventually, plates of food started to be prepared and ferried out to tables. Mum was urged away, dabbing at her brow and still volubly expressing her dissatisfaction. 'That woman in the kitchen has just asked me to keep your mum out,' said my cousin, Tokunbo, appearing at my side and striking a note of puffed-cheek exasperation at being caught in the middle rather than any sort of personal annoyance. It is about as perfect an illustration as you could wish for of the furious intensity of feeling that Nigerians have when it comes to the business of eating, the keeping up of appearances socially, and the enervating drip-drip of a society that can send you half crazy with its slow-moving incompetence and dysfunction.

More than that, perhaps, it was another example of the way that Nigerians problem-solve and commune with each other. During that trip, I was reacquainted with the performance of Lagosian interaction – an innately understood lingua franca of Nigerianness that has only a passing connection to language, class or ethnic grouping. To accomplish things in Nigeria, to get by at all, is to have your foot all the way down on the behavioural accelerator pedal. Conversations are conducted in a barked, bluntly direct form of the creolised language, Nigerian pidgin. To be understood and respected is to embrace coarseness and operate on the assumption that absolutely everyone you engage with is trying to cheat or scam you in some way. What you must not be, as I can attest, is a determinedly polite and soft-spoken British-Nigerian, stammering through some Hugh Grant-ish version of the Queen's English while you try to buy a meat pie. After the third or fourth time of some perplexed Nigerian looking at me as if I were speaking Esperanto, I had become a partial mute, reliant on the interpreters in my family who were able to code-switch more convincingly. Nigerian interaction comes with certain high-decibel codes, symbols and expectations. It is a dialogue of extremes, speed and respect won through mutual willingness to escalate a disagreement. But my mum's run-in with the catering staff at my uncle's seventieth showed that even these attitudes and expectations have their limits. There was, it seemed, a way to be *too Nigerian* in any given situation. And now all Mum could do was sit at the table and let the bubbling pan of her righteous irritation subside.

Despite this scene, the rest of the seventieth passed by without much more in the way of incident. Champagne flowed and flowed. Halting speeches and presentations were given, as foil-scrunched cobettes of barbecued street corn were nibbled. Sugar-drunk children careened around a crèche area hemmed in by multicoloured balloons and cutouts of pre-school cartoon characters. My mother, who had apparently been able to shake off the earlier incident, danced and posed at the centre of a 360-degree photo booth as a camera whirled around her.

In the midst of all this, I remember feeling a freeness and comfort that had, up to that point, eluded me on the trip. I think part of this was just the familiar focus and pull of a party. Not to mention the safe harbour of abundant alcohol and a tableful of younger people – Folarin, my three cousins, Tokunbo, Tenne and Bade, plus two of their on-off girlfriends – who could share in my sense of dazed bemusement. There had been, from the Doomed Cow outwards, something about this trip to Lagos that had felt a little cloistered and frustrating. The days leading up to the main event had generally involved my brother disappearing off on mysterious errands and my mum delighting in the familiar behavioural atmosphere of Lagos, while I looked on from the periphery; an honoured but mostly ignored guest. Accustomed to the easy liberty, authority and confidence of my life in London, gadding about to different restaurants on my Brompton, I struggled with the restive rhythms of Lagos. We sat in darkened rooms. We visited family members. We waited on drivers or house staff or miscellaneous other helpmeets and handlers if we wanted to move, eat or accomplish almost anything. There was still a tug of recognition and awe; still the daily thrill of being in an environment where I wasn't defined by difference or my status as a minority. But many of the early days of that 2019 return, not helped by the fact I had restaurant writing work to do on my laptop, were coloured by the distance and displacement not typically associated with a supposed homecoming. Everyone around me seemed tuned to a frequency of enjoyment or ease that I couldn't quite lock into.

Until, that is, a couple of turning points. The first was the party: an event that not only forced me to literally don the cultural costume that I had once been so fearful of but also, in each precisely symbolic moment – the dancing into the room and the outfits, the spraying of dollar bills, the specificity of the food and those pre-colonial gourds of palm wine

– helped me to realise that so much of Nigerian identity and lineage was a kind of joyful, collective performance.

The second occurred the next day, during a trip to one of Lagos's beaches. The day after the seventieth, a little wearied but perhaps still riding the adrenaline high of those festivities, we formed a plan to head out to Elegushi beach: one of the privately requisitioned parcels of the sandy Atlantic coastline that bounds Lagos's city perimeter. It happened to be a public holiday: National Democracy Day. And so my mum, Folarin, another cousin, Femi, and a driver who had seemingly appeared out of nowhere negotiated the long, potholed road out across the well-heeled district of Lekki, through a payment gate where multiple outstretched palms needed to be greased, and into the ragged car park that heralded the vast stretch of sand and roaring ocean.

As a patch of seaside, it was both strangely familiar and acutely Nigerian. Bars, restaurants, hawker stalls and manually operated, rickety metal Ferris wheels dotted the shoreline. Young men in begrimed football shirts galloped lean, hireable horses along the sand. A few families and young children dipped cautious toes in a body of water that is locally regarded as more of a source of terror than Dryrobe-wearing enjoyment (if you are a Lagosian without a story of some sort of an oceanside drowning befalling an acquaintance then you are hardly a Lagosian at all). Jostling party music blared out from big speakers.

After a while of snapping photos, labouring across the sand, and looking out towards a becalmed tanker, as flags and tattered parasols flapped in the wind, hunger struck. Unanimously, we decided that the moment called for suya (pronounced soo-ya): the fiery, peanut-laced form of Northern Nigerian roadside barbecue that is both a ubiquitous way of life and a sort of impossibly addictive, edible narcotic. We found a stall; an open-air affair, billowing smoke and the scent of sizzled animal fat, and manned by a barrel-chested young man in a counterfeit Fendi T-shirt. After my mum had given him what was becoming her customary dose of hell over both the price and the quality of the food – 'Ah, it's not cooked yet,' she said, gesturing towards a piece of meat, with a puckish grin, as the young man's spirit left his body – we left with steaming parcels of orange-tinged, fire-kissed chicken and thin pieces of steak, chopped and pulverised almost into a ragged, beefy crumb. Soon, we had made our way to the balcony of a deafeningly loud beach club, and were all looking out towards the setting sun, pulling clumps of meat from damp paper and cooling the lip-singeing burn of the suya with urgent, bitter gulps of cold beer.

The notion that we might visit something as purely pleasurable and faintly touristy as a beach in Lagos had never ever occurred to me. The thought that there would be such ease and distinctly African contentment in this apparent land of armed robberies, power cuts and old-fashioned, thick-accented elders was brand new. Here, shamefully, was my narrow and oblivious view of the country and the culture laid bare. Elegushi beach was rough around the edges. Yet it solidified my feeling that, by degrees, I was making my way back to something important and revelatory. That there were lessons to learn from the crab-apple tree, the chest freezer of lollies, the Doomed Cow and all the complications of an eating life shaped by both Nigeria and Britain. I reached back through the opening in the soggy paper, teased a scrap of spice-dusted chicken thigh away from the bone and watched as my mum danced contentedly, her eyes looking out to the Atlantic. It was one of a number of completely new, utterly bizarre Nigerian experiences I had that week. And yet, there I was, feeling strangely at home.

2

Pain is a Pocket of Mashed Potato

In keeping with the transience of diasporic Nigerian lives, I had many primary schools rather than one. From the moment of my birth in an Edgware hospital – an event that was partially shepherded, as my star-struck mother would go on to relate to basically everyone she met, by moustachioed celebrity physician Dr Robert Winston – our parents zigzagged across continents and let their children reap the educational whirlwind.

My eldest brother, Folarin, had a brief enrolment at a boarding school in Nigeria's south-west, where, as he told Mum with a mixture of horror and astonishment, some of the other eleven-year-old boys already had pubic hair. My other older brother, Ray, went to both a Kent fee-paying school and a Lagos primary where students wore natty scarlet shorts. Meanwhile, I spent the unremembered entirety of what would have been my reception year at a Nigerian school and the bulk of Year 1 at a Chatham primary where my only real recollection is of charging through a friend's patio door, knee-first, and ending up with six stitches and a scar that still glimmers on my knee to this day.

Among this frantic early movement, the place that I see when I recall my earliest years is Gallions Mount: the primary school in Plumstead, south-east London, where I learned and grew and ate for much of my life between the ages of seven and eleven. Set near the top of a steep hill like a giant, stalled funicular, it was a place of progressive early 1990s values – there was no uniform and the headteacher was a crop-haired 'Ms' who always ensured that even confused five-year-olds got the buzzing pronunciation of her preferred prefix correct – and architectural contrasts. Ornate entrance arches at the roadside betrayed its past as a Victorian girls' school, while stepped, fully glazed, 1970s-era classrooms traced the incline of the building's old bones. There was a vast playground, dotted with jutting water fountains and chipped football goals, accessed by a grand double staircase. The freezing outdoor toilets were still in use and all stocked with Izal Medicated Toilet Paper, a notorious brand of abrasive bathroom tissue apparently designed by malevolent aliens who had never seen, nor wiped, a human backside. What's more, if you ever forgot your PE kit, it was always decreed, either through pure necessity or a kind of punishment, that you would have to do it in your vest and pants – a rule that I remember occasioning more than a few moments of inadvertent flashing from male classmates in overly roomy Y-fronts.

Nowhere was this collision of the old and the new, of Victorian rectitude and modern expectations, more pronounced than in the dinner hall. This was a time of sweeping change in the field of school lunch provision. Almost ninety years after the Liberal party first encouraged local authorities to provide meals of porridge and bread with dripping to deprived children, the incumbent Conservative government scrapped nutrition standards, nudged councils towards outsourced catering, and created an on-ramp to the looming age of shovelled chips and turkey twizzlers. Of course, we children had no sense of this, and it seemed that the powers that be at Gallions Mount had not fully got the memo that the early twentieth-century approach was out of step with the times.

My memory of that primary school canteen is that, like a repurposed stage set, it was an altered version of the assembly hall. Sometime amid the thick, late-morning miasma of gravy, lamp-lit warming cabinets for food were wheeled in and arrayed around stunted sets of tables and chairs, wiped and bleached to a municipal shine. The wooden fold-out climbing apparatus of those PE lessons would be stowed away and paper cutouts of giant peaches and leaf-fringed harvest festival displays still adorned the walls.

That gleaming space was, in my memory, a monument to strangely comforting British culinary traditions. Thickly chunked, slightly watery beef bolognese would billow steam from a metal basin beside a great, pale wodge of tangled spaghetti. Dimpled, faintly brown garden peas and soft, hot slices of carrot would be spooned into a subdivided tray-plate beside cauliflower cheese or an arid wedge of quiche Lorraine. Coconut-flecked sponge cake would nuzzle beside chocolate custard, liberated from a clasped metal contraption that hissed open like an air lock, and anointed with a thick, wrinkled floe of congealed skin that would be stirred in with a wrist-twirling flourish.

Growing up in a Nigerian household, this sort of post-Beetonian British canon was completely non-existent. If you asked us about béchamel, we would probably have guessed it was a ski resort. Which is to say: this would have very much been my first time encountering these dishes. My first time experiencing flung fistfuls of pale, grated cheese-like product, syrupy, suet-laced puddings and tinned pineapple rings anointing thin gammon steaks.

By this point I already knew, through self-perpetuating family lore and my own instincts, that I wasn't the sort of child to compliantly devour whatever I was presented with. Even familiar foods could be a source of repellent worry and fear. The scent and spectacle of an aunty extruding tangerine pips into the cupped spittoon of her hand; a crustless cheese sandwich, terminally contaminated by slices of leaching tomato. To first experience food constructed with such a different culinary toolkit was to fretfully venture into the unknown.

This newness meant that there was also the capacity for delight – be it through an Arctic roll's brain-jolting chill or the additive-heavy hit of a soft, neon-crumbed puck of fish-cake on a Friday. But it also meant, as I would learn one fateful day, there was the potential for an especially forma-tive, absurdist disaster.

I think I would have been about seven or eight and early on in the repeated daily patterns of primary school life; cross-legged mornings on the scratchy carpet, frenzied games of British Bulldog in the playground, thin blue straws plunged through the foil into glass bottles of milk that Thatcher had not yet totally snatched. There was some sour folded in with the sweetness. I have a fixed memory of a red-headed girl at school, let's call her Cassie, who was bullied horribly by the more volubly cruel kids in the school. A large part of the pile-on was that she ate a chilled beetroot salad from the dinner hall that apparently contained some indeterminate 'lurgy' – a word that, in the parlance of 1990s south-east London was used more in the sense of having 'cooties' than being ill. It was a grim, inexplicable bit of mob rule meanness that nonetheless cemented the link, in my mind, between food and public perception.

At this point, exposure to more of these new forms of eating – to children's parties where there was the whiffy terror of beef-paste sandwiches and concerningly pink, cold chicken legs served at a temperature that was especially mystifying to a Nigerian – sharpened my fussiness, but also gave it a new complexity. On the one hand, there was the creeping sense that I should try to overcome some of my reflexive disgust in order to fit in. On the other, there was the very real fear that dallying with some weird, lurgy-coded repast would lead to the cruel victimisation that Cassie experienced.

I'm sure similar scenes were playing out in draughty Victorian halls all across the country. If the image conjured is of miniature inmates in a sort of benign penitentiary then, well, it is not only correct but was very much reinforced by the presence of one group: the dinner ladies.

Generally kindly but with a brisk, hassled air, these women may not have fitted into the natural power hierarchy of the school like our teachers, but they ruled that daily pop-up cafeteria like hair-netted autocrats. Never mind that the approach within school dinner provision was, at that time, shifting from the matronly instruction of the post-war era to a more individualistic future of self-serve decisions. The dinner ladies controlled portion size but they also took it upon themselves to impose shape, structure and some semblance of nutritional balance on our meals. This meant you could not merely come away with a double shovelling of chips on Fish Fridays; you could not pair a veg-less serving of sausage plait with a thick wodge of jam roly-poly and double custard. But above all else, and most challenging to wrap our little pleasure-seeking minds around, was one unbreakable, sanctified rule: no pudding or, for that matter, freedom until you were deemed to have finished enough of your main meal.

There will be entire generations that have their own tales of bumping up against the iron will of these joy-bouncers; of smiling fifty-somethings called Jan and Barbara who would frown at untouched carrots or broccoli and send you back, enforcing nebulous shared ideas about 'a balanced diet' with Dickensian rigour. On my particular fateful day, it concerned a portion of mashed potato. The parts of the meal that I had actually wolfed down are lost to history – sausages and some of those garden peas, maybe – but I remember that, as the clattering hurricane of conversation and knives and forks could be heard around me, I looked down at the gathered, cooling clump of pale mush with a mounting sense of dread and apprehension.

Smash – the powdered, reconstituted potato product and mainstay of talking-head nostalgia shows – comes together with a whipped smoothness and evokes the addictively bland, processed sense memory of deliquesced crisps. At the other end of the scale, pioneering 1980s-era French chef Joël Robuchon revolutionised this broad field with a pommes purée where the ratio of delicately riced potato to chilled butter was an ambrosial, indulgent 2:1. The unappetising mass that looked back at me that day resembled neither of these. Riven with huge, lumpy pustules of scantly cooked starch, pappy on the palate and oddly dry, it felt closer to the school of East End mash-making that regards oil, animal fat, or seasoning of any kind as an un-English frippery to be avoided at all costs.

I had an exploratory tongue-dab of a taste, to see if I could put some away. Bleurgh. Not possible. Yes, there would have almost certainly been other children in the dinner hall who had happily wolfed down double portions, who would have been perplexed by my extreme reaction to this most uncontroversial of carbohydrates. But the combination of taste, texture and increasingly chilly temperature was a particular trigger to my pickiness. The foods that I loved at that point tended to be either sweet, piquantly savoury, fried to a tensile crunch or (preferably) some combination of all three of those things. This mashed potato, possessed of the same gloopy mouthfeel and unmasked vegetal hum that always seemed to activate my gag reflex, had none of those properties. Beyond that, my hesitation was just as much about a strong suspicion of anything that was even slightly unfamiliar. These were potatoes, yes, but they were not potatoes in the way my mum would make them; nor were they the synthetically yellow chips, waffles or machine-formed smiley faces that had a uniformity I interpreted as a sign of safety and trust. Add in my extreme squeamishness and sensitivity to food decay – the squelched, rotten produce that would lurk at the edge of my vision during Mum's Saturday expeditions to Woolwich Market – and I think you have more of a sense of it. It wasn't just that I felt incapable of forcing down something unfamiliar or fleetingly unpleasant – though this was both true and a reality of life that I simply hadn't really experienced before primary school. It was also that an active imagination and long memory for instances of revulsion whipped the *idea* of a hazardous food-stuff up to a grotesque point that far outstripped its reality. They were just workmanlike mashed potatoes. They were also the psychically daunting, combined essence of the few, haunting occasions that food had made me feel stressed, bewildered or bilious.

I tried to return my unfinished tray-plate, in the faint hope one of the dinner ladies would be distracted or look the other way. No dice. I moved the mashed potato around, muttering well-worn prayers to the patron saint of fussy eaters, in the hope that a bit of dispersal might make it look like I had put a small dent in it. 'Come on,' said the dinner lady, sending me back to my table with a tone of head-shaking, gentle exasperation. 'Just try a little bit, please.'

So, fresh out of viable options, what did I do? Did I just hold my nose, open the hatch, and grimly suck it back, like an *I'm A Celebrity* contestant chewing on the sphincter of some blameless marsupial? Well, no. What I did was the same, completely logical thing that any innately duplicitous, incredibly stubborn child would do. I made sure no one could see me, picked the clumps of mashed potato up with my bare hand and, one compacted gobbet after another, stuffed them into my trouser pocket. 'There we go,' said the dinner lady, as I came back up wearing a shifty look. My scraped plate was taken with a smile and a satisfied head nod.

That I don't recall what the resultant pudding was, or whether I even chose eating it over scurrying straight out of the dinner hall as potato flecks spilled guiltily from my pocket, tells you everything about my mind state. The adrenaline must have been off the charts. I am also not sure why I seem to have thoroughly memory-holed an entire afternoon of school where I wandered around and sat through lessons with a malodorous blob of fetid, squished mashed potato in my pocket. (Equally, that I escaped this incident without it being the creation myth of a cruel life-long nickname – Tater Trousers, say, or Spud Bum – feels genuinely miraculous). Regardless of all that, the next significant memory I have of this day is, a little later, a fuzzy picture of my mum discovering the trousers I had worn that day in the laundry, calling me over to the washing machine to explain myself, and then being uncharacteristically understanding and unbothered about it. Although, I do not remember any future incidents of having to secrete subpar vegetables about my person, so maybe she had a quiet word with the school about getting the dinner ladies to soften their demands.

This story burns bright in the memory, and its light illuminates plenty about my nascent relationship to pickiness, appetite and identity. On the one hand, it's an instructive portrait of my early struggle with British food culture. For all that my early life involved me committedly trying to define myself somewhat in opposition to Nigeria, not just through how I acted but through what I ate and desired, the pocket mashed potato incident showed that it would not be straightforward.

The robust soups and stews of my elders and ancestors, the pieces of offal and mounded heaps of whipped tuber flour, might have struck me as perplexing. But, in the simplest terms, the vagaries and expectations of English culinary traditionalism had shown me they could be just as bewildering and terrifying. Even a palate willed to assimilate would not always play ball. As later interactions with all sorts of foods and dishes – blancmange, the mere scent and thought of Marmite, any cheese more pungent than the mildest, bendiest supermarket Cheddar – would show me, an uncritical headlong dive into the larder of early 1990s Britain did not seem to be the answer. My troubling contact with the less obviously appealing aspects of the country's post-war gastronomy had not fully resolved the conflict in my food identity.

Separately, that day in the Gallions Mount dinner hall had highlighted another piece of cultural dissonance related to eating. Stuffing unwanted mashed potato into a pocket is quite an extreme reaction. And I think part of the reason that my response was so dramatic was the pure shock of being forced to finish food. This, in my experience, was an extremely alien piece of behaviour within West African eating culture. The strictness of Nigerian parents, authorities and elders is rightly legendary. Beyond the expectation to always show respect and bowing fealty to those of advanced years, there is also an ingrained, quite puritanical assumption that children will not talk back, that they will cooperatively complete household chores, that they will be ever ready to suffer all manner of arcane punishments for naughtiness – being smacked; facing the corner of a room – without complaint, and that, fundamentally, the family units we belonged to were functional dictatorships rather than democracies. Throw in the sense that these self-defining traditions were doubly important in diaspora, and I think it's safe to say that my brothers and I were raised in an atmosphere where there was a healthy amount of fear and a high behavioural bar.

However, this world of strictness, order, rules and the figurative taking of unpalatable medicine never really applied at mealtimes. There is a folkloric story within my wife's family about her elder sister stubbornly refusing to finish her peas and then, later that same evening, being presented with an entire bowl of them. Nigella Lawson has spoken about the fact that, growing up, for her or her siblings to fussily refuse anything on their plates would be to ensure that they would be served the same, congealing remnants of it at the next mealtime.

Nigerian parents are not always known for their emotional empathy, understanding or softness; it is arguable that many second-generation kids have felt the particular sting and harsh expectations of elders who understandably let the stresses and frustrations of starting a new life in a foreign country seep into their daily interactions. My mum and dad were imperfect because all humans are. But the notion that any of us Famurewa kids would be forced to eat something we didn't like growing up, the idea that there would be any instances of brinkmanship over uneaten vegetables, is, for better or worse, just unthinkable. Food may have been vitally important to us, a sanctified communicative tool and form of cultural expression, but it tended to be experienced in an atmosphere of pointed comfort and light chaos.

Dinner would rarely happen at exactly the same time two nights in a row. Meals would be taken, not at the dining table but on laps in front of the blaring television. It was not unheard of, at weekends, for my mum or a benevolent aunty to suddenly fry up a batch of midnight pancakes or fluffy, liberally salted lengths of yam chips. What's more, for a period that stretched long into my adolescence, my favoured way to eat spaghetti bolognese was to languorously pick at it with my fingers while never once taking my eyes off *Top of the Pops*.

I don't doubt that my mother despaired at the nose-wrinkling revulsion I exhibited when in the vicinity of certain traditional Nigerian dishes; I'm sure the very short list of vegetables I would countenance was, at best, quite frustrating. But her attitude, as a maniacally committed feeder, was always to try to elicit the joy of the things that I did like rather than attempt to eradicate the dread of the many, many things I didn't. This is probably part of why she shrugged off the discarded mashed potato in the pocket of my trousers that day. Cooking was about meeting specific need wherever, or whenever, it happened to emerge; food was pleasure rather than punishment. Though it wasn't a fantastically wealthy upbringing, we were, in this respect, very much indulged.

And so, I think it's safe to say that this pandering was part of why both elements of the food and the general approach at Gallions Mount proved such a shock. It is also an unavoidable reminder of the conflict at the heart of the person and the eater I was becoming. There was Cassie's shameful bullying, and an emerging, fearful understanding of how food could shape identity and social status. There was the joyous, anarchic Nigerian approach to food and feeding that I was more attached to than I perhaps realised. It was, as that image of a little boy with a plateful of mashed potato in his pocket proves, more than a little bit confusing.

I should say, at this point, that to characterise my mother's approach to food as totally permissive and laissez-faire would not be accurate. She had her limits and a particular code. And, to better understand it, the best place to start is with the woman who made me perhaps the most consistently satisfying snack I've ever had. My time at Gallions Mount brought refreshing structure and reliability to the convulsions and continent-hopping movement of our early lives. After periods living in Wembley, Chatham and Lagos, we had settled in our house on Littledale: a pebbledashed semi-detached in another suburban corner of south-east London called Abbey Wood.

Lying a fifteen-minute bus ride from my primary school and on an attractive circular loop of homes that nuzzled up beside dense woodland, the Littledale house had an especially positive energy; a handsome idyll perched on the shoulder of Kent and representative of a period of contentedness and stability for the Famurewas. I say that. Though things had slowed, settled and simplified for me, the family was still a little atomised. My brothers were at different boarding schools. My father, in the process of establishing an engineering business back in Lagos, was still based in Nigeria; a spectral presence who would waft in and out of our lives, often with little notice. Mum, meanwhile, had by then started working in an administrative role at the Commonwealth's grand offices on Pall Mall in London. The absence of anyone to actually look after me when I came home from school meant we had a problem. It meant, after a few stints of being deposited in a clamorous Plumstead gymnasium for an after-school club, that I needed the reliable care of a childminder.

Charlene was of Caribbean heritage; statuesque, light-skinned and doe-ish, with a businesslike but not unkind demeanour and a small, trinket-stuffed house a short walk from Gallions Mount. In truth, I cannot remember much in the way of specifics about the afternoons that I would spend at her place, alongside her six-year-old daughter, before my mum appeared at the door, poised and trench-coated, in a waft of Trebor Extra Strong Mint scent. What I can recall, what I can practically still taste, is the toast that Charlene would make me as a snack not long after we had all shuffled in through her front door.

Some toast feels special because of the bread that's used, the liberal application of a certain form of fat, a particular presentational flourish or some ineffable, mysterious quality related to mood and timing. The toast at Charlene's seemed to somehow alchemise all of these. It wasn't that the bread, bog-standard supermarket white but notably thick sliced, was especially unusual; it wasn't that the spread – which, this being the early 1990s, would have absolutely been margarine rather than actual butter – was all that delicious. It was just something about the specifics of it: the abundant stack of four slices, the fact they had been sliced into neat quarters, the way there was the dripping melt of liquified spread but, also, audible crunch and the sort of just-popped freshness that nips the fingers and warms the spirit.

Maybe what I'm remembering is just the ravenousness of a growing boy who had probably spurned a good amount of what was on offer at school; maybe almost anything halfway bland and edible that was put in front of me at Charlene's would have sparked the same lustful focus. Similarly, my mum still talks about the transcendent nectar that was the little cup of instant hot chocolate a kindly midwife made her the morning after she gave birth to me. All I can say is that when I think of safety, simplicity and comfort stripped down to its most basic, elemental and unadorned form, I think of losing myself to a high-piled plate of toast in Charlene's dining room.

To be clear, it was not the enormous rounds of toast that my mother had an issue with. It was what Charlene chose to feed me later that evening. Following a few hours of watching *Newsround* and *Blue Peter*, Charlene's daughter and I would be called back to dinner and, similarly to the toast, it would pretty much be the same thing every time. It was large, waxy potatoes, bisected and steam-boiled to soft submission, tumbled with rice and, if memory serves, maybe a wisp of some sort of seasoning or stock cube to add a smidge of interest. It was not the most exciting of meals but there was no need for me to stash part of it in my pocket. It was fine. The other side of the ascetic coin when set against the beautiful restraint of the toast. Mum asked me what we had had for dinner one day and so I told her. Rice and potatoes. Same as we have every day. My hesitant attitude to food and culinary discovery, that I was happy to cling to the rocks of what I knew rather than set sail for thrilling new gastronomic lands, meant that this had hardly registered as unusual. The monotony of rice and potatoes was preferable to the potential discomfort of a more varied diet. Maybe boredom was the price I would have to pay to feel safe from watery salad vegetables, the faint armpit-scent of cumin, and other lurking horrors.

To say that my mum did not share this view is to perhaps undersell it. I wasn't privy to the exceptionally Nigerian tearing-a-new-one that Mum engaged in, but if it was anything like the apoplectic preview I had heard her work-shopping during irate landline calls to relatives – essentially, 'Can you believe I'm paying her that much money and she's just feeding my child rice and potatoes every day?' – then I imagine Charlene would have been suitably chastened. It's worth pointing out here that my mum's issue, as I understood it, was not with the distinct lack of useful nutrients in Charlene's double-carbed house speciality. (Although, genuinely, the more of this I write, the more I wonder how I didn't have scurvy by the time I was eleven.) For Mum, it was the lack of imagination and roundedness that was the issue. The fact that someone would not just make something so insultingly two-dimensional – where was the focal point in the form of a couple of roasted chicken legs? The stew? The fried plantain? – but make it repeatedly, every night, made no sense to her. Yes, as a gifted and innate cook, throwing creative and dynamic, robustly seasoned plates of food together was something that came to her easily, but this was about her deeply held beliefs when it came to food and feeding; the paradox that underpinned the relatively relaxed, appeasing nature that seemed to colour all those family TV dinners. A proper, belly-filling hot meal was, in her eyes, a non-negotiable. To not have the instinct or acumen to create meals with real colour and variety, particularly when you were being paid to do so, was an unforgivable failing.

This is not to say that Mum completely disregarded the convenience solutions of the day. As a working woman in her early forties who was a single parent by proxy, she had no qualms about embracing the frozen chips, burgers and garishly packaged crispy pancakes that could be clanked into a baking tray and whacked in the oven. However, when there was ample time and availability, you could be in no doubt about what she considered 'real' food. Even on weekday mornings, I'd be directed away from the cereal boxes and towards bacon, faintly charred frankfurters and an omelette, paved with peppers and onions, keeping warm beneath an upturned plate.

In this, she was merely finding another way to forcefully press home the importance of our culture. We may have counted our blessings to be in this land of beef-paste sandwiches and cold, monochromatic buffets. There may have been both an implicit and explicit onus on fitting in and getting on. But there were limits to our culinary integration. It should be noted here that these ideas around Nigerian food traditions very much came through the particular filter of my mother. She was a Yoruba heritage, nakedly aspirant, upper-middle-class woman born in 1950, with her own gustatory biases and personality quirks; a typically Nigerian, indefatigable force of nature in the kitchen, with little patience for people – and, truthfully, women especially – who couldn't match her pace, pride or creative fervour as a cook.

She was also, rather than a flag bearer for an entire culture, just one, fallible person with a particular viewpoint. Years later, my brother Ray sent a panicked message to our family WhatsApp group. 'Have any of you guys heard of Indomie noodles??' his query began, referencing the Indonesian instant noodle brand that is a meme-worthy obsession among modern Nigerians thanks to its status as cheap, umami-laden sustenance. 'I've just been told that I'm a "posh Nigerian" because I'd never heard of it.' Indomie had never blipped on our collective radar until adulthood, both because none of us had been students in Nigeria for an extended part of our adolescence and because it was not something Mum or other relatives ever meaningfully engaged with. Here, again, was a sign of what can happen if you are reliant on your elders to be the sole access point to ancestral cuisine and culture. Our perspective on Nigeria may have been sharply defined but it was also, as we would consistently learn, restrictively narrow.

Beyond the pocket mashed potato and the mild friction between my mum and Charlene, this broad era in Abbey Wood is one I regard as being an especially happy period for both my life and my diet. It is a time that flickers back as a soft-focus haze of boundless freedom, easy contented-ness and, frankly, abundant E-numbers. Elder millennials can get tiresomely wistful about the particular freedoms of a pre-internet childhood in an economically prosperous and relatively safe society. I am here to tell you that even the most misty-eyed recollections barely do justice to the miraculous wonder of coming of age in that generational sweet spot between healthy parental ambivalence and a helpfully barren landscape of home entertainment options.

In our time at Littledale, my best friend in the world, a boy at my school called Gary, happened to live just around the corner. My typical days at weekends and holidays would involve me whizzing to his place on my bike, knocking to ask his mum if he was 'playing out', and then heading off to join an amorphous pack of grubby-cheeked neighbourhood kids. We would race around the block in prolonged Le Mans-level competitions, play games of football on a tufty nearby rec, or explore the woods behind our houses – a mulch-scented network of tree hollows, shaded glens and bramble-fringed dens where it was said notorious highway-man Dick Turpin had once hidden out in subterranean caves – with time slowing to a molasses crawl, before some-one would be sent out to tell one of us that our dinner was ready and we needed to head home.

You will have heard some version of this before. The

highly selective, it-was-better-in-my-day reveries about endless summers, grazed knees, white dog poo, and parents that only ever saw their children when they briefly dashed in for a frenzied gulp of Robinson's Fruit & Barley. They are the staple of an entire genre of rose-tinted collective remembrance. Even so, it was a form of unencumbered playfulness that felt especially key to my development as a person.

I had always been a child with quite a smart mouth, precociousness edging towards outright cheek, plus an impressionable streak and an often wilfully loose grasp on reality. The absence of my older brothers engendered a need to make my own fun and a knack for make-believe. Not to mention, relatedly, a credulous obsessiveness with television. In those primary school years, our sunken, patterned sofa was never just a sofa; it was a gator-infested swamp to be jumped across, a teetering Gotham City ledge negotiated by Batman, the wrestling ring I would elbow-drop on to, muttering excitable commentary to myself. There is a photo of me at what looks like my sixth birthday, completely lost in the moment, as I smash two action figures together with a fervour and intensity that is both cute and lightly concerning. This solitude, a deep yearning for acceptance in the promised land of Britain, and the capacity for adventurous pretending made me especially receptive to those days playing out. To swagger among a group of other begrimed neighbourhood kids was to feel tacit approval for the persona I was tentatively constructing.

Those days were an early, affirming rush of independence, novelty and self-expression beyond the stew-scent and cultural responsibilities of home.

This tendency very much carried over into my relationship with food. By the time I was about ten, the daily fact of a long parental leash – as much a product of my busy mother's necessity as of the cheery negligence of the era – freed me up to make the kind of irresponsible dietary decisions you'd expect from a pre-adolescent. Away from the paced drumbeat of Charlene's toast, Mum's cooking and the school dinners that, beyond Friday fish and chips, were still a challenging, gravy-fragranced obstacle course of mushy carrots and custard skin, I remember this era as a technicolour whirl of sweetness. It was thick, corner-shop 'Ice Berger' popsicles in lurid toilet-cleaner blue and twist-tied paper bags of 30p pick and mix, heavy with white chocolate mice and cola bottles that I pretended to drink from. It was different chocolate bar experiences – the snapped, gooey segment of a Cadbury's Caramel, a fingernail piercing the foil of a mini KitKat, a Twix nibbled and scraped down to a soggy, denuded girder of shortbread – as distinct and exciting as their glinting wrappers.

Perhaps more than anything, though, this period was the dawning of my love for things dipped into sugary tea. By this I mean biscuits, of course – custard creams or ravishingly salty Digestives or raggedly broken petticoat tails of Scottish shortbread that I would plunge, to the point of disintegration, into a milky bucket of Typhoo. But I also, oddly, mean toast: generously margarined triangles that I would furtively dunk in my brew to the point that there'd be a speckled oil slick glistening the surface. (Aeons later, when I had a Dishoom chai and buttered roll breakfast based on this combination, I felt a throb of nostalgia and belated vindication.) My dining universe, beyond the expectations of set mealtimes, was confectionary, convenience foods and the companionable burble of Saturday morning television. Having reached a point where my pickiness was never challenged, I could let my freak flag fly and be a boy of strange culinary kinks and snack proclivities. There were no dinner ladies insisting I at least try a few more oddly powdery peas. No well-meaning friends' mothers presenting me with browning apple slices or crab sticks that struck me as looking more like disrobed highlighter pens than food. No sense that I had to in some way comply with the world's idea of what constituted a rounded or healthily varied diet. When I was not playing out, those languid hours at Littledale would involve my rapt face absorbing the anarchy of *Live & Kicking* or *Fun House*, in between mouthfuls of silty biscuit remnant dredged from the bottom of my mug with a teaspoon.

If I was especially sugar-obsessed then it was to be expected. Not just because of the way English school dinners – very much in a continuum with the wartime rationing of sweet things – presented pudding as the dangled reward for forcing down lumpen vegetables. But also because of a

Nigerian cultural prizing that encompasses everything from the natural sugars of groundnuts to the sweet, refreshing jolt of a cold Fanta. Not for nothing is the Yoruba word for sweet – *dun*, pronounced more like 'doohn', with a bassy whump – the same as the word for delicious.

Nonetheless, my junky obsessions extended to savoury food too. To burgers and crinkle-cut oven chips and, occasionally, the fibrous, deeply satisfying planks of fried yam that my mum would emerge from the kitchen with if the mood struck. And it is this broad category that occasioned what we might term the frozen pizza experiment. It is a central, usefully illustrative piece of family lore that has been repeated so often there is now a recollection of it permanently implanted in my mind.

It was summer at Littledale, perhaps a couple of years before that golden era of freedom around my tenth birthday, and both my brothers were back from their respective schools. Mum was at work and the house was, in all likelihood, a chaotic morass of discarded Penguin wrappers, drained cans of Sainsbury's own brand Classic Cola and slumped bodies distracting themselves with portable tape players or a roll around the block on a shared pair of Bauer roller skates. We were latch-key kids living an extended latch-key existence. Sallow-eyed Lost Boys subsisting on frozen burgers, ultra-processed snacks and, if we were lucky, a reheatable tray of chicken and oven-baked onions that Mum had left out.

Remember I mentioned how obsessive I was about television? And how that obsessiveness could somewhat scramble any connection to reality or common sense? In this era, I, like lots of other impressionable children, had a particular mania for Teenage Mutant Hero (né Ninja) Turtles: the parodically of its time animated series about a gang of amphibian, sewer-dwelling martial artists eating junk food, cracking wise and beating up bad guys in New York. For some early 1990s kids, an intense love of the show meant the purchase of a pet terrapin turtle procured on a new, highly contentious black market. For me, it meant emulating the turtles' Italian-American diet with one thing and one thing only: crap 1990s pizza.

The current pizza landscape in Britain thrums with once unimaginable breadth, craft and creativity. Big-city restaurants and takeaways meticulously channel the specifics of Chicago deep-dish, crisp, Newhaven-style pies, or rapidly fired Neapolitans made with flavoursome ancient grains. Even rural pizza vans and arse-end-of-nowhere pubs send out crisp, dramatically blistered margheritas without giving it much thought. It is hard, then, for those of us who were there, to accurately conjure how objectively bad most mass-market pizza used to be. The supermarket pizzas of this time were particularly egregious: dimpled frisbees of inexpensive bread, hosed with sweet tomato sauce and flaked cheddar cheese product, and designed in such a way that cooking didn't bring textural crunch so much as a boiled, mouth-scalding softness.

Despite this, and perhaps because it blossomed in a more innocent time, I maintain that crap 1990s pizza has a charm and appeal independent of actual pizza. It was an act of imitation performed with such slack ineptitude and disregard that it had accidentally created a separate category of quintessentially British food. For a period, this precise genre of crap, blandly soothing pizza was all I wanted to eat.

On the day of the experiment, Mum had stocked the house with a few frost-furred cheese-and-tomato specimens. While my brothers were otherwise engaged, I reached in to liberate one from the icy maw of our old chest freezer. The only issue with my plan to sate my craving – and, in doing so, cosplay as a monstrously anthropomorphised turtle named after a Renaissance artist – was the significant wrinkle that I was a tiny child without the first clue how to operate the oven (not to mention a nagging sense that this appliance, as a demarcated part of my mum's culinary fiefdom, was not something I should even be touching).

So what did I do, presented with this dilemma? Call for one of my brothers? Wait until later, when there was an adult who could cook it for me? In a move that has always been presented as a strangely revealing character moment, I climbed up on to a chair, shoved the pizza into the toaster, and waited to see what would happen. Sadly, the precise results of this first experiment in toaster gastronomy are lost in time. I have faint memories of pluming smoke, an unappetising smell, and a dripping first bite into something that was evidently still quite cold in the middle.

Somehow, perhaps because my digestive system had been mutated by all the additives in my diet, there were not the dire gastric consequences you might anticipate. My brothers, on belated discovery of what I had done, responded with head-shaking disbelief. My mum, meanwhile, surprised me. Once she had trudged in from work and been told what had happened, there were no recriminations about physical danger, or mess, or the potential ruining of an important kitchen appliance that would need to be replaced. She just laughed and smiled at my bloody-minded ingenuity; gleefully told everyone who would listen about the chaotic ridiculousness of it. Food to her was about pleasure above all, cracked resourcefulness and the sanctified importance of hot food. She may not have understood Ninja Turtles, crap 1990s pizza, Charlene's rice and potatoes, or toast dunked into tea. But she knew the burning, intractable intensity of appetite and so she did not really judge. To Mum, the fact that I could content myself for hours with just television, cups of sugary tea and a dwindling sleeve of Digestives was a mark of self-sufficiency and industriousness, rather than a sign of limited impulse control. That some of the ways we ate were so different – me, a fruit-phobic, junk and convenience food obsessive; her, a hardy, hands-on lover of offal-laden stews who had once wrung chickens' necks and saw best before dates as a challenge – tickled rather than tormented her. She knew her son perhaps better than he yet knew himself. And she knew just how important food, no matter how ridiculous, could be in loudly proclaiming who you were.

If there was Toblerone, then he was back. For months at a time during those golden days in Abbey Wood – first at Littledale and later at a perhaps slightly smaller place, near the railway station on Sydney Road – my father, Olumide, would be our Yoruba Godot: the perennially discussed off-screen character whose very absence shaped and defined our lives. He was the gravelled voice at the end of the phone; the person sending what money he could; the parent that I would insist, with a slight air of tetchy defensiveness, was not actually absent so much as tragically tethered to a Lagos-based engineering business.

In the moments that he would come swaggering back into our lives, often at short notice, his trademark would be the gift of a duty-free Toblerone: that impossibly glamorous, segmental pyramid of Swiss chocolate, and totem of the harried international traveller, that came in a flashing gold box and somehow always carried the faint taste of inexpertly removed foil wrapping. These sporadic returns would bring a familiar shift in the energy, a realignment of demeanour and sensory environment. Dad would be sprawled on the living-room floor with his push-broom moustache and yuppy-ish Filofax. Mum would be in the kitchen, saucepan held at an angle, as she

Picky

once again made one of her wayward husband's favourite dishes: the taupe-coloured *amala* swallow that none of her children had inherited a taste for. Our atomised family would stumble towards temporary nuclear status. And, for me, the precise taste of it was the peace and pleasure of a part-melted hunk of nougat-flecked confectionary.

Am I mentioning this to better explain why sweetness has always felt like an especially significant and emotionally charged form of reward? Sort of. Associating Toblerone with the much-longed-for presence of my father only exacerbated my growing sense that joy and refined sugar went hand in hand. But the particular significance of mentioning Dad's sporadic returns is to underscore an important truth: my recollection of this period as completely idyllic is not the full picture. In fact, to look a little more closely at the years leading up to my transition from primary to secondary school is to see dark clouds gathering overhead.

This applied, around the mid-1990s, in a broader social sense. As jittery mutterings about IRA bombings grew, there began to be an unavoidable sense that a violent racism that many hoped had been left in the last decade was bubbling over again. Somali refugees arrived in south-east London only to face prejudice and ostracisation from established white and black communities alike. I remember being herded into the house at Littledale so a group of anti-racist protestors could march on the headquarters of an emboldened BNP in nearby Welling. In

1993, Stephen Lawrence – a young man from a family that attended the same Plumstead Methodist church as us – was killed in a manner that shocked a nation, illuminated the malevolent institutional racism that lurked beneath supposed British civility, and manifested the palpable fear of every black parent.

I think, even as I whizzed around on my bike or spent entire days in a breathless blur of cage football and den-building, I could sense something of this volatility lurking at the edge of my vision. Our corner of south-east London was an increasingly ethnically diverse area; a patchwork of verdant commons, futurist housing estates and dormant munitions facilities seasoned with West Africans, Caribbeans, South Asians and more. But, amid whispered conversations about the Lawrence family and the Gallions Mount kids occasionally parroting slurs they had heard at home, I began to discern glitches in the outwardly multicultural matrix.

From one angle, my fondness for escaping into the protective fantasy of television and imaginative play was merely a mark of my young age. From another, my particular hunger to flee my surroundings – through food, especially – betrayed a desire for a protective cocoon against the increasingly troubling realities of the world.

This applied on a smaller, family-specific scale too. Dad's absences became more frequent; his financial support, as far as I can tell, became more erratic and unreliable, which had growing consequences for my older brothers' school fees. The fact that I didn't go to private school (apparently a result of my typically headstrong opposition to the idea) was also a probable reflection of our new economic reality. For a while at Littledale, I remember that we had a lodger – a chewing-gum-smacking Gambian man called Lamine – who, as well as being a fellow African benefiting from her bottomless well of generosity, helped Mum make the domestic sums add up on a single wage that was around £10,000 a year. Later, at Sydney Road, there was muttered talk of an intractable private landlord and preliminary plans to move somewhere where the renting situation was more manageable. My eldest brother, Folarin, on his own questing journey of self-discovery, had fallen in with some of what was always euphemistically termed 'the bad element'. A development that I'll never forget was apparent in Folarin's sudden taste for odd, squat-ready dishes – tinned pilchards, sugar spooned on to bread and then grilled to a crisp – that seemed to prove that Mum's dwindling influence over us extended to appetite as well as behaviour.

At the time, I regarded these proposed changes and wider concerns as frustrating inconveniences. Impertinent attacks on my happy life of TV shows, knockabout neighbourhood friends, and kitchen cupboards groaning with an inexhaustible supply of multipacks of Walkers crisps, Clubs and toaster waffles. But now, of course, I have a greater sense of the difficult decisions my mum was having to make. And the added challenge she must have felt of having to put a positive spin on all this tumult for the benefit of her spoilt, snack-addled youngest child.

Irrevocable change was everywhere. Age was shifting my perception of who I wanted to be and reality was intruding on the sweet, soft-focus haze of childhood. The Toblerone, for better or worse, would never quite taste the same.

3

Power, Politics and Party Rice

To be the youngest in a family is to occupy a strange perception paradox. On the one hand, life plays out to the steady soundtrack of siblings loudly explaining that all the ease and privilege you enjoy – the extravagant generosity at birthdays, the later curfews, the softer punishments from parents who have mellowed with time and experience – was built on the backs of their comparative suffering. On the other, you are rarely trusted with anything because you are seen as fundamentally incapable.

If my family perennially saw me as the baby then I was at least partly culpable. There was the love of make-believe and the long-maintained habit of waking up extra early and claiming the remote control for Saturday morning cartoons. Relatedly, there was the strange tendency I had, when the late, undefined hour of my weekend bedtime approached, to simply nod off on the sofa and wait for someone to sling me over their shoulder and carry me upstairs. And then, perhaps still most uncomfortable to admit, there was the fact I was a pretty prodigious bed-wetter until I fully kicked the habit in that last year of primary.

Now, look. I do not want to apportion any blame to the people around me for failing to help me manage a hair-trigger bladder. But when I think about my many, on-off periods of piss-drenched pyjamas, hot shame, bed-sheets bundled into the washing machine and the excruciating monument of a damp mattress, stripped and propped up so it can dry out again, I think of it as being directly connected to the decidedly hands-off, relaxed attitudes to food, drink and pleasure that I grew up around.

Put simply: I would be allowed to guzzle late-night cans of soft drink and great whacking flagons of squash, and then wonder why the inevitable would happen. The bed-wetting was, in my memory, regarded by my family as an annoying fact of my existence; a commonplace, babyish trait to be brack-eted with thumb-sucking or secret adolescent devotion to a special blanky. I was never really shamed for it, beyond some understandably exasperated, light teasing. All the same, the feeling seemed to be that it was something I would naturally grow out of rather than a source of deep embarrassment that could probably be solved with a few weeks of committed parental intervention. Starting, at minimum, with a blanket ban on all those late-evening Fantas, Sprites and Lilts. Decades later, as a dad pursuing quite a different, concertedly hands-on parental path, I can't help but think of the long period nudg-ing my children awake in order to train them to take themselves to the loo in the middle of the night; the slightly neurotic, house-wide zero tolerance policy on consuming any drink over about 300ml after 8 p.m. This is not to say that one approach is right and one isn't. It is just a realisation, with the benefit of hindsight, that the pleasure-forward freedom of my youth was its own double-edged sword.

Anyway, I am telling you about my rubber mattress era to better help you understand something else: the private misery of my first camping trip away. I think I would have been about nine years old and it was my membership of Cubs that, ultimately, would have been to blame. My general memories of this glorified after-school club, the bridging designation between Beavers and fully-fledged Scouts, are happy. We would all gather in the chilly glare of a church function hall, little neckerchiefs tightly woggled, and either kick a football around on the squeaking parquet, recite Baden-Powell's nonsense incantations like unquestioning child soldiers (dib dib dib, dob dob dob) or train towards badges in arbitrary things like key ring collecting. My mistake was to let this ambient feeling of positivity distract me from the fact that the forthcoming camping trip to a site just outside Tunbridge Wells would – given I hadn't really had all that many sleepovers at friends' houses – present quite the challenge for my recalcitrant bladder.

Right from the start, it was an especially isolating and dispiriting experience. For some reason, none of my regular friends from Cubs had gone along, and so I was placed in a miserable, chilly tent with a horde of unfamiliar, grunting lunks who would either roundly ignore me or make some great show of having noticed that I'd had an accident in my sleeping bag and tried to hide it. 'You smell that?' one would say, sniffing the air theatrically. 'Urgh, it's like someone's come and dobbed something on him in the night.' (Unclear if the Cubs-specific wordplay usage of 'dob' was intentional here but, look, fair play if so.) I have faint, unfortunate memories of wet pants and nightclothes stuffed into plastic bags and shoved to the bottom of a rucksack; an own-brand Lynx derivative sprayed everywhere to try to neutralise the smell. I cannot really say why I tried to just pretend none of it was happening. Or why there wasn't some form of help from a vigilant scout leader or grown-up who must, surely, have been alive to the possibility of nervous primary school kids having accidents at night-time. All I could do was content myself with morning bowls of Frosties with a sugary splash of UHT milk and count down the days before we would be piling back on to the coach and driving back to south-east London. The faintly chemical, watery sweetness of the long-life milk slightly reminded me of the tins of Carnation that my older relatives favoured in their tea. As I had grown up in an environment where refrigeration was so prevalent as to be taken for granted, this evaporated, shelf-stable simulacrum of fresh dairy always seemed a strange generational quirk. Yet this was a small reflection of the extent to which our family identity had shifted across this relatively brief period of migration. To me, that processed milk was a cloying holdover from an unfamiliar place and time. To them, it was pure nostalgia and cultural connection through habit; the momentary relief and sweetness of the home they still longed for.

Regardless of the reminder of my family, those slurps of UHT cereal milk only affirmed my unhappiness. Then, a few days later, my misery deepened. Our Cubs pack had gone on an excursion to The Rocks: a cluster of gnarled sandstone formations and walking trails with an adjacent playground, a famous boulder that supposedly resembled a squatting toad, and loosed hordes of feral local kids clambering over everything in sight. This being the period of the early 1990s where the Batman symbol was a pop cultural ubiquity, I happened to be wearing a faded T-shirt with the black-and-yellow, Tim Burton-era logo at its centre. 'Hur hur,' said one white kid, part of an unfamiliar group, as he gestured to me. 'It's Black-man.'

Now, I must have heard stray racial slurs before. This was an era of proudly racist 'jokes' and the casual hate-speech that meant certain people couldn't even reference a South Asian-owned corner shop or Chinese takeaway without recourse to some breathtaking offensiveness. I have vivid memories of another black boy at my school explaining, slightly absurdly, that the best way to combat a white racist was to compare them to something else white, like a football goalpost. I was familiar with small-mindedness and the supposed problem of my skin colour from a very early age. But, I think, the fact that I was at a particularly low ebb made this feel like the especially painful puncturing of a protective bubble. That I also remember the bullying lunks from my own Cubs pack surprisingly leaping to my defence – more a tribal act of fending off outsiders than any sort of gesture of apology or acceptance towards me – is only partly comforting.

As a relatively popular and robustly cheery kid, this was the first time I had experienced bullying, ostracisation and people directly picking on me because of how I looked and where I came from. It was a visceral, haunting moment at the end of quite a challenging, homesick trip. Which makes it all the stranger that, as I handed over my stinking bindle of dampened pyjamas and bedding, I didn't really speak a word of my difficulties to my mum. From an early age, I had absorbed the lesson that it was important to not burden her with any extra worries. As middle-class Nigerians we had been taught that racism was a fact of life, but it was some-thing that we were to overcome with undeniable excellence and a kind of quiet fortitude and superiority. How these moments of prejudice made us feel was not something we ever openly discussed.

That camping trip is difficult to relay, obviously. Difficult to hear about too, I imagine. Yet, I think the memory of it is so deeply burrowed both because it was a rare moment of isolated vulnerability in this period and because it probably marked something of a turning point in terms of identifying the kind of treatment I wanted to avoid at all costs. It was a particularly unique and extreme weekend of feeling adrift and singled out. But, I think, coupled with those lingering memories of Cassie and her apparent beetroot-derived lurgy, and with the truly heinous, xenophobic things that people would say about supposed 'curry smell' and the South Asians in our community, this feeling attached to my innate pickiness and created a conformist approach to both food and life.

Never mind the conspicuousness of my Nigerian identity. Never mind the fact that I still adored heaped plates of the half-mushed yam dish we called *pottage*, or the sweetly enriched *agege* bread and beef stew that was one of my grandfather's favourite combinations. I never stopped eating these dishes, but they were not something that I would proudly or publicly proclaim as some sort of cultural birthright. Like the fact I understood Yoruba or had village-style bucket baths rather than showers, the devouring of these meals was something hush-hush, taking place behind closed doors. My ardour was a private affair and fearfulness meant that I was especially committed to fitting in as best I could. This spilled out into an incuriousness about not just my own cultural traditions, but any that sat outside the white-centric norm of the day and my environment. Throughout our Sydney Road era, we lived next to the Roys, a Filipino family that we were all very close to; there would be friendly interaction, a shared, immigrant affinity between my mum and the elder Roys, and, in the holidays, games of tennis played over the garden fence with the kids.

But do you know what I never did? I never once had a taste of the chicken *adobo* or crackled slices of the fragrant, roast pork belly known as *lechon*, or the deep-fried, spring roll-ish *lumpia*, that I now know were part of what was probably being cooked next door. Obviously, I could hardly have invited myself over for dinner. And I probably had a reticence that was typical of many ten- or eleven-year-olds. But I always think this oversight – which I retroactively curse, now that, in adulthood, I have fallen hard for the polyglot dynamism of Filipino cuisine – speaks to all the culinary brilliance I was missing throughout this period. The memories of that camping trip had solidified my goal. In my palate and my personality, I would do whatever I could to try to pass.

This muddled, lowbrow and decidedly Anglocentric food identity would only be heightened by my arrival at secondary school. Having failed my eleven-plus – an outcome that my mum blamed squarely on the fact that my recently rematerialised father had dropped me off at the examination hall mere minutes before it was due to start – it was decided that I would go to what was then called Bexleyheath School: a sprawling, outer-London-based but suburban Kent-coded mothership with a giant Asda next door and around 1,200 pupils split across two separate sites.

BS, as we called it, had been a rag-tag, poorly regarded comprehensive of ill behavioural standards and innumerable uniform combinations before a newish Scottish headmaster had succeeded in remoulding it into an institution that was all about standardisation, modernity and thrusting blue-blazered ambition. 'Pride Through Achievement', as the new-minted motto on our school badge had it. Though the old, unruly school was talked about in the past tense of something that had been recently vanquished, there was always the sense that this message hadn't quite got through to the student population. BS may have told itself it was on a path to greater things but it still felt like a place dominated by violent confrontations, ribald tales of sexual conquest, and young, hoop-earringed men in lowered Vauxhall Novas waiting at the gates for girlfriends who were in Year 10. The feeling of unimaginable scale and an old order colliding with a coldly corporate future carried over into what we might call the school's dining offering.

The contrast between the Gallions Mount dinner hall and the canteen at BS could hardly have been more stark. Where that primary school dining space was all homely amateurishness and the repurposed gleam of an assembly hall, at secondary school the general vibe was of a vast, mechanised processing facility for a trudging, endless wave of hungry children. Based in an older, single-storey building on the senior site of the school, it was a clamorous indoor arena with dwarfing stacks of damp trays, roughly split into a long procession of both self-serve and manned (or, generally, womanned) food stations, plus a dining area of neatly ordered long tables.

Food-wise, if the sprinkle cakes, custards and lumpy mash of primary school felt like terrestrial TV, then this was the equivalent of full-package Sky. Neon-orange chicken curry and mounded hillsides of white rice. Formed 'rib' cutlets of pork complete with drawn-on grill marks, plus individually wrapped hamburgers where the meat patty was, for reasons unknown, a grey, wet paste. A largely ignored salad bar and a station where you could grab thick, fridge-hardened triangles of chocolate Rice Krispie cake or white polystyrene cups filled with thin, bubbled milkshakes. It was autumn 1995 and the faint wholesomeness and guiding nutritional hand of primary school had disappeared. Here was a free market of catering contracts, illusory individuality and empowerment through dining choices that, away from the strictures of home, could be as baroquely unhealthy as you wanted them to be. None of it was especially good but there was so much to choose from.

Having said all that, my first significant memory of that BS canteen didn't really have anything to do with food. Though there must have been terror accompanying my move to this biggest of big schools, my sense of it is that from the moment I first walked through the gates, fresh from a morning prayer session led by Mum and a photo shoot in my cavernous blazer and stiff shoes, I felt content and happy. I marvelled at the bomber-jacketed mass of unruly, moving bodies and lavishly gelled fringes, our charismatic, young and bracingly sarcastic class tutor, the anarchic games of football played with a scraggy tennis ball. I had already met a boy called Mark – a tall, olive-skinned kid who lived near me – and my recall for pop culture and knack for mimicry had given me a confidence that begat a group of fast friends. I still remember the precise feeling of doing a campy, hand-waving impression of Jarvis Cocker to a laughing audience of mates and having, for perhaps the first time, the realisation that my private, living-room capering may have a public currency.

The thing that disrupted this initial wave of happiness was the reality of the school's coalescing male hierarchies. This was a time and a place where there was a particular onus on 'hardness' and family reputation; on playground scuffles, a byzantine whisper network of wilfully exaggerated third-hand insults, and the pervading feeling that the most character-staining thing you could do as a boy was refuse an offer to fight.

I should note, also, that Bexleyheath in the 1990s was a place of strange contrasts. Ostensibly a cosy, suburbanite nowheresville of shopping precincts, chain pubs and the newly prosperous diasporic white working class, the encircling presence of other groups – striving ethnic minorities, economically disadvantaged council estate kids, a sprawled Romani community – made for a volatile combination. I felt this volatility, one day during that first term, in a confrontation with a kid who had seemingly picked me out at random. He was, I later learned, from a traveller family of such terrifying local renown that, like Beetlejuice or the Candyman, his was a name best not said out loud. Even now, I'm hesitant to even hint at it. Not so much out of a cautious sense of legal propriety as the very real feeling that some middle-aged former neighbourhood hard case might suddenly appear, put me in a headlock and demand my dinner money.

Anyway, my memory of it is that the member of this mythical clan – who was about twice the stature of us other Year 7 pipsqueaks and had stiffly gelled spiked hair that only accentuated his size – had cornered me in the playground one day and commenced accusing me of some apparent insult or just a funny look. As I gibbered a nervous response, he whipped a jutting, open-palmed blow, like something from a Bruce Lee film, towards my temple and knocked me on to my heels. 'Yeah? Yeah?' he said, goading, 'you think you're hard, boy?' Things didn't develop much beyond that; either the bell or the presence of a teacher caused a quick dispersal of nearby kids and there was the impression that I'd fled by proxy. Decades later, I can still feel the particular shape and texture of the thudding headache that was my companion for the rest of the day's lessons.

Now, I am decidedly more lover than fighter. I think of myself as someone with a hyper-measuredness and borderline cowardly aversion to conflict and confrontation – a need, really, to always maintain the moral high ground – that is its own issue. A childhood largely free of grappling with siblings is another symptom of those long stretches of youthful solitude. However, for a reason I can't fully explain, the throbbing sense of injustice was something I couldn't shake. I found myself craving the sort of vengeance that I was generally too much of a scaredy-cat to even imagine. And so, a few days later, I was rising up from my lunchtime tray of chips, striding over to my spiky-haired tormentor and then, somehow, ending up in an odd clinch where we both gripped each other's blazer lapels, sent cups and cutlery flying from the long tables, and heard the excited shrieks of our bloodthirsty peers.

That this scuffle barely qualified as a fight and was over as quickly as it began (one of the teachers in the canteen came over to break it up and warn us both about future conduct) did not diminish its legend. Afterwards, I'd have strangers approach me in the playground to ask if it was really true that I'd engaged one of the hardest kids in our year in a prolonged bar-room brawl that was all flung fists, trays cracked over heads and flailing bodies? Not fighting especially well on two separate occasions was beginning to reorient people's perception of me. And nowhere was this more true than in the mind of the aggressor that had set all this in motion.

After the incident in the canteen, he approached me again in the playground. I think I probably flinched in anticipation of a more decisively wounding and painful round three, or the threat of some reprisal off school grounds involving one of his legendarily violent relatives. In fact, what he wanted to do was give me grudging respect for the fact I hadn't totally capitulated. For the fact that I had passed some test of character that he hadn't even set all that consciously. 'To be fair,' he said, with a nod of respect and newfound kinship, 'you're not as much of a pussy as most people here.'

If apparent fighting ability was one way to establish and define identity at BS, then food was very much another. School dinners in the 1990s delineated class and social status in a manner that was always obvious without ever being openly discussed. Today, free school meals are a useful demographic indicator and a means to talk more generally about childhood poverty and economic disadvantage. Back then, at my secondary school, there was just an innately understood hierarchy that put those on school dinners – denoted by thin, matte-silver tokens that were either provided via government assistance or paid for by parents – at the bottom and then, at the top, the pampered nobility enjoying the ambrosial, high-status delights of a packed lunch at the fag end of the Major government.

I am being overly simplistic here. I'm sure plenty of children brought in prepared lunches that consisted of, at best, rudimentary, foil-bundled sandwiches, reconstituted leftovers and soft, overripe pieces of fruit. It should also be noted that one of the reasons packed lunches proliferated from the 1980s is that, thanks to inflationary pressures, they were suddenly a cheaper option than school dinners. Regardless of this, even as someone who mostly didn't mind the junky eccentricities of the food provision at BS, kids who had packed lunch just seemed to have ascended to some shining social pinnacle.

This, remember, was an age of corporate hyper-material-ism and largely unregulated food advertising. Generationally, we were all in the grip of conglomerates flogging masterfully marketed lunchbox products – packets of Peperamis and Cheesestrings; pale, foil-wrapped triangles of Laughing Cow cheese; subdivided plastic trays of Dairylea Lunchables, primed with slimy pink counters of formed ham – that often looked more like the toys in a toddler's play kitchen than anything resembling useful sustenance. The anarchic, earworm theme tunes, tag lines and jingles for Clubs and Tango and Trio biscuits were new anthems for doomed youth, imprinted on to our collective consciousness. In fact, as a Nigerian kid, the faintly racist idea that a Nestlé-owned, tropi-cal fruit juice drink called Um Bongo was especially loved by Congolese people was about as close as we got to anything like positive mainstream representation of African culture.

It all feels quite quaint and naff, looking back from the vantage point of an era of consumption and materialism supercharged by social media. But in what felt like an espe-cially brand-obsessed era, in a time when a pair of Kickers shoes or an official Alpha Industries MA-2 bomber jacket conferred unimaginable status and sexiness on the wearer, the flex of a packed lunch thickly stocked with recognisable brands was a legitimate one. And, of course, the perceived privilege of being among those who toted lunchboxes to school went beyond what they were actually eating. As with the divide between kids who made their own way to school – often getting more than one unreliable bus from less salubrious neighbouring towns – versus those who were chauffeured there in the family Mondeo, it was really a matter of parental availability and labour.

My mother had a fanatical dedication to hot, belly-filling food and what felt like a tireless capacity to sate our culinary appetites. Now and again, if we left at the same time in the morning, she would press a warm, foil-wrapped egg and bacon sandwich into my palm. This revering of 'proper food' almost certainly contributed to her feeling that school dinners would be the best option for me. Yet the idea that, amid the kinetic whirl of our lives, she'd have either the time or the inclination to carefully concoct a packed lunch for me every morning seems laughably far-fetched. A thoughtfully curated packed lunch always seemed like an expression of loving, parental supplication, casual wealth, and the nuclear domesticity of families with 2.4 children, a present father, and a homemaker mum. To covet a friend's lunchbox – the Rolo yoghurt, the neatly sliced ham sandwich on grain-flecked Mighty White, hell, even the little pot of Dole pineapple pieces in syrup – was, I now realise, to slightly covet the settled 'normality' and inconspicuousness of their lives. That I never once had packed lunch spoke to the stubborn fixedness of my identity and family situation. So all I could do was carry on lusting after the entombed glamour of those sandwiches, yoghurts and miniature biscuit bars.

Some took this covetousness to extreme lengths. Another slight blot on those happy first months at BS was the presence of Sabrina: a bullying Jamaican-heritage girl who ruled the classroom with an iron fist and a lacerating wit. I was a constant target – my apparently conspicuous Nigerianness and intolerably large 'African head' having marked me out for a regular torrent of abuse – but I was not the only one. And one of the other people in my class, a boy called Sean, had to deal with the persistent torment of Sabrina taking a particular liking to the packed lunch that he brought in. For almost every day throughout at least that first year at BS, Sabrina would demand that Sean hand over his lunchbox, on punishment of violence if he didn't and if he told anybody, so that she could have her pick of the sandwiches and snacks that his mum had prepared for him. In my memory of it, just to underline that this was about power as much as the taking of possessions, Sabrina would even offer up leering reviews and commentary on what she liked or didn't like about that day's particular purloined bap or multi-pack bag of Mini Cheddars.

Even writing it down now, I'm still taken aback by the breathtaking malevolence of it. It's an inexcusable, almost comically over-the-top piece of bullying. Sean, who became a close friend in later life, still vibrates with disbelieving rage when he talks about it. But in recent years, I have come to think there is something especially sad about the bald details of the whole affair. One eleven-year-old stealing another's food could just be a remorseless act of childish cruelty. It could also, given the daily repetition of it, be desperate hunger dressed up as blustering aggression. Sabrina was taking Sean's packed lunch, but she also seemed to be trying to take some of the parental thoughtfulness and care that he had and she plainly didn't.

Stealing sandwiches was extreme but, really, it was just one of the ways that food defined character and demarcated tribes at BS. Packed lunch kids would trade chocolate bars and throw the healthy pieces of fruit their mothers had given them straight into the bin; some sandwiches would be devoured during morning break long before lunch; there was, I now remember, a thriving black market for free school meals dinner tokens sold by kids who either pocketed the coins or shovelled them into the vending machines that dotted the school's senior site. Without the nudging influence of Gallions Mount's dinner ladies, I could encounter something that particularly spiked my fussiness – springy button mushrooms, lurking in a bolognese like discarded pencil erasers; the stray loop of black olive that rendered a final bite of crap margherita inedible – and simply chuck it. We had slipped the field of parental influence and been entrusted to make our own nutritional decisions. That we consistently made quite terrible ones should probably not be such a surprise.

This period was, on reflection, especially damaging for me. Innate pickiness, the largely unchecked freedom of secondary school and my tendency to emulate whatever shiny new behaviour I was presented with was a combination that wrought functional chaos. Though I'd been happy enough with the unchanging rhythms of the canteen, with a shuffled permanent playlist of rib cutlets, paste burgers and pallid-battered Friday fish, I sensed things begin to shift around our mid-teens. Where previously, as whelpish Year 7s, most of us on school dinners embraced the novelty of the canteen with excitement, now there seemed to be a collective affected disdain for anything that qualified as a vaguely nutritious or balanced meal. Cans of fizzy soft drink, which would thunk satisfyingly out of the belly of an ancient, Pepsi-branded vending machine, would be slurped out of the tiniest opening in the can. Grubby fingers were permanently coated in Wotsit particulate, beef flavoured Monster Munch dust or the wincing remnants of Brannigans thick-cut beef and mustard crisps. Roustabout lads with fat, stubby ties were always either chewing away at a sickly scented wad of Hubba Bubba bubble gum or spitting it out so they could theatrically volley it into a bush. (I once attempted this

Fonz-level move, completely missed my kick, and was swiftly given detention for littering by a passing PE teacher.) By the time we got to sixth form, the tow-rope of bakery scent from the Asda next door would reel us in for mid-morning bags of warm, sugar-heaped jam doughnuts. It's hard to fully do justice to the vast quantities of processed garbage that were either close at hand or being stealthily hamster-pouched into our mouths during lessons.

I gleefully went along with pretty much all of this. What's more, even worse was to come. I remember a particular preposterous period around fourteen where, inspired by a friend, my entire lunch would consist of two chocolate Rice Krispie triangles alongside a strawberry or chocolate milk-shake for dipping purposes. That would literally be it. No embellishment in the form of a starter course of chips or even the addition of a pappy 32 per cent pork hot dog for some much-needed protein. It was, I think, a form of self-punishing recklessness and rebellion. To those justifiably wondering why I wasn't constantly ravenous during this portion of my schooldays, the answer is that, of course, I absolutely was.

My response to that hunger would be to turn my journey home into a sort of Dionysian, additive-laden food crawl. Getting back home – first in Abbey Wood, and later, deeper into Kent in a house near the Dartford Tunnel's southern entry – would be at least one thirty-minute bus ride and a fifteen-minute walk, or a ninety-minute meander on foot.

Occasionally, I'd just do the long walk and use the money my mum would give me (a combined pot for both bus fare and the occasional after-school snack from the corner shop) to max out on food. That could mean shuffling into the fish bar near Bexleyheath bus garage for a golden heaping of vinegar-doused chips and an indecent, priapic length of saveloy. It could mean chewy, Barbie-pink strawberry bon-bons in a rustling paper bag. It could just mean an idle browse in a newsagents – complete with a surreptitious peek at the glamorous, titillating fantasy world in magazines like *The Face* and *Sky* – before a fractious exchange with a reflex-ively suspicious shopkeeper, and the capture of a king-size Yorkie.

I was not unique in adopting an after-school diet almost entirely shaped by the corporate whims of Mars, Rowntree, Cadbury and Trebor. Those hours on the premises at BS were really just the hors d'oeuvre for a looser but no less important session of off-site learning among kids from other schools; a third-space blur of buses, takeaways and shopping-centre interiors that were soundtracked by the hungry guzzling of pickled onion Space Raiders and Yazoo milk-shakes. Yet I think there was something about the mecha-nised consistency of these snacks that I was particularly attached to – reliant on, even. A burger from an unfamiliar place might occasion the need to slide a damp, unwanted slice of tomato out of the bun. Fruit's innate instability and decay – the browning apple core in a teacher's hand, say

– still felt unutterably frightening and disgusting. But the enticing, lipped seam on an unwrapped Mars bar was always there; the flashing black and orange of a packet of Nik Naks Nice 'N' Spicy promised a pacifying rush you could bet your life on. Fear of new experiences, the ostracisation I had felt on that Cubs camping trip, and the itinerant instability of the Nigerian home had turned monotony into the most precious of security blankets.

I look back at this period, from the vantage point of an era dominated by rightly urgent conversations about childhood obesity, with a kind of awed horror. It is a little like watching back footage of my younger self hopscotching blindfolded through a clogged minefield. However, if there was a single thing that saved me from myself, and my apparent desire to alter my biochemistry to the point that Tizer was my official blood type, then it was the quality and range of the food I would be eating at home. And, more specifically, the fact that my mum would, either by accident or design, find some democratic sweet spot between the hearty meals she saw as especially culturally important and the ever-shrinking list of things that my fussy little tastebuds would countenance.

Family meals in those days are so vivid I can almost still feel the nose-tickle of their scent. On a weeknight, hours after I had finished my sugary fetch quest home from Bexleyheath and probably also put away a half packet of bourbon biscuits in front of *The Simpsons*, my brothers and

I would hear the click of Mum's key in the door, her court shoes being kicked off. That would be my cue. As she trudged in from a long day of work at the Commonwealth, it would be the expectation that, once I'd said hello, I was to retrieve her slippers and supplicantly pop them by her feet. Some people change into elasticated loungewear and reach for the remote when they get in from work; others pour a big, glugging measure of Chablis into a wine glass and run a bath. My memory of almost every evening during this time is of this little, stoic woman stepping into those slippers and heading straight to the kitchen to make us all dinner without breaking stride. It was an almost superhuman act of ritual-ised generosity and sacrifice; Mum's particular emotional toughness and mania for feeding amplified by the cultural context she grew up in. I like to think that those of us that benefited – me, my brothers, the endless procession of cous-ins and relatives that would pass through our house – at the very least appreciated it at the time.

And so what would Mum cook for us, in this doubtless weary state, as 9 p.m. approached? It was not, as would have been completely understandable, something mostly oriented around a jar of Dolmio. On weeknights, this would mean chicken thighs and drumsticks, all blistered, oven-blackened char and barrelling Maggi cube marinade; supermarket burgers alongside a tangled, zhuzhing wreath of onions and split lengths of potato sizzled in the residual beef fat; a tangy tomato and red pepper stew (the ubiquitous, Nigerian equivalent of a mother sauce), either from the weekend or her extensive freezer archives, spooned over fluffy white rice. At weekends there would be stewed beans, maybe a baked horseshoe of bone-in trout with peppers, and an ever-present accompaniment of Green Giant tinned sweetcorn: the plant kingdom equivalent of confectionary that was about the only vegetable I would tolerate. My picture of this time is of the warmth of both the immersion and the electric heater – complete with its backlit frieze of ersatz glowing coals – and a drifting plume of fried plantain; Mum yelling out some Yoruba exhortation to come and grab our plates while a Gladiator on television prodded some hapless, leotarded contestant with a giant cotton bud.

It was a comforting space but also an idiosyncratic, palpably African one. The fact that I ate so differently when I was at home enforced the growing sense of a split personality and bifurcated identity. At school and out in the world, I was Jimi: a vaguely academic but reliably motormouthed, cosmopolitan tyro, all sharp skin-fade and scuffed Reebok Classics, who spoke in the same sweary, Roma-inflected Estuary dialect as all his mostly white friends. At home, meanwhile, I was JJ. The wisecracking, eye-rolly baby of the family who, nonetheless, was still very much a Nice African Boy who never swore, fetched slippers, got drinks for visiting elders and knew, amid the hail of spoken Yoruba, drifting King Sunny Adé CDs on the stereo and brimming bowls of shelled monkey nuts, that the expectation was that I be polite, obedient and respectful.

All children code-switch, and that is especially true of second-generation immigrant children. But to cross the threshold into the Famurewa house was to enter a world within a world; an annexed Nigerian protectorate where different behavioural and culinary rules applied. Even the name that I had chosen to adopt recently – 'Jimi' being a shortened form of my birth name, Olufolajimi, and a conscious shift from 'Roger', the fig-leaf of a given English name that I had used at primary school – felt like an attempt to better reconcile these two selves; to gather up the disparate threads of my identity. To further complicate things, my pickiness around food was probably less of an issue at home. Mum and the rest of my family knew that someone peeling an orange would get me grimacing and shifting awkwardly in my seat; they knew that I would avoid springy, fragrant portions of the steamed bean cake, *moin-moin*, or side salads of shredded lettuce and faintly desiccated grated carrot. It was a safe environment where my prissy culinary foibles were not just tolerated but hardly noticed. Yes, there may occasionally be a visiting relative who was taken aback by, say, my visible revulsion when asked if I wanted some sliced banana alongside my rice (that this union is not all that different from the jollof and fried plantain combination that I adored is just one of the many illogical mysteries of my particular form of pickiness). But the relaxed, pronouncedly Nigerian atmosphere of home was, for the most part, a sanctuary of understanding. A place where I could drop part of the performance, and slightly unclench, safe in the knowledge that some of the baffling culinary realities of the outside world – the pungent, yeasty whiff of a classmate's cheese and Marmite sandwiches, say – would never intrude.

Still, to say that I appreciated this atmosphere at the time would be to put too much of a retroactive gloss on it. The default setting of every home we had was a happy chaos that seeped into the aesthetic. Though Sydney Road and, later, the house in Crayford glowed with textured cosiness, they both always seemed to teem with a physicalised non sequitur of unrelated objects. There were boxes and files and suitcases from recent trips to Lagos that hadn't yet been taken upstairs; abandoned desktop computers, Nigerian folk trinkets, and glass-fronted display cases stuffed with photos, knick-knacks and school certificates. Our navy, leather-effect three-piece suite clogged the front room and was dominated by a sofa that sagged at one end, having been broken not long after it was purchased (this may or may not have been one of my WWF elbow-drops). There never seemed to be enough rooms to fully accommodate the constant procession of siblings and relatives and outright strangers, and I remember a particularly strange period when the kitchen – a zone of happy lawlessness dominated by Mum's hood-less gas cooker, her ever-replenished mug of sugary Kenco, and a little radio tuned to Capital FM – was ornamented by two microwaves, one working, one not, stacked one on top of the other.

I'd like to believe that I wasn't embarrassed by the deranged reality of all this. Yet it is perhaps telling that I spent more time at the houses of friends – generally, tranquil, ordered and uncluttered spaces that smelled of liberally applied Shake n' Vac and had a spotless living room that nobody was actually supposed to go in – rather than at mine. The unruly noise, heat and definably Nigerian smells of our home were just another thing that affirmed the fact I was fundamentally different to my none-more-Bexleyheath pals; another unavoidable barrier to the frictionless assimilation that I was still dumbly pursuing.

That said, even at this adolescent phase of shaky self-confidence, I was still able to recognise that the specific assemblage and attitude of our home may carry some positives. Midway through my teens, I remember going round to have lunch with a friend I'll call Adam. His family's house was the quintessential mock-Tudor palace: a double-drive-wayed four-bed with an air of precise spotlessness, a huge, sitcom-style kitchen flooded with sunlight, and a second front room with soft furnishings that sparkled. The meal was cold cuts of an indeterminate grey, roasted meat – among the first times I'd been presented with meat that was deliberately served cold – and scantly seasoned, almost lethally underdone potatoes. The atmosphere at the dinner table was clenched and formal, the ring and scrape of cutlery and an occasional cough the only thing punctuating the funereal silence. I used every ounce of resolve to nibble a bit of the food and thought of the pleasure-forward riot of conversations, colour, thrumming spice and jostling bodies that characterised our dinners at home; the ease and comfort of it. And for maybe the first time, I recognised the gift of the dining environment I had grown up with. We may have wanted for outward grandeur. But when it came to joy, generosity and warmth, our lives were absurdly privileged and vigorously seasoned.

For this, I was grateful to the older generation. It was Mum and my elders who ruled and maintained the Little Lagos of our home. They were the ones with the knowledge and wherewithal to cultivate links to our ancient culture through language, environment and food. Though I had an unchained freedom and agency when I was retrieving a bag of Spicy Tomato Wheat Crunchies from the maw of a vending machine or sliding change on to the counter for a Twirl, I was reliant on the older generation for the more foundational pillars of my diet. Whenever one of us was sick and delicate of stomach and appetite, Mum would inevitably give us *garri*: a faintly saline, tolerably bland, miracle elixir of fermented cassava flour and water, sweetened with a little sugar or maybe some roasted peanuts. It was a dish among many that was ostensibly simple but spoke to Mum's gastronomic sorcery and our feckless reliance on it. If channelling the tastes and

energy of our home felt like a sort of magic that was inacces-
sible to me, I was soon to realise part of the reason why.

Yoruba lives begin with sweetness. Exactly seven days after a
child's birth, at the family celebration known as a Naming
Ceremony, the baby is held up and given little symbolic
tastes of foods they are not technically meant to consume for
months. There will be a blotted pinkie of salt, to signify a
well-flavoured existence, a dab of palm oil to embody good
health, and some form of hot pepper, which usually elicits a
squalling cry and is administered to help engender a life full
of excitement. And then, often near the end, this newest
member of the wider family and community will be soothed
with a spoonful of honey; a sugary totem to better manifest
hopes for a charmed, long life filled with joy and pleasure.

In 1996, at the age of twelve, I looked on from the corner
of a flat in Streatham, south London, as my newborn cousin's formal entry into the world was marked by this meaningful tasting menu. This was the first child of my Uncle Jibola:
an urbane, hugely likeable gentle giant who also happened
to be second youngest of the nine siblings on my mother's
side and had, alongside his wife, Yemisi, yearned to start a
family for some thirteen years. These combined facts meant
that, even in the context of the Nigerian tendency to treat all
social occasions like a building occupancy record attempt, it
was a standing room only affair of bodies sprawled on floors
or perched on sofa arms. I remember looking on, through

the doorway, as a gathered prayer circle of grown-ups formally gave the baby his names – mainly Demilade, though, in truly extra Yoruba style, there were at least a dozen other, unofficial names offered – and my mum praised the Lord and proffered the honey like a sacrament. Demilade wriggled as Mum's pleas to God were punctuated by amens (always pronounced, by Nigerian congregants, as a see-sawing mutter that sounds more like '*ah-mee*').

If this ritual hinted at food's importance to our culture, if it brightly illuminated its status as a way that we marked significant moments and symbolically expressed the inexpressible, then it was of a piece with the broader context of the day. I remember Demilade's Naming Ceremony because it was a significant date and waymarker for our family. But I also remember it because it was one of the more unforgettable examples of the events that punctuated our lives in London and seemed like a crucial part of how I came to understand and appreciate Nigerian food, traditions and cultural duality. This, despite the domestic setting, was an especially vivid example of the phenomenon known as a Nigerian Hall Party. And there really isn't anything like one in full flow.

After those ceremonial prayers had been said and Demilade had been given his many, many names, things took a familiarly ragged shape. The crowd in the living room dispersed and an event that had begun with a morning of separate arrivals – relatives, friends and vaguely acquainted church hangers-on, hefting cases of stout and scenting the possibility of a free meal – would reorganise itself again. My vision of the rest of the afternoon is of something a little like a low-budget, Yoruba version of the Copacabana scene in *Goodfellas*. Blaring music competed with a swarm of voices and younger cousins, faces vigorously moisturised to a mirrored, cocoa butter sheen, whooping and shrieking as they bumped down the stairs on their backsides. Just above them, an impatient, jittery queue waited to use the single toilet. A side room had been requisitioned by the men: uncles in open-toed leather sandals and unbuttoned shirts who, when they weren't sending passing children off to get them something from the kitchen, were having deafening, cross-talk-heavy conversations about the dark joke of Nigerian governance or some percolating, Lagos-based business idea that could yield an instant fortune.

Follow your nose to the high nimbus of sizzled palm oil in the galley kitchen, beyond a hallway lined with plastic cool boxes of overflow dishes, and you would find perhaps half a dozen women squeezed into a space hardly bigger than the span of a bus shelter. Spearheaded by my mum, prowling around like the self-appointed chef-patron, it was a blur of aproned church attire, merciless teasing and enough well-drilled cooking ability to shame the toqued brigade at a multi-starred temple to French gastronomy. The dishes and the work of creating them had a processional discipline. A blipping, carmine stew was tended by one aunty; another was slicing plantain, with just a dextrously angled knife and a calloused palm standing in for a chopping board; one younger female cousin was washing up (and perhaps lightly cursing the accident of birth that had landed them in a service-obsessed Nigerian family) before the rising steam of the sink; an especially formidable matriarch was responsible for policing the highly snafflable, burnished pieces of tender stewing beef that tiptoeing uncles and children alike would try to pilfer without being detected.

Over the course of the day, every bite in the expansive celebratory canon – the steamed leaf-parcels of gently spiced black-eyed bean slurry known as *moin-moin*; the sugar-rolled, *puff-puff* drop doughnuts that would be skilfully plopped into a roiling pot of Crisp 'N Dry; the special designation of jollof, known as party rice, that had a pronounced, crackled smokiness to conjure the musk of ancestral village feasts cooked over glowing pyres – would get its moment in the sun and on our laden paper plates. My memory of the food at Demilade's Naming Ceremony, as at almost every Nigerian party I have been to, was of the cooking never really having a natural end-point.

This was a category of West African diaspora celebration where food was the gravitational focal point of the event. Satisfaction drawn from its preparation almost existed independent of that taken from its actual consumption; the whole thing, a time-honoured ouroboros of infinite toil scrambling to meet infinite need and desire. The dishes, both in terms of preparation and ease of enjoyment, ran the full difficulty spectrum of the culture's culinary canon. You'd be forgiven for assuming that this would be a nightmare for my fussiness. That the presence of *amala*, infernal, green-pepper-laden *ayamase* stew, and other expressions of Yoruba cooking at its most full throttle and uncompromising would have induced some anxiety. Yet the chaotic, judgement-free abundance of a true hall party feast – a spread with the same choose-your-own-adventure spirit as a hotel buffet – provided the perfect cover. Chicken legs and sugar-dusted *puff-puff*; three consecutive servings of fried rice; a muddy tricolour of stews spilling into a pale clump of coleslaw. The spread was a rejection of judgement, an embrace of dining individuality, and another, pandering expression of the specific ways that Nigerian culinary culture could inadvertently enable pickiness.

On that day in 1996, as all this tireless labour was occurring in the kitchen on our collective behalf, my most pronounced memories are of larking around out front with my brother, Ray, and my closest cousin, Tenne. We clambered on to walls, did languid keepy-uppies with balloons ordered to herald Demilade's birth, posed for photos with big, liberated grins on our faces and, most unforgettably, invented Guinola: a lavishly foamed cocktail comprising Coca-Cola and a slopped measure of African Export Guinness.

Can you spot what's especially glaring about the scenes I've just described? What might have turned it into a core memory when it came to how I perceived Nigerian culture, food, and my relationship to both? Yes, there was the fact that the grown-ups in my life had a decidedly lax attitude to underage drinking, as long as the alcohol involved was Guinness (the Nigerian belief that stout is basically a kind of godly, vitamin-rich medicine is proven by the fact my paternal grandmother would give me little consoling nips of it when I was still in nappies). However, more than that, this was the first time that I truly noticed and contemplated an essential truth about the cooking and serving of traditional Yoruba food: it was subject to a wild, pointedly patriarchal gender imbalance.

At every party and in every domestic space, there was a strictly observed divide. The oldest and most respected guests would be granted the best available armchairs. Fathers, uncles and men of working age would congregate in some prized spot near a television, or disappear to a vacant box room, two-day-old *Daily Mail* clamped under an arm, to read and, perhaps, sleep off a formidable portion of pounded yam and *egusi*. We boys and young men would be either sullenly looking around as the grown-ups spoke, or tearing about outside with bottles of Supermalt gripped in our palms.

Meanwhile, all the women, aunties and female relatives old enough to assist would be expected to make their way, at least momentarily, to the kitchen to start chopping and stirring, or snap on some Marigolds to help with the washing-up.

This is not to say that my brothers, male cousins and I were completely indolent – there was a whole range of front-of-house duties, including ferrying drinks to our elders and entertaining toddler-age relatives, that we were coached to perform without complaint. But we were all implanted with the sense, from an early age, that the kitchen wasn't really a place for us. A traditional indoctrination of sorts was taking place and the gossipy sorority of those little spaces might as well have been protected by a force field. I even remember, at a later family party, a more traditional aunty insisting that, rather than fixing my own plate of food, I was served by Kemi, a slightly older female cousin. I don't think the transfer of a portion of party rice and chicken has ever been freighted with quite so much sheepish bafflement (me) and justified rage and simmering resentment (her).

All of this was, of course, the rank sexism of the era, super-charged by a culture that put a particular emphasis on tradition and the man's sanctified role as provider and high-status alpha. It was the strict upholding of a labour gap between the sexes that was both wholly unfair and, it always seemed, ran contrary to the glaring fact that our family was a matriarchy ruled and sustained by smart, strong-willed women. But it was a status quo that imprisoned all parties. A tussle of power and control. Girls with no real interest in cooking or serving were expected to fall in line; men who, for all manner of reasons, could have done with learning to make their own damn stew were kept at a deliberate remove. This food, so important to our culture and sense of self, was a power that our mothers, grandmothers, aunties and elder female cousins were the sole custodians of.

In one very simple sense, this form of cultural programming had a lasting impact on mine and my brothers' sense of privilege. We were, as Mum's slippered walk from the front door straight into the kitchen proved, pampered little princelings. Years later, my wife, Madeleine, would look on with disbelieving horror as she watched me morph, within seconds of crossing the threshold in the family home, from a capable, industrious father of two into a slumped, lordly layabout, happy to grunt out requests from the sofa while Mum scurried over with plates of food and drinks. This was just another way that the codes and traditions within a Nigerian household could transmogrify the diaspora kid who entered it.

However, beyond the shameful laziness that these defined gender roles helped inculcate, they also shaped my relationship to Nigerian food. I should note that we young boys were not totally useless when it came to feeding ourselves. This, after all, was the era when my mum's generous spirit and the sheer quantity of Lagos-based relatives and family friends who had children attending British boarding schools turned Sydney Road into an oversubscribed flophouse, groaning with the bodies of unfamiliar cousins. Through a strange genetic quirk, almost all these temporary house guests – who could pitch up for days or even months at a time – were other boys. And duly, because of our limited collective cooking ability, summer holidays and weekends during this period could feel like a chaotic, testosterone-scented social experiment exploring junk food's long-term effect on the adolescent body. Amid the fights, noxious farts, and complex rota system detailing who was next on the N64, there would be mounded, mid-afternoon serving bowls of Crunchy Nut Cornflakes, steaming plastic flagons of chicken and mushroom King Pot Noodles, and hillocks of unnaturally yellow vanilla ice cream heaped with spoonfuls of Ovaltine. That these days felt forever perched on the edge of a *Lord of the Flies*-level moment of violent collapse did not diminish the pure anarchic thrill of them.

Which is all to say that, as young boys, we did have some agency and independence. Having sprung from diaspora environments where adultification was a reality, there was an expectation that we would be self-sufficient, durable and streetwise. Yet when it came to proper sustenance, when it came to the vitally important, meticulously spiced starches that kept us healthy, happy and connected to the bigger, anchoring story of the culture we came from, we were useless. Completely reliant on our elders doing the work for us.

It was a two-way street. The importance placed on dishes being made a certain way and to a certain standard, the secret, recipe-less, oral-cooking traditions that were passed down and perfected through practice, represented a power that our female elders did not necessarily want to relinquish.

To ask my mum for a stew or jollof rice recipe is to get what can feel like a deliberately bewildering set of lengthy, arcane instructions attuned to her particular skills, unteachable instincts and 10,000 hours of experience at the stove. But, again, it was another example of how fraught it can be to rely on elders and family as the sole source of connection to heritage. As I shuffled between worlds and personas – trying very hard to be British at school while dutifully attempting to be Nigerian at home – this only deepened the feeling of a scrambled identity. To be consciously separate from the labour of food production was, in lots of ways, to be let off the hook. To both become complacent – assuming that understanding the intricacies and significance of the cuisine and culture is merely the work of grown-ups or some put-upon future wife – and slip the moorings of a vital part of your wider story. Demilade's Naming Ceremony was a reso-nant, happy waymarker; a day that showed the strength, significance and continued relevance of communal Yoruba culture in our diffuse, metropolitan lives. It had important lessons to teach me. But, as befits a stout-addled twelve-year-old on his own haphazard path of self-discovery, I wasn't yet ready to learn them.

4

Say It with Pancake Mix

Heathrow in the 1990s crackled with life, blinding light and a variety of hustling tribes. There were families wheeling baggage trolleys past the Rothmans waft of the smoking area and glamorously attired Virgin flight crews swaggering out across the polished floor; business travellers sneaked a complimentary, last-minute spritz of duty-free Kouros while Lagos-bound matriarchs heaved bulging cases on to bag drop scales, muttering desperate prayers to the gods of mysteriously sanctioned oversized luggage. Ceiling fans whirred and red-waistcoated porters loitered by the check-in desk. There were, of course, errant fathers hurriedly grabbing Toblerone and toy aeroplanes.

However, one of the most intriguing groups in this morass of bodies were the Unaccompanied Minors. Both a symptom of internationally dispersed family units and a reflection of an era of extreme parental trustfulness, these were the junior air passengers – generally aged five to sixteen – who were lavished with attention and preferential treatment because they happened to be travelling without an adult guardian or caregiver. To be alive to their presence was to be endlessly fascinated. They were the backpacked ladies and lordlings being driven to the departure gate on beeping electric wagons; the Game Boy-clutching adolescents strung with identifying lanyards, furnished with laden activity packs, and taken up to meet the captain. Occasionally, they may even be bumped up to first class. To be a UM was to be a continent-hopping Paddington Bear of the sky; both a pitied symbol of a very modern temporary abandonment and a piece of precious human cargo who had attained a covetable level of privilege by way of a technicality.

In the high summer of 1993, at the age of nine, I stepped on to a Miami-bound plane with my two older brothers and crossed over into this strange, sanctified firmament. Specific recollections of that exact flight have been fogged by time. But what I do remember is fidgety excitement amid the strange hums and hisses of a plane being readied for take-off; the coddling attention of perfumed American Airlines hostesses; a PJ & Duncan tape loaded into an off-brand Walkman with a rudimentary LCD game built into its hot-pink fascia; an endless flowing river of Canada Dry ginger ale poured over ice as we pushed on through wisps of clouds, borne by something that felt as much like magic as aeronautical ingenuity. The three of us were off to spend the entire summer in the US: a city-hopping six weeks of visiting relatives that would culminate in the final flourish of our paternal uncle's wedding in a Detroit suburb. It was, at nine years old, the first time in living memory that I had been on a plane, travelled to America, or gone on anything that could be plausibly described as a holiday. It was also, significantly, the first of a series of subsequent adolescent trips across the Atlantic – practically every summer from the age of twelve to sixteen – that would come to have a lasting, transformative impact on my appetite and nascent sense of self.

The queue-jumping American Airlines 'blue lane' sticker from that trip is still, more than three decades later, neatly affixed to the back of my old Nigerian passport. I can still remember the blue chequerboard of swimming pools viewed from above, the feeling of emerging from Miami International's arrivals terminal into a wobbling gust of Floridian, oven-door heat. Nine hours after we had boarded that plane at Heathrow, we three unaccompanied minors were jointly stepping out into a new country and an uncharted universe of seductive possibility.

To say that I was excited about this trip doesn't do justice to my mental state. From early consciousness in Lagos to childhood in London, America's culture, environment and supersized possibility had been the thing firing my youthful imagination. Michael Jackson's helium squeal and Michael Jordan's protruding tongue; *Saved by the Bell*'s cackling studio audience and the dad rocking Americana of a Wrigley's chewing gum advert. Levi's and *Ghostbusters* and the pixellated red drop-top tearing down a highway in *Out Run* on the Sega Mega Drive. I vividly remember being so entranced by Kris Kross, a manufactured tween hip-hop duo who wore their clothes backwards for reasons that were never fully explained, that I once hobbled awkwardly into the front room at Sydney Road with my jeans on back to front, almost certainly causing my family to wonder whether I was experiencing some form of mild mental collapse. Even allowing for the fact that many British children of this era were under the spell of American entertainment, I was, I think, especially and indiscriminately obsessed.

Throw in the reality that this was a pre-digital age when the cultural radio delay between Britain and America was a lot more pronounced – a time when films, music, fashions and more would proliferate in the US months or even years before they dribbled across the Pond to Britain – and you perhaps have even more of a sense of it. My dominant memories of those first few weeks in Florida, with my mother's younger brother, Uncle Gori, are of a land that was simultaneously familiar and possessed of a hyperreal, super-charged quality. From the climate-controlled chill of Uncle Gori's capacious SUV, my little gaping face would take in a daily bombardment of vast, palm-fringed byways, mini malls clogged with intriguing, faintly recognisable brands (K-Mart, Jiffy Lube, Dairy Queen), movie theatre marquees advertising films that I knew we wouldn't get a sniff of in the UK for months, if at all, and condo apartments with a clean, factory scent and armoire-sized refrigerators that dispensed thundering pellets of ice at the nudge of a trigger.

To go to America at this point of the early to mid 1990s was not just to feel, rightly or wrongly, that you had journeyed to the centre of global monoculture. It was to be puffed up by the sense that you had managed to journey into the actual future. We were there to see relatives, have a good time, and ease the parental load on my mum. We were also, in a more urgent sense, there to trolley-dash through giant stores like Ross and TJ Maxx grabbing the US-only CDs, ostentatiously labelled sportswear and other exotica that would serve as proof of our time-travelling voyage. Access to tangible American culture, and realising I had a rare, credible claim on it, was huge. A crash education that hit my suburbanite, British-Nigerian brain like a reorienting bomb blast.

This was especially true when it came to food. Never mind the repertoire that I thought I already knew, the burgers, pizzas, hot dogs, fries and sundaes that I had experienced ham-handed facsimiles of in the UK. Forget the smuggled grocery store snacks and convenience foods – the crumbled packets of Chips Ahoy! cookies, the bottles of Aunt Jemima syrup in knotted plastic bags, the especially precious, dented boxes of Bisquick instant pancake mix – that sprang from the suitcases of the visiting relatives who would come to see us in south London. By this point, my fussiness around eating and aversion to any of its messy, unpredictable realities was as pronounced as it had ever been. (My mum still grimly remembers my nose-wrinkling, aristocratic disdain whenever she had to take me along to buy stewing beef amid the pungent scrum of Deptford Market.) Ditto my prizing of a nebulous, western-coded idea of what constituted 'normal' or high-status food. In this context, the United States' larder of standardised, corporation-controlled products was like a kind of full-throated siren song; a ready-made intensifier for my existing belief that almost everything I ate should be hyper-satisfying, visually soothing and broadly familiar. However, to experience a prolonged flavour of actual American cuisine in its proper context was to be confronted by how little I actually knew about it.

Here, across the course of that first trip, were heightened, steroidally huge iterations of things I vaguely recognised. Here were heaped breakfast bowls of rainbow-hued Froot Loops cereal; square-edged paving slabs of Little Caesars pizza, emerging from beyond the billowed steam of a lifted cardboard lid; a compacted verge of chilli con carne on the forearm-length hot dog at a diner. But here too, thanks in part to the fact that my Uncle Gori's wife – Aunty Della – was an American, were things I had never previously seen and did not fully understand. Plates of 'grits' that were a sort of claggy, vomitous spill of savoury porridge. Servings of 'biscuits' that, rather than crumbly, McVitie's-branded snacks to be dunked in tea, were warm, buttery scones served beside fried chicken. Kool-Aid, as well as being quite an apt nod to the manner in which I took deep, uncritical gulps of every bit of American culture offered to me, was also a powder-based soft drink, cloyingly sweet and served in iced pitchers.

It was like learning an interrelated but distinct culinary language. While I can now see that I was interacting with complicated gastronomical histories and traditions – most pressingly, the Deep South foodways and cooking techniques that were themselves descended from my own West African roots – it all just registered as life lived at the correct scale, volume and confronting colour vibrancy. Uncle Gori took us for breakfasts at IHOP, or rather, the International House of Pancakes: a grandly named 24-hour chain where, rather than scrawny, lemon-squidged crepes, the pancakes came as a fluffy, Bible-thick stack with the sour twang of buttermilk, a melting pat of pale butter, and maple syrup poured out in glossy, striped ribbons.

Throughout the six weeks of that summer in 1993, via stints in Florida, Missouri and Michigan, we were spoiled and indulged like competition winners; paraded through an interstate smorgasbord of warm, cinnamon-scented mall pretzels, refillable two-pint flagons of root beer, and cinema trips fuelled by rattling boxes of caramel-filled Milk Duds chocolates. Our lives in London were, generally speaking, happy and safe and full. The fact this was an era with an emerging emphasis on kid-centred, family-friendly entertainment, a time of video game arcades and sprawling waterparks, has undoubtedly put an additional rose-tint on my memories. Equally, the fact it was the summer holidays and we were unburdened by the demands of school will have played its part. Nonetheless, everything about what we were experiencing in the US – the condo apartments with shared swimming pools; the abundant stream of TV commercials – was impossibly seductive. In later years, Mum would reveal that she had toyed with choosing North America rather than Northern Europe as the place to settle after leaving Lagos. And so, to spend those weeks gadding about America was to float through a hypothetical life. There is a picture of me, Ray and Folarin at Disney World, early on during that holiday. We are huddled together, decked out in brand-new baseball caps and basketball jerseys, and my mouth, partly occupied with the straw of a gigantic soda, is bent into a blissful smirk. It's almost a parody of commercialised, gaudy western consumption and excess; the sort of thing that might have been used in a recruitment video designed to stoke anti-American senti-ment in insurgent foreign groups. But it illustrates just how willingly, how completely, we embraced this new temporar-ily American life. We felt, through it all, that we had crossed over into the bigger, more prosperous version of existence that we'd always wanted and felt we deserved.

These feelings of Americanised self-fulfilment only acceler-ated when I returned to the country on my own. That initial trip was formative. It was a series of firsts that I experienced alongside my brothers and a period that, barring quite a few seminal moments – the arrival in Florida, those unforgettable meals, riding to the top of the arch in St. Louis, my Uncle Joseph's wedding – I remember more as a bone-deep feeling rather than a specific series of events. Yet, it was when I began going back solo, starting with a trip taken as a twelve-year-old in the July of 1996 (just after Demilade's Naming Ceremony), that the memories attained a particular adhesiveness and significance. These were languid, happily indolent days of drift, self-discovery and a summer that felt like it would never end; an infinite supply of Oreo cookies dipped into a bottom-less glass of milk. Occurring in parallel with my first years in secondary school, it was also another occasion of the rubber of my persistent pickiness meeting the road of a junky, indi-vidualistic food environment. There would be no watchful policing of root beer consumption. No kindly exhortations to eat my broccoli or maybe not put away an entire packet of Twizzlers. The decadent holiday mood combined with a highly literal kid-in-a-candy-store freedom. If my bifurcated eating identity in London – paste burgers, rib cutlets and paper 20p mix-up bags when I wasn't at home; jollof rice, varying forms of fried starch and sugary teas when I was – enabled a life untroubled by the unfamiliar, stigmatised foods that scared me, then this was doubly true across the Pond.

What's more, the absence of my brothers – who were, by this point, older teenagers who didn't necessarily want to spend their entire school holidays visiting theme parks and arcades – meant a degree of extra independence was thrust upon me. With bored isolation as the only alternative, I fell in with my American cousins and the neighbourhood children they hung around with in picture-perfect suburban cul-de-sacs, playing games I only partly understood.

Days were punctuated by the thunk of a basketball hitting the backboard above my Uncle Deji's driveway until long into the evening; there were exploratory tastes of Skippy peanut butter and Smucker's strawberry 'jelly' sandwiches, oddly powdery, pink discs of formed bologna on pronouncedly sugary white bread, and neat spoonfuls of Fluff: a jarred marshmallow gloop that, even then, seemed to me in possession of a synapse-frazzling sweetness that wasn't necessarily all that enjoyable. I wore chunky basketball high-tops and absorbed a world of black middle-class self-possession, cool and prosperity – sitcoms like *Family Matters*, magazines like *Ebony* and *Jet*, clothing brands like FUBU (aka, the overtly African-American-coded For Us, By Us) – that were as novel as they were empowering.

I think, mercifully, I stopped short of affecting an unconvincing Midwest accent, but that summer in 1996 marked the beginning of what would be a habitual transformation. Life in Bexleyheath, its friendships, routines and anxieties, felt a world away. Any private worry or shame related to Dad's dwindling presence in our lives – and by that point, we had not seen him for at least two years – dissolved somewhere over the Atlantic. And so I threw myself into the task of eagerly cosplaying as just another child in suburban America. To assume a new role and embrace the shift in my psyche as well as my palate.

There is a particularly strong, sharply defined memory from this period. It was late on in the August of 1996 and I had followed the established visitation path from the maternal connections down in Florida up to the paternal ones in Ann Arbor, a tranquil, comparatively tiny university town on the outskirts of Detroit. I was out in the mystically carless, sitcom-perfect cul-de-sac of huge houses that lay beyond my Uncle Deji's place, playing a game of touch American football with a rag-tag group of local children. If memory serves, my grasp of the actual rules of the game was loose, and I was generally mute in conversation; thrilled to be involved but self-conscious about the conspicuous, apples-and-pears-level Englishness that would betray me whenever I opened my mouth. Yet I can still picture the moment that I looked up at the perfect, spinning arc of a pass aimed in my direction, the dimpled, precious egg of the football nestling safely in my hands, the sprint to the designated end zone as grasping fingers from the other team tried and failed to catch me.

'Dayyum,' said one of the more garrulous kids on my team, stretching out each syllable with relish. 'JJ got some wheels!' To have been praised for my innate, Forrest Gumpish running ability by a stranger might not seem like much. But the fact that I still remember this moment, and the warm glow of acceptance, decades later tells you everything about what those summer odysseys had given me. And maybe, also, how much I needed them. Much of my young life had involved a nagging sense of identity crisis that manifested in the contradictory nature of my appetites; a feeling that neither British nor Nigerian culture felt like an accurate embodiment of who I was. Well, in that moment in Michigan, a third option presented itself. In its food, its cartoonish abundance and its confident swagger, America offered a compelling, shiny personality alternative.

Whether given infinite guesses or strapped to a primitive torture device, I don't think I could reliably tell you the specific style of cake at my Uncle Joseph's wedding. Was it chocolate? Red velvet? An unnaturally yellow pound cake, thickly daubed in frosting? The truth is that the specifics of its flavour are beside the point. Because, really, the thing that I absolutely can vividly recall – more than thirty years after the ceremony my brothers and I attended in the late summer of 1993 – is the precise, ceremonial and, frankly, deeply weird manner in which it was first cut and eaten.

After a long day of festivities, I remember all of us in the vast wedding party – including me, Ray and Folarin, in our rented tuxedos and buffed, painfully tight dress shoes – being gathered around my uncle and his new bride, Aunty

Tina. Amid lascivious whistles and whoops of encouragement from the crowd and the flash of multiple camera
bulbs, I strained to watch as my uncle stooped to reveal a
frilly garter beneath his new bride's hitched-up skirt, before
removing it with his grinning teeth.

Next, the happy couple were manoeuvred behind the
multi-tiered cake, where they cut slices and then, just as you
thought they were about to have a conventional taste, they
instead playfully pushed the slices into each other's faces
like the custard pies on a Saturday morning TV show, their
eyes laughing as they scooped fingers of pale, fluffy butter-
cream from each other's noses. Again the cameras flashed;
again the ribald cries and applause told everyone that this
was an important and satisfactorily observed piece of tradition. I was too young to know all that much about sex, let
alone the overt dance of purity, fertility and impending
consummation that still shapes so many wedding traditions.
But, even then, I had the idea that this was both the kind of
adult impropriety that children shouldn't be watching and
also, perhaps more lastingly, a deeply un-Nigerian waste of
a good cake.

Why, then, does it feel like such an apposite memory in
relation to my experience of America throughout this period
of near biennial visits? The first reason relates to that continued idea of cultural performance. And, more to the point,
the realisation that a mutable identity in relation to nation-
ality and tradition was something that even the elders in my

family were having to deal with. I may not have been able to articulate it this way at the time, but to see Uncle Joseph – a personable but quite typically conservative Nigerian who worked with computers – embrace this suggestive American wedding tradition showed just how easy it was to defy one's cultural programming. It showed, bluntly, that I wasn't the only one trying on tendencies, personalities and behaviours that strayed beyond the Yoruba norm. To fit in was to be valued. To put the people around you, in a new land, at ease was being modelled as an important quality.

Separately, this moment underlined the encroaching, unavoidable reality of the adult world. My summers of escapist, American indoctrination had begun as exercises in childish wish fulfilment. That first trip especially felt like a candy-hued, extended daydream of IHOP pancakes, sight-seeing tours, souvenir-buying trips, amusement park visits and the near-infinite buffet of television options. Age and inclination never really caused me to question the broader context of the country I was in, its dark side, or any wider ramifications for the people who were taking care of me. Those summers, like my preferred diet at the time, were all about unbridled pleasure and a long sugar rush with no recourse to forms of nourishment that I found unpalatable. But, as prefigured by my aunt and uncle removing garters and smushing cake into each other's faces, these grown-up realities would soon become unavoidable. As my returns to America coincided with puberty and the social shifts of the late-1990s, I was, metaphorically at least, going to have to force down some vegetables.

A post-war housing shortage in Britain gave rise to all sorts of creative solutions. Prefabricated bungalows sprang up; abandoned army bases were commandeered by the newly homeless; New Towns were planned and built, and entire families squatted in hotels. In Crayford, a rapidly modernising and expanding town on the shoulder of north-west Kent and Greater London, this meant a vast hamlet of prefabricated BISF houses; uniform in their semi-detached, two-storey layout, characterised by reinforced concrete walls and hard-pitched, corrugated roofs, they were an easy-to-construct, flat-pack solution to a growing epidemic.

By the mid-1990s, these emergency houses had passed into council ownership, still provided a home to hundreds of families, and had collectively acquired a local nickname: Tin Town. Now, not long after I had started at Bexleyheath School, I fell in with the Jarretts, an unruly rabble of charismatic siblings who lived nearby and taught me the hierarchical nuances of the area. To be brought up in these odd, utilitarian grey homes, among a preponderance of low-income families, was, I soon learned, to be on the absolute lowest rung of the social ladder in the status-obsessed, hyper-materialistic atmosphere of suburban Kent at that time. The Jarretts lived in a council house and their parents were both on benefits; they did not have much or ever claim to. And yet, my memory of it is that they would always console themselves with the simple fact that, whatever happened to them and whatever cruel things people might have said in the playground, they at least didn't live in Tin Town.

Can you guess yet, where my family and I ended up moving to, as the summer of 1996 tipped into autumn? Is it obvious where fate conspired to land us, after my mum announced that the Famurewas would be swapping Abbey Wood for a rented council property in Crayford? I can still remember the precise, self-pitying misery of looking out of the front door of our new prefabbed, BISF home on moving day, as the sun set behind the banked rows of uniform, asbestos-covered roofs. 'So where's Tin Town, then?' said Ray, from over my shoulder, brightly oblivious to the fact that we were very much in it.

Adulthood brings perspective and appreciation for the financial stresses and general life fissures that parents artfully conceal from you. Selling us on the sudden move from Sydney Road to Crayford – a decision hurried along by both an inflexible private landlord and, I'd wager, the fact my dad's dwindling support had turned us into what we might euphemistically call a more budget-conscious, single-income household – must have been incalculably difficult for my mum. I see that now. But, of course, back then, my youthful myopia caused me to process this upheaval as a personal attack; an irreparably embarrassing, wholly unfair tumble down the social pecking order that I had not got to have any sort of say in. I still have a clear image of the 'cele-bratory' KFC that we ordered that evening – the paper bucket of fried chicken and the sweaty, plastic-bag-sheathed corn cobettes eaten among unpacked boxes and a television we couldn't get to tune. I glumly dipped soggy fries into a tub of barbecue baked beans and felt, with typical adolescent level-headedness and restraint, that my life was basically over.

This, then, was the atmosphere of destabilised flux that coincided with all those defining trips to America. A time when the natural tumult of puberty was magnified by constant, whiplashing movement between different worlds and distinct tribes. Crayford, even beyond any perceived social regression, was a subtly different environment to Abbey Wood, somehow both just a twenty-minute drive and a total lifetime away. Where south-east London had pointed multiculturalism, angular, grey housing estates and cage football, north-west Kent had sprawled green fields, traveller kids clip-clopping down the street in horse-drawn wagons, and the cultural homogeneity of suburban white flight. One of my prime memories of our early months there is of logoed Nike and Adidas sports clothes being pilfered from the washing line by our neighbours.

Furthermore, to move into an area where we were suddenly one of only two black families on the street was to experience that central paradox of ethnic minority life. Namely, simultaneous hyper-conspicuousness and virtual invisibility. This led, from my early teenage years onward, to a period of trying on different obsessions and subcultures like outfits. It was chameleonic behaviour – self-preservation through camouflage – in the purest sense of the word. Muddy-kneed football-obsessive. Budding theatre nerd (like all serious actors, I began this journey with about three lines as Mayor of the Munchkins in a BS production of The Wizard of Oz). Chain-walleted skateboarder. I oscillated through all these personas, often to the point that they overlapped. They all felt true and representative of who I was or aspired to be. Yet the added fact of being a British-Nigerian in an environment where that wasn't the norm, the added fact of those lurching instances of code-switching, could lead to a kind of disorienting rootlessness.

This sense of experimentation, or perhaps merely of unquestioning emulation, extended to my appetite. Food, again, like hobbies, music and clothes, seemed to be a means to demarcate self. Away from the Nigerian comfort dishes that were the soothing constant of home life, proximity to people like the Jarretts opened up new worlds, words, and tastes. I caught lifts home, wedged into the boot of their stepdad's dope-scented estate, listening to Frank Zappa cassettes and nibbling on bread pudding: thick paving slabs of a dense, damp fruit cake, anointed by a healthy sprinkle of glistening caster sugar. On the days we'd get the bus home, Carl, the brother I was probably closest to, would explain that what I knew as a gherkin should in fact really be called a 'wally'. Despite the fact that their parents had three teenage siblings plus two other younger children, all crammed into a four-bedroom house, their home had the open-door policy of a youth club and the thrilling lawlessness of a commune. At weekends especially, the bedroom all the older kids shared was a kind of anarchic, pubescent nirvana. Beneath a cloud of acrid spliff smoke and to the hectic crackle of jungle on a pirate radio station, packets of value custard creams would be passed around. When we bunked the train into London, to skateboard and infuriate security guards in the echoey, clattering surrounds of the South Bank, they made peanut butter sandwiches and stashed their bags with 20p Smart Price bottles of cola, and so I watched and did exactly the same.

These food traditions emphasised stolid, English functionality rather than the laborious, deeply seasoned ceremony of Nigerian cuisine. Even so, there was a thread of connection and communication that I recognised. I have a clear memory of the Jarretts' mum, a small, twinkly lady with a high, parched cloud of peroxide hair, calling a whole horde of us down – her actual children and about half a dozen pimpled hangers-on – for dinner: a vast tangle of spaghetti, an enormous, blipping cauldron of very wet bolognese, and grated cheese that we were all to help ourselves to. It was like a soup kitchen crossed with feeding time at Fagin's hideout; an act of pure, welcoming generosity that I still think about and appreciate.

The issue, insomuch as there was one, was that the cultural and culinary exchange only worked one way. As established, I had my own self-conscious reasons for not necessarily wanting to invite friends into the distinctly Nigerian chaos of our home (a feeling that was only compounded by the move to Crayford). But, more than that, the onus was generally on me to adapt to the gastro-nomic proclivities of my friends, rather than the other way around. Britishness was the prized default setting to adapt to. Relatedly, there was always the hovering implication that everything that sat outside a western norm was inferior. I distinctly remember sitting in the Jarretts' living room during this time, silently letting whatever was on the TV wash over us. Their youngest sibling, who was about five or six, turned my hand over in theirs, again and again, mesmer-ised by the fact that the contrasting, blushed peach skin on my palms was essentially the same tone as all over their body. 'This bit's lighter,' they said, wide-eyed, as I nodded and tried to brush off the awkward prodding. 'See,' said one of my friends from a neighbouring armchair, not taking his eyes off the screen. 'At least some bits of Jimi are white.'

Presented with the options of fight, flight or freeze, I very much chose the latter. Dumbfounded and disbelieving, I stayed rooted to the spot and kept my eyes forward as my chest tightened, not quite knowing how to react or whether I had misheard. It was such a shocking, unexpected thing to hear that I questioned whether it had really happened. I may well be the only person in that room who remembers it. Yet all the same, despite the unexpectedness, it seemed to confirm some hunch or deeper reality. Even spaces where I felt welcomed and safe were not adequate sanctuaries. Racism and ostracisation could strike at any time and from the unlikeliest of sources. And no matter how much I felt that I fitted in, no matter how convincingly I played any given role, there was always the lurking threat that I would be reminded that I didn't quite belong.

This was the reason, perhaps, that I was so entranced by the dangled possibilities of American identity and consumption. It wasn't just that my relatives' houses, with their spacious interiors, snug, clubby basements and shared tennis courts, were the outwardly lavish antithesis to our unruly but loving, insalubrious domestic environments in the UK. It was that American culture felt like something I could claim with confidence and impunity. On the face of it, this did not translate to much of a material change in my attitude to food. Mine was still a closed-off eating philosophy predicated on ultra-processed pleasure, a suspicious attitude towards the unfamiliar, and shredded burger lettuce as a primary vegetable source. Relatedly, the fact that the dining I experienced during that time reflected a kind of American exceptionalism (notable: this was an era when fewer than 20 per cent of US citizens had a passport) probably only exacerbated my resistance to broadened culinary horizons. But those summers were mostly about feeling like I gained desirability through access to a highly desired environment. It was self-esteem through osmosis. After that adolescent period of confused weathervaning, after hopping from tribe to tribe, those flights to the States signified both escape and education. An experience that was mine and mine alone.

One of the consistent lessons of my later American summers was this: I would have to make my own fun. While there was novelty and shape to the 1993 holiday, a packed itinerary formed by the fact relatives were excited to show off their country and culture at its best, there tended to be a formless drift to those subsequent trips. The aunts and uncles tasked with looking after me – my Aunty Sade and Aunty Tele in St. Louis, my Uncle Gori and Uncle Kalia in Florida and my Uncle Joseph and Uncle Deji in Michigan – were all working adults, at various stages of trying to establish themselves personally and professionally within the country. As I pitched up in the summers of 1996, 1998 and 1999 it became more apparent that I was, well, not a burden exactly, but someone who would have to fit around their lives rather than the other way around. A deal that I was happy to accept because it also meant multiple opportunities to continue my full-immersion introduction to American snacks and the TV networks that would try to sell them to viewers every ten minutes or so.

In Miami, I provided entertainment for younger, toddler-age cousins and gloried in the convenience miracle of Eggo waffles: frozen, manila-yellow, gridded frisbees that popped up from the toaster as a warm, appealingly bland vessel for far too much drizzled syrup. In Fort Lauderdale, while my uncle worked, I walked through the pummelling heat and alongside a highway to get peppery, cinnamon-scented Big Red gum from the 7/11. In St. Louis I was taken to the cinema and introduced to American popcorn – which, rather than the salty or sweet styrofoam pellets found in British concessions, seemed fresher and warmer, slicked in a pump-gunned dousing of intensely perfumed liquid butter – but only so my Aunty Sade could watch *Dave*: a political comedy starring Kevin Kline that I mostly remember as the absolute apogee of a soporific, explosion-light film for grown-ups.

Don't get me wrong. There were still moments when my aunts and uncles clearly strained to do the sort of pandering, touristy things that would make my time special; there were hot dogs and paper bags of sugared peanuts at a memorably interminable baseball game in Missouri, plus oily pizzas, cacophonous arcade games, and the ticker strips of pink winners' tokens whirring from Skee-Ball machines at a child-oriented restaurant called Chuck E. Cheese. Yet I was never that far from an indolent, shapeless couple of days in front of the television or a reminder, never in anything like a pointed way, of the slight hassle of having to accommodate and entertain me and the other younger children. In 1996, a coterie of us drove up from south

Florida to Orlando for a couple of days of snaking queues, pummelling sunshine and chlorinated log flume spray at Disney World and Universal Studios. Beyond the associative dread of the words 'Space Mountain' and some of the ridiculous food – particularly, the hulking, thickly glazed giant turkey legs that were equal parts renaissance fair and *The Flintstones* – my prime memory is of my Aunty Tayo frantically calling back to Miami so one of the uncles could grudgingly use Western Union to top up our depleted funds with an emergency wire transfer.

In recent years, I have thought about the fact that these temporary caregivers were youngish adults in their late twenties and early thirties with their own needs, whims and sense of what an ideal summer might have looked like. This almost certainly didn't include a nephew who needed entertaining and, in one way or another, nourishing. Yes, there was the occasional detectable moment of strain or awkwardness caused by my presence. But mostly I was made to feel welcome, pampered. Adulthood has only brought a heightened appreciation for the pure, selfless generosity of this.

And it was, I think, a generosity tied completely to culture. Though these moments played out in America, they were very much shaped by the obligations and traditions of what it is to be a Nigerian. It was another reflection of non-traditional, globally dispersed family units and the sense that any prosperity, privilege or good fortune was a collective possession to be shared among all of us. It was its own sort of transatlantic trade. Just as we had no say in whether to welcome the Nigerian relatives who pitched up at Sydney Road or Crayford, my American elders wouldn't have regarded my summer trips as something they could opt out of even if they wanted to. To show me a good time in the consumerist theme park of the USA was a kind of cultural obligation; payback to my mum for meals, labour and care she had given them in London or Lagos. A kindness extended to a distant corner of our family's global compound.

What's more, it became apparent that there may have been another function to these summers, beyond my mum's chance to have something of a rest (the image of her actually sitting idle is, of course, basically impossible to conjure). Particularly for my uncles. Though the fact that I was essentially living without a father was never verbalised or acknowledged, during those later trips I had the feeling that a degree of urgent paternal guidance would be part of the syllabus at my informal summer school. Some of this was the unspoken instruction of modelled behaviour; the sharp-dressed, good-time generosity of my Uncle Kalia, or the ritual of IHOP breakfasts with my Uncle Gori (not to mention the way that he would flirt outrageously with the waitresses serving us). But, elsewhere, some of it was more pointed and direct.

Uncle Deji seemed, perhaps understandably as my estranged father's older brother, particularly intent on offering some of the instruction he thought I might be miss-ing out on. Memorably, he once chided me for wearing my jeans sagged halfway down my backside – explaining that my skater-ish fashion choice had actually originated from prison inmates who had their belts and shoelaces taken from them as a safety precaution. Elsewhere, when I returned as a fourteen-year-old in 1998, there were a memorable few days accompanying him on a business trip upstate. We ate thick trenchers of diner French toast, got bags of Ruffles potato chips from gas stations and, thrillingly, I got to ride a jet ski across the inky, bracing murk of Lake Michigan.

However, the thing I most remember about it is the moment my uncle gave me an unexpected warning. 'You need to make sure you don't go out alone after dark up here,' he said, his usual sing-song delivery suddenly grave, and his expression stern beneath the thick, neatly trimmed moustache. 'Some parts of this place are still Klan country.' The words hung there like gunshot echo. I don't recall whether he elaborated further, or simply left me to imagine Ku Klux Klan groups roaming around northern Michigan in the hope of visiting violence upon the bodies of unsus-pecting British teenagers. Either way, the message – of care-fulness, caution, and maybe some of the active, racialised terror that my US-based relatives lived in fear of – hit home. And if this was a window into the dark side of the American dream I had long been so drunk on, then it wasn't to be my only one.

I have another image, from the same summer, of my Uncle Kalia having a loud conversation with a friend about Monica Lewinsky and the ongoing saga of President Clinton's impending impeachment. 'He got caught with his hands in the cookie jar,' he barked, the curious mix of Americanised phrasing and Nigerian directness echoing out into the cool, white-painted space of the family's open-plan apartment. On another day, one of my young female cousins and a similarly aged boy who was a family friend – both of them perhaps seven or eight years old – were loudly upbraided for privately acting out some approximation of the lewd, '90s-era bump and grinding they'd seen in a music video.

This was the age of oiled bodies on MTV and The Box, stray cable news items about the Lewinsky and OJ Simpson scandals, Schwarzeneggerian big screen blood-spatter, and furtively glimpsed adverts for something called Girls Gone Wild. As the Y2k anxieties of the new millennium approached, my initial image of America as this benign, harmless dreamland of cultural abundance and improbable portions had begun to be corrupted by glimpses of sex and violence that were terrifying and tantalising in equal measure. This was a function of the particularly brash and contradictory social inflection point of late-1990s America. Yet it was also, as presaged by the perplexing sight of my Uncle Joseph's cake- and garter-play, a symptom of the fact I was growing old enough to register these things. Those solo trips to America punctuated my stumble through puberty and late adolescence. Roiling emotions and chin-pimples tentatively dabbed with Clearasil? Furtive late-night flicking through scrambled adult channels at very, very low volume? The precise moment that skateboarding lost its obsessional, all-consuming appeal? All of these teen-age waymarkers would, in later years, remind me of Florida and Michigan and the associative sense-memory of crunched Jolly Rancher candies. I counted out my young life in Unaccompanied Minor activity packs and just as my relatives' circumstances seemed to change – life shifts marked by new houses, the birth of children and, in the case of my Uncle Gori, the never-to-be-explained dissolution of relationships – each American summer would see me arrive as a slightly different person.

One flip side to these convulsions of personality was a broader shift in my appreciation of these regular excursions to the US. More simply, the longing, self-consciousness and anxiety of adolescence had somewhat taken the shine off American culture's bombastic overload and dark edges, its indifference to my British life and the odd, babied power-lessness of navigating an environment where I couldn't just jump on a bus or a train like I could back home. I still thrilled at my regular reunions with Wendy's fast food, for square-edged burger patties and jolting, malty slurps of Frosty milkshakes; I still gleefully filled my suitcase with all manner of limited-edition Oreo packets and rattling grab-bags of Reese's Pieces candy.

But then there were the drifting, lonely journeys down to the communal tennis courts at my uncle's condo in Fort Lauderdale; there was the almost painful yearning to meet some other similarly aged kids that I could befriend, having only had relatives and cable TV for company for days; there was the mounting frustration that every time I opened my mouth – asking a gas-station attendant for a 'water' but making the grave, terminally English error of actually stressing the 't' – I would be met by genuine bewilderment, the look of people struggling to categorise a boy who looked African-American but sounded, perhaps, like a white English minor character in *Mary Poppins*. Then there was the knowledge of the summer holidays my friends were having – the Jarretts would go to Great Yarmouth and send me very sweet postcards that normally alighted on exactly how many girls in bikinis there were at the beach – and that particularly teenaged sense that everyone else was having a more exciting time than I was. Memories of one of my last school-age trips to the States, as a fifteen-year-old, are a little hazier and flatter. It comes to me as the clack of Parental Advisory rap CDs in plastic cases at Tower Records, my aunty making me a very sweet 'grilled cheese' toastie, rigged with molten Kraft singles, and a church service in a sweltering Floridian shack, where faith healers caused congregants to shudder and convulse.

Maybe it was just the novelty slightly wearing off. Maybe it was ageing out of certain experiences or just a nagging homesickness for British culture. Whatever it was, though America had had a permanent impact on me, those summer visits did also feel like a passionate love affair that had faded slightly. Life was not a suburban game of touch football and, however much I willed it, America was not a place where I would find real belonging. It may be that, in many ways, that was the thing my Uncle Deji was trying to impress on me with his warnings related to safety and appearance. What, really, all the US-based grown-ups that took on those surrogacy roles were trying to tell me about behaviour, appetite and its impact on self.

Years and years later, my ardour for American culture and cuisine remained just as strong – even as adulthood and the oppressive dread of the Trump era tarnished my glossy, simplistic view of it as this shining, seductive example of humanity at its biggest and best. In 2014, I returned to Florida – diverting my flight home for a brief layover following a work trip to a movie set in Atlanta – to visit Uncle Gori. Recently dogged by a period of extremely ill health, he had just undergone major surgery and was still edging towards recovery. Nonetheless, he roused himself to pick me up from Fort Lauderdale airport. The plan was that he would take me out to breakfast and so, by association, the effect was of the twenty or so intervening years since my first trip to the country being suddenly collapsed. Here was the blinding glare and oven-door swelter of Florida heat. Here were the palm-fringed highways, innumerable drive-thru businesses, and breathlessly delivered terms and conditions on radio commercials. And here too, as we arrived at a vast, air-conditioned chain restaurant, was my uncle flirting shamelessly with a waitress that he seemed to know well.

'Good to see you, Gary,' she said, briefly resting a hand on his shoulder as she set off to log our pancake order with the kitchen. The question of whether she had simply misheard my Uncle Gori's name or had been specifically invited to use a slightly Americanised version dangled there, unaddressed. All the same, I felt in that moment that I understood a little more about the social costuming and cultural performance of immigrant life; about the unseen, similar journeys of discovery that my elders had been on long before my own struggles. A later trip to my uncle's small apartment, where the palm-oil scent of a recently made stew hung in the air and plantain loitered on a counter, only cemented this feeling. There was, it seemed, a way to be palatably American where necessary but proudly African where it counted.

Though we Nigerians in the US ate a certain way, though we gorged on diner chilli dogs and pancake breakfasts and peanut butter and jelly sandwiches, we were never to forget who we really were. Because America, and for that matter the world, absolutely would not.

5

Big Macs, Fries and Edible Bribes

C ar rides were the measurement unit of a vast portion of my childhood. Back in the everyday rhythms of London after those stateside holidays, mine was an automotive life that was a simultaneous reflection of Mum's twitchy adventurousness and the dispersed nature of our family network. Adolescence flashes back as a series of upholstered interiors and swinging air-freshener trees. A Tupperware of steaming chicken warming my lap as we inched around Elephant and Castle roundabout. The roar of rushing, chilly wind and a beam of pride viewed from the passenger seat of Ray's ice-blue cabriolet Golf. Faint snoring and the scent of Juicy Fruit chewing gum, as Mum's Sierra swept down a darkened country road to deposit a snoozing cousin back at their prestigious private school. Particularly in the teenage years leading up to my departure for university, life was either buses, trains or shuffling from one cadged lift to the next.

But few of the vehicles of this broad era are as clear in my memory as Chris Dickson's dad's car. Chris occupied a strange nexus between friend and de facto relative; an impish, Ghanaian-heritage kid who was a year or two younger than me, had a God-fearing, gold-toothed mother who was one of my mum's closest friends, and – through primary school, youth clubs and football teams – always seemed to be close at hand. His dad, Charles, was of the same roguish, swaggering stock as my own father, a man of smirking good humour, backless leather sandals and occasional, unexplained disappearances. However, he was enough of a present figure to be the person who would pick me and Chris up from weeknight football training when we were about twelve or thirteen – a hulking, benevolent figure behind the wheel of an idling German saloon. The reasons that these trips, an everyday kindness in a life littered with them, left such an impression are probably threefold.

First was the particular luxuriousness of the car: a cavernous, low-slung spaceship with muscular bodywork, buttery, cool leather seats in Murray Mint cream, and a glowing blue switchboard of electronics a world away from the hand-cranked windows and tape deck of our family's succession of functional, second-hand runarounds. Second was something called 'zigzags', an odd, never-explained father-son tradition where, at Chris's whispered urging, his dad would swerve the car from side to side, creating a very mild, somewhat reckless lateral see-saw that would elicit screams and giggles from the back seat.

Third, and perhaps most pivotal, was this: Chris's dad almost always showed up with McDonald's. From the moment we scampered over in our shin pads and muddied socks and heaved the door open, we would know. Wafting out from the interior would be the familiar gust of gherkins, fryer fat and the sweet, bovine grunt of quarter pounders steaming up in their polystyrene clamshell boxes. There would be paper cups of cola, edged in the familiar brown and yellow insignia, and oil-glistened paper sleeves of fries; there would maybe be a box of uniformly cragged, straw-gold McNuggets alongside a colour wheel of sugary dips, and, to finish, the spurting, fryer-bubbled lava bomb of an apple pie or two.

Given the fearful cocoon of my pickiness, there was always something about the bland, pleasure-forward uniformity of McDonald's that particularly spoke to me. Yes, this was hardly rare sentiment for an Americana-addled '90s kid; yes, I was experiencing this happiness, safety and affection from within the targeted marketing crosshairs of a ruthlessly effective Big Food giant. But my devotion to the abiding treat of a McDonald's was practically sanctified. The Golden Arches might as well have been the pearly gates. And there were foods I wouldn't really countenance in real life – wrinkled, warm gherkins under the lid of a burger bun; lacy clumps of shredded lettuce remnants plucked up from the corners of a McChicken sandwich carton – that the world's biggest fast-food chain magically emboldened me to accept and even enjoy. So, yes, as undoubtedly aided by both an increasingly pronounced paternal void and the ravenousness of having just finished playing sport, nothing signalled happiness, generosity and a sort of everyday decadence like a McDonald's in Charles Dickson's car. Mine was a purchasable affection at a reasonable price-point. Buy me a Happy Meal in a moment of need, remind me implicitly of all the times I had self-soothed with syrup-drenched morning 'Hotcakes' or the little gluey nubbins of cheese peeled from a waxed burger wrapper, and I was yours.

Again, you could justifiably say that this level of maniacal love was not all that surprising – particularly given the pervasive hypnosis of fast-food advertising and the brutal efficiency of dishes laboratory-engineered to flood every possible pleasure centre. On top of that, it could be argued that my McDonald's worship was, alongside my unbridled America-lust and those junk-heavy grub crawls after school, just another means of trying to affirm a western identity through appetite. Yet there was always an added cultural charge and significance to this particular fast-food giant. And it was evident in the fact that this was something that Charles Dickson always got for us, with no sense of guilt or shame, and with a palpable appreciation of how grateful we would be.

McDonald's in particular, and multinational fast-food businesses in general, occupied a fascinating space within West African families like mine. Put simply: these businesses were revered by adults almost as much as they were by children. They were a point of generational crossover and communion; a silver bullet to our elders' hard-wired aversion to eating outside the home. My mother was perhaps the best case in point. I often say that she used to be mystified by the entire concept of going out to eat at a restaurant, but this feels like not quite doing justice to the burning intensity of her scepticism and scornful bafflement.

The rebuffing line that diaspora kids were accustomed to hearing, as they gazed longingly through the glass of a high-street Pizza Hut, was that 'there is rice at home'. I am sure I heard versions of this sentence. But Mum's reflexive resistance to restaurants seemed linked to her own cooking ability and preferred mode of eating as much as a reluctance to fritter away hard-won and limited financial resources on unnecessary, less-than-reliable sustenance. Why, she would often ask, would she take a chance on handing over money for something that she could have made a better version of at home? Why did these places have such constricting rules around reservation times, the number of people at a table and menus that offered a finite number of dishes, rather than just whatever people wanted? Why would she roll the gastrointestinal dice on some begrimed, probably salmonella-ridden mom-and-pop operation? Nigerian dining, particularly at this point in the 1990s, was very much a home-centred affair. Mum's class, generation, temperament and natural facility at the stove meant that she was especially primed to view heading out and coughing up money for a substandard kung pao chicken, a drab penne

arrabbiata or, God forbid, a slapdash jollof rice as a peculiar lunacy.

This allergy to restaurants is something that I've generally brought up in relation to the ironic reality of my eventual career as a restaurant critic; something that helps to
explain the autodidactic approach I've had to take to hospitality and dining culture. Yet it is only really writing it now
that I appreciate how much I must have unwittingly
absorbed some of these attitudes to eating out. How, as a
picky child, this background scepticism and negativity in
relation to restaurants would have only confirmed my
worries about tastes that sat outside my specific, hugely
contradictory idea of 'safe' and 'normal'. Mum saw the bulk
of independent restaurants as overrated scams; she didn't
always have the most generous things to say about other
immigrant cuisines that had punctured the British
consciousness. And so it's reasonable to infer that some of
these biases were passed on to me.

Of course, the intriguing aspect of this is that McDonald's,
and businesses that were broadly similar, got a special
dispensation. For all her wariness about buying food in
dining establishments, there was a certain kind of bright-lit,
faintly Americanised 'restaurant' that Mum pedestaled as
especially glamorous and seductive. Simply put: they were
as much of a treat for her as they were for us. Part of their
mystique and invincibility in her eyes was, I think, the sense
that these places trafficked in something that even she

couldn't hope to replicate. Ask her to make you some chips and she would conjure a kind of ragged magic: thick-cut, burnished potatoes, pale yellow, shallow-fried with fragrant slivers of onion and perfect in their finely crisped, stratified imperfections. But the slender, elegant uniformity of McDonald's fries in a pillar-box-red sleeve? The thick, syrupy glaze of baby back ribs at TGI Fridays? The dramatic wave of fryer-bronzed batter encasing a large haddock from our favoured Friday night fish bar in Abbey Wood? These were prized marvels of craft and consistency, a standardised, reliable and replicable high, that she spoke about in hushed, reverential tones. This affection would have almost certainly transferred over to me and helped stoke the intensity of feeling I had during those trips to the US.

I would probably never regard a steaming parcel of good *moin-moin* in the same way as my mum; she would almost certainly never share my conviction that thin canteen milkshake and a single chocolate Rice Krispie cake constituted a proper lunch. So our rapt, shared appreciation of these chains became a meeting point and a kind of common tongue. After I had accompanied her for a full Saturday of errand-running, an interminable programme of visits to food shops, banks and mysterious side quests that would require me to wait in a radio-less car feeling for all the world like I'd been abandoned, the dangled prize would be a trip to Wimpy. Liveried plates and plump, lettuce-frilled burgers; blue sachets of punchy tartare sauce and a kite-shaped piece of formed, orange-crumbed cod like a giant fish finger. We would sit amid the bright, yellow and red hubbub with sugary teas in proper mugs, food shopping bags pooling at our feet, and broad smiles on our faces. I realise now that what felt like a reward for me was really a ritualised treat and some respite for both of us.

I suspect there was more to it than the food. McDonald's in particular is a corporate behemoth built on conformity and the elimination of human error; on the promise of an experience and environment that, from a precisely meas-ured squirt of mustard to the dead-eyed stare of a smiling clown mascot, will be exactly the same no matter where in the world you encounter it. Nothing in a fast-food chain is incidental. Not the scrupulous, scrubbed cleanliness; not the egalitarian, bolted-down seating; not the hyperreal, sharply defined menu photographs of the burgers, with their coquettish, drooping neckerchiefs of melted yellow cheese product. Few subsections of British society, particularly in McDonald's mid-1990s heyday, were immune to this allur-ing display of corporate might and rigorous, gleaming consistency. Even so, I think there was something about this attainable, inexpensive display of order and abundance that spoke particularly to migrant families who were familiar with atmospheres of scarcity and chaos. The cookie-cutter glow of a McDonald's or a Wimpy or a KFC or a Burger King symbolised an ease and a welcome we wouldn't neces-sarily find in, say, a pub or caff.

There was an unavoidable transience and disorder to our lives. The roots we had in the country were shallow and so, through food and life, we were trying to meaningfully impose ourselves on the environment. This came through clouds of *egusi* scent, billowing out into the atmosphere above a Kentish commuter town. But it also came in finding moments of constancy and new forms of western-coded, inexpensive indulgence. And so that, I think, was why those post-football meals in the back of Charles Dickson's car were so special; that is why I still remember, another time, being in tears because my hands were so cold after a match, only for Ray to slowly bring me back to life with the cupped warmth of a hurriedly purchased McDonald's hot chocolate.

This business and its spiritual antecedents have come to permeate every corner of my life. McDonald's is the bolstering reward, in a car bursting with suitcases and Christmas presents, for an early-morning grapple with the M5. It is swaying at a touchscreen order console near Charing Cross, gilding the lily of drunken regretfulness after a night out. It is the paper-bagged, illicit surprise in my mother's hands as she nudges through the front door and induces grinning bedlam among her grandchildren. McDonald's in our family remains a bridge across generations. In later years, with kids of my own, I would realise that the thing I was ordering at the crackling speaker of a drive-thru was not a Happy Meal or some Chicken Selects or a McFlurry but, rather, the silent contentedness that would descend in the car; the sigh and release of that first, hot fistful of rummaged fries.

This is the result of that early programming and indoctrination. The combined forces of my forcibly constrained palate, those trips to America and the complicity of elders has engendered a lifelong fixation with a certain kind of Golden Arches-adjacent restaurant experience. It was a full-blown obsession. It just wasn't, as I would come to learn, a particularly healthy or nourishing one.

It's important to remember the origins of McDonald's dominance as a business. We revere the precise interplay of diced onions and cheese-melt beneath a glossy, enriched bun; we rhapsodise the unique, soaring bliss point of spurting tartare sauce within a Filet-O-Fish. But it was speed and efficiency, rather than any kind of special culinary aptitude, that turned McDonald's into such an all-conquering corporate monster.

Founding siblings Richard and Maurice McDonald were, above all, inveterate tinkerers. In 1948, conscious that their hit San Bernardino hamburger and barbecue stand (itself a product of Californian suburban prosperousness and the burgeoning, hard-charging freedoms of the automotive age) was bedevilled by operational issues, inefficiencies and loitering delinquents, they realised they needed to make a change. Successful but dissatisfied, they detonated a popular business and reimagined it as something new entirely: a

leaner, simplified operation built upon a rigorously choreographed production line kitchen and unusual points of
difference – disposable crockery, self-service, warming pens
for racks of pre-prepared burgers – that would go on to
become industry standard. Soon, Ray Kroc, a maniacally
driven catering equipment salesman, would encounter this
revolutionary, space-age business and the rest would be
world-bestriding, indigestion-giving history.

The McDonald brothers, then, were able to discern an
unglimpsed future of human dining and behaviour at a time
when their competitors were still running their businesses
like the misbegotten cross between a sprawled outdoor diner
and an insalubrious parking lot. But I'm not sure that they
could have envisaged the scene across the Atlantic, around
fifty years later, when a group of friends and I huddled in the
chaos of the Leicester Square branch of McDonald's. It was
a Saturday afternoon, when I was about fourteen years old,
and we had just met a group of girls from some other far-
flung part of suburban Greater London – a situation that
was very much the desired outcome whenever we sprayed
our puny bodies with Lynx, buttoned up a Ben Sherman
shirt and went off on these weekend jaunts into the formless
part of Zone 1 that we all unthinkingly referred to as 'Town'.

We called this practice 'chirpsing' (basically, 'chatting
up'), with varying levels of seriousness, despite the fact it was
mostly just a few hours of hormonal meandering and hesitancy that very occasionally led to the desired end-point: the

exchange of landline numbers and a clumsy, teeth-clanking snog on a train platform. As I remember it, on that day, things were not going especially well. The hopeful gang of us – likely my friend Mark and a couple of assorted Jarrett siblings – had probably started chatting to the girls in the cacophonous, darkened spaces of the Trocadero before, through hunger or boredom, drifting towards the glow of this supersized version of the Golden Arches: a bright-lit commissary of familiar brown, yellow and red accents, loitering beef scent, and hundreds of tourists all clamouring for a pot of barbecue sauce at the same time. We pecked at some fries and nuggets until money and conversation dwindled, glumly accepting that this would probably not be an encounter that lingered in the memory.

Until, that is, one of the girls did something that I still think about over a quarter of a century later. 'Right, wait here,' she said, as we all perched mutely at a table near the counter. In my memory she is blonde, slight, and puffa-jacketed, with her hair swept up into a tight, botoxing pony-tail . She approached the thronged crowd, all placing orders at the till, tetchily pointing out errors or asking for removals and substitutions, and edged her way to a vacant space by the zone where orders were being bagged. 'Excuse me,' she said, aggravated and forceful. 'I'm still waiting for my McChicken Sandwich and I've been waiting for about twenty minutes now, so it's really taking the piss.' I saw suspicion flicker in the male server's eyes as he continued clamping lids on to fountain drinks while a many-headed beast of customers swarmed the tills. A wordless snap judgement was made. And soon, in palpable pursuit of an easy life, the server was handing over a chicken sandwich that he probably knew to be completely purloined. I can still picture the shrugging, unbothered way that the girl came back to the table and tucked into her artfully hustled snack; the mixture of shock and awe that we lads wordlessly transmitted to each other with a wide-eyed look. It was as if she were Rizzo from *Grease* lighting up a cigarette; a streetwise femme fatale who sparked fearful desire because this was extremely cool. But also, maybe on my part, a degree of tutting judgement and pity, as it was the move of someone accustomed to not having much money.

I think there are a number of reasons why this observed piece of teenage misbehaviour has stayed with me for so long. The first is the lasting sense it gave me of the broader ecosystem that high-volume chain restaurants were built upon, and the mutable nature of perceived value. As evinced by those consoling trips to Wimpy and the wafting quarter pounders in Chris Dickson's dad's car, these dishes were, to me, the pinnacle of preciousness; the rare, covetable pleasure point on which an otherwise miserable day or week could turn. But that Leicester Square girl's enterprising scam – which, through either cunning or fluke, exploited the overrun chaos and bewildering economies of scale that are an inherent part of the fast-food formula – turned all this on its head. Later, Ray getting a part-time job at a local branch of McDonald's – where staff ate as much free food as they wanted and constructed monstrous, hybrid Frankenburgers spilling McNuggets and squirted dribbles of McRib sauce – only extended this transgressive peek behind the curtain. Mine and my family's sanctified treat was a corporate insignificance; a decimal point on an enormous global ledger that could be given away to a scheming adolescent and written off as the kind of wastage that, economically speaking, wouldn't even touch the sides. The burgers, fries, pizzas and formed poultry remnants I projected so much feeling and happiness on to were, really, just the chosen instrument for processing people and their wallets. Chain food, in my mind, had a sheen of near-holy specialness. This moment showed me that this allure was as flinty and brittle as an overcooked French fry.

The second point of relevance for this memory is how it signals a particular phase of my teens – and the clinically bright big-brand spaces where these defining moments would play out. From around 1998, as I hit fifteen and those transformative summers in America continued to take hold of my consciousness and sense of self, there was a noticeable and wholly predictable shift in my social patterns and priorities. A big part of this was my dwindling interest in skateboarding. My standard line has always been that, by the time I hit my middle teens, the lurking temptations of that particular era – girls, misbehaviour, the time-honoured practice of swigging Merrydown cider at a bus stop daubed with crude, graffiti penises – overrode my passion for ollieing up kerbs, scrawling the logos of Californian skateboard companies over my school textbooks, and sneering at the grunting, mainstream awfulness of almost everyone else at school. Narrative expediency demands a hard stop: a ritual conflagration where I threw all my chain wallets, capacious hoodies and blocks of kerb wax on to a giant pyre. But I think it was probably more of a gradual shift than that. Skating gave me a creative outlet, fellowship through rebellion and a portal to permissive cultural worlds beyond the macho closed-mindedness that tended to dominate in Bexleyheath; to rumble down the middle of an emptied street with a crew of friends, after a day of landing tricks, bunking trains and raising a modest amount of hell, was to feel ten feet tall. Regardless of that, skateboarding eventually became just as much about youthful hanging out, just as much about underage drinking and impressing skater groupie local girls, as it was about hurling our scrawny bodies down the steps of outdoor shopping precincts.

Slowly, imperceptibly, this appropriated child's toy shrank in prominence. And what replaced it? Well, scenes very much like that one in Leicester Square McDonald's. We drifted around the Trocadero's noisy attractions, its bumper cars, cinema screens and beeping arcades, before picking the olives and peppers off squishy takeaway slices from the late-night Pizza Hut hatch near the Odeon. We rode rattling, late-night trains, sharing a bottle of lurid MD 20/20 flavoured tonic wine and the earbuds of a Walkman, out to underage discos in Maidstone and Gravesend. We journeyed to Birmingham, to meet a group of palpably disinterested girls who the Jarretts had got to know on holiday, and ended up having to bed down on the frigid plastic seats of an abandoned bus station, having missed the last coach home. The core drivers were an acutely '90s blend of the nascent UK garage scene, the prospect of meeting girls, and some nameless, wild-eyed desire for whatever legally opaque mischief we could find. The settings for these misadventures were shopping centres, unpeopled children's playgrounds, laser tag facilities, multiplexes, waterparks and fast-food restaurants: the garish, commercialised leisure environment that was our explorable urban wilderness.

This gently feral exploration carried over into appetite. The 20p ice-cream cone nursed next to a McDonald's window flecked with discarded burger gherkins. The dense, unsold egg mayo subs that a chain called Benjys would give out for free at the end of the day. Softened bars of Cadbury's Dairy Milk, swiped from Woolworths by an acquaintance with undercut curtains gelled down into thick, wet leeches and an especially prodigious shoplifting habit. There was one time where, for reasons that were never obvious, we 'camped' in the wooded interior of a recreation ground behind Crayford's greyhound track – a completely tent-less experience that mostly amounted to us setting a mass of discarded pallets on fire, inexpertly cooking some value sausages on the end of gathered sticks, and shuffling back to our houses in the middle of the night. It was a kind of anarchic, suburban foraging; a form of hunter-gathering for commuter belt kids.

That I was engaging in such wild behaviour would have probably been news to my mum. Here, again, was a sign of a fractured personality, split across cultural lines. Yes, my weekends were now often a caffeinated megamix of nocturnal train rides, distant house parties, and breathless sprints to evade the rolling cast of violent lads who always had it in for the Jarretts (and us by association). But as I was still a pretty diligent student and a well-mannered kid when I was at home, there was nothing to really shatter the image of the quintessential Nice Nigerian Boy. Occasionally, there would be slippage. On one occasion, a friend and I were given a scare-them-straight warning from police for setting off smoke bombs inside Bromley shopping centre – I can practically still feel the hot, instant tears as the squad car screeched up, blaring its siren. Mum's message that it was unacceptable behaviour – delivered with chilling calm following a silent drive out to a remote location that gave me the distinct impression I was a soon-to-be-whacked mob informant – did not need to be repeated.

More frequently, the fundamentals of my Yoruba upbringing stopped me straying too far into misbehaviour. I knew that I could not afford to behave in exactly the same way as the friends I was tearing around with; that she had neither the patience nor the capacity to deal with a son in any sort of unnecessary trouble. And the result was a sort of protective force field of scaredy-cat obedience. There is a clear picture of a sweltering, high-summer day near a murky, hidden lake at the base of a vast Kentish quarry. As my friends leapt in from the chalky, crumbling cliffs, whooping and flailing before the giant splosh of the water swallowing them up, I couldn't quite bring myself to do it. Couldn't shake the terror of the water's uncertain depth or my body impaled on the end of some unseen, submerged scaffolding pole. And so I looked on from the edge. Accustomed, in more ways than one, to going right to the brink without ever fully making the leap into the rebellious unknown.

And of course, this inherited conservatism was evident in the dishes that I ate and the spaces that I gravitated towards. On the one hand, my adolescent fealty to the iconographic Huts, Colonels and Hamburglars of the high street was another form of deliberate identity-building; a chance, away from the adult chaperoning of family trips to the West End or those American summers, to cultivate a gleefully unhealthy culinary independence. However, on the other, I was merely succumbing to the cultural programming doled out by my elders. Mum and my brothers; my aunts and uncles; the parents of friends: all of them had a particular trust and affection for the sort of hyper-standardised, conglomerate food scene that the McDonald brothers revolutionised in post-war California and brought to my native Woolwich in 1974.

And then, once I progressed to sixth form and, inevitably, on into the world of menial Saturday jobs, this Americanised eating landscape was still ever-present. At Tiger's Eye, an endearingly shonky soft play and children's activity centre, I corralled misbehaving kids from within a dense, hovering nimbus of chicken nugget smell. At H&M, in the glossy, space-age expanse of the new Bluewater shopping centre, I ended almost every shift with a messily dispatched Zinger Tower Burger. Behind the bar at my local five-a-side centre, I would occasionally have to break off from making Foster's tops to lift a flopping, shelf-stable 'brockwurst' sausage out of a murky jar like something at the Wellcome Collection and into a long-life hot dog bun (that, to this day, this is pretty much the grand sum of my food service experience will never not be funny). Whether at school, at work, or at play, and bar the odd nourishing interruption from something home-cooked and Nigerian, dishes drawn from this processed, pappy vernacular increasingly became my every-thing. And I really wouldn't have had it any other way.

This unquestioning love and fetishisation – aided by the ambient hum of hypnotic marketing – was a product of the fact that my family and social groups all occupied a particu-larly convenience-drunk, late-90s food environment. Yet my animating desire to fit in, and some of the scepticisms to 'unfamiliar' cuisines that I had absorbed, led to an acutely limited view. To have swerved into such a gastronomic cul-de-sac was to deny myself all manner of potential pleasures. Something that, by degrees, was only going to become more of a glaring issue.

By the time GCSEs were diminishing in the rear-view, both my friendship group and my primary interests had shifted again. This was around the year 2000; the fresh, unblemished page of the new millennium and the dawning of a UK garage scene – flashy, futurist, hedonistic – that was like the Summer of Love in sockless Patrick Cox loafers. My friend Mark and I, physically dissimilar but spiritually aligned, had grown a little tired of nocturnal wandering and purposeless evenings in skunk-filled rooms. From the moment we bought our first underage alcoholic drinks from an unscrupulous off-licence in Bexleyheath (inexplicably, two warm bottles of Newcastle brown ale), we both had a pronounced thirst for more. Specifically, it was a thirst for two to three syrupy alcopops, lots of muttered conspiring about attractive girls, and an occasional bit of self-conscious shuffling, on a dry-ice-fogged floor, to a specially booked DJ and MC combo who had some tenuous affiliation to So Solid Crew.

We rarely had more than £20 in the pockets of our snug catalogue jeans. There was almost always a lurking air of violent suburban menace. The fact we didn't have reliable fake IDs, and so were heavily reliant on a lax bouncer or a workaround where we got to the venue before security arrived and then hid in the loos, meant the night could often be over before it had really begun. Nonetheless, exploring this strobe-lit, late-night playground of Versace jeans, glinting zirconia earrings and boob-tubed girls dancing around gathered piles of handbags held a transformative excitement. By some fluke of geography and history, it truly felt like we found ourselves lurking at the edges of an emergent cultural moment. Not as cool as grime, nor as cultish as jungle, this faddish wave of soulful two-step is dismissed by some as a vacuous musical and subcultural footnote. But, for a certain generation who grew up in and around London in this era, there is a certain level of ownership and attachment; a certain pandemonium that breaks out if Sweet Female Attitude or Wookie or MJ Cole gets dropped at a wedding. And so whenever I think of the sweet ridiculousness of that time – the iridescent, ill-fitting Next shirts, the polite guilelessness of our chat-up lines ('Hello. Can I have a kiss please?'), the spittle-flecked, scream-rapping along to an MC Neat verse – it hits as a joyfully nostalgic gratitude; we were clumsily vaulting the barrier between innocence and adulthood, grit and glamour. And the soundtrack could hardly have been more perfect.

Although, for a long time, food was not an especially significant part of these evenings. True, there would occasionally be a tipping-out time stumble to KFC or a kebab shop. An extended section of the evening where we would pool funds for boxes of wings, shiver with the other jacketless ravers on a patch of glowing pavement and chat, with generally misplaced optimism, to girls with bits of masticated chip swarming their tongue piercings. But eating always felt secondary, incidental even. An enterprise that ran counter to the clear, prevailing motivations of the night. No one ever literally used the words 'eating is cheating' but it was a sentiment that hovered beside the shared feeling that whatever nutrients we needed for the night could be found in either a Malibu and Coke or a bottle of Reef.

But then, out of nowhere, one of my friends started to institute the ritual of a post-club curry. It was another learned piece of adult cosplaying, I'm sure; an attempt to emulate the hallowed, decidedly white English practice of 'going for a Ruby' that I sensed was an important social tradition among my friends' uncles, older brothers and dads. Either that or a desire to prolong the evening in a venue where we at least knew we'd be permitted entry. Whatever the root cause of it, soon it would be customary for a staggering gang of us, glassy of eye and breathing out the mentholated heat of two-for-one Aftershock shots, to troop into the flock-wall-papered interior of a nearby tandoori house for a South Asian repertoire garbled by British sensibilities. These days, I realise that this occasionally derided subcategory of 'inau-thentic' restaurant (often Punjabi-owned but run by those in the Bangladeshi community) is its own fascinating expres-sion of immigrant hustle and a culturally fluid, Anglo-Indian culinary vernacular. However, back then, at the early noughties dawning of lad culture, they always seemed like quintessentially English arenas of machismo and boorish male performance. Gary and Tony in *Men Behaving Badly* crushed drained cans of lager on their foreheads; Lister from *Red Dwarf* dove into a tray of vindaloo. Every young boy seemed to know innately that this was a place where you karate-chopped a thick stack of poppadoms, ordered something 'really hot' (a national tendency fatally skewered by *Goodness Gracious Me*'s 'Going for an English' sketch) and likely treated the harried staff with a patronising and racially loaded dismissiveness.

Though I had good friends who were South Asian, my recollection is that, perhaps understandably, none of them came along for late-night curries, amid the spice-fragranced air, all-male bellowing and spattering sizzler platters of those chintzy rooms. And so it tended to be me and a few white pals who all regarded the semiotic language of the environment – the giant bottles of Cobra, the microwaved lemony hand towels, and the colour wheel of fluoro gravies mined with suspiciously cuboid pieces of meat – as one they were fluent in. The problem for me was that this was a culinary tongue that I simply did not know. In fact, more than that, I had made a firm point of never learning it. The picky, chain-obsessed contortions of my palate, my mum's inherited gastronomic hang-ups and, lamentably, some of the prejudiced stigmatising of particular foods that I'd overheard growing up, had all combined to convince me that 'curry' was to be filed away in the padlocked cabinet marked: 'not for me'.

Never mind that the Nigerian tomato and pepper stews that I had loved since infancy were basically a few sprinklings of turmeric, cumin and coconut milk away from being plausibly categorised as curries. Never mind that one of the essential ingredients of any half-decent jollof rice recipe is a small measure of literal curry powder. My particular social conditioning had convinced me, to my eternal shame, that even this heavily westernised and watered-down interpretation of South Asian cuisine was not something I was willing to engage with. The cracked logic of it only serves to illustrate how wrong-headed some of my rules around food had become; how narrow and chain-focused my gastronomic horizons had grown. And so, each of these post-clubbing meals would feature the grim spectacle of my English friends availing themselves of jalfrezis, bhunas and Peshwari naan while I – product of a spice-prevalent household and culinary culture – tentatively flicked through the sticky leatherette menu in search of just about the plainest and most inoffensive thing I could find. I want to assure you that this wasn't one of the omelettes or plates of chips that were always listed near the back, like an especially implausible plot twist. No, I would, in those early visits, go for a training-wheels preparation that was listed only as 'chicken curry', hinting in its own way at a patron so terrified of spice, seasoning and perceived 'foreignness' that even the mere sight of some descriptive Bengali might cause them to faint or run howling into the night.

Bright orange, chip-shop adjacent and offering scant heat, this central casting 'curry' was always perfectly nice; not the cumin-heavy, sickly challenge I had imagined and a small but lasting crack in the armature I had built up against unfamiliar tastes. All the same, I always had the haunting sense, as my friends ordered and ate with confident abandon, that I was missing out on something.

Let us not kid ourselves: the sickly sweet kormas, leathern lamb chops and oily bhajis of a suburban curry house in the early-2000s were hardly representative of commendable culinary daring. In later years I would, thankfully, come to appreciate the manifold pleasures of both Anglo-Bengali curry houses and the enlivening biryanis, chaats and niharis of restaurants trafficking in more region-specific expressions of the subcontinent's interconnected cuisines. But those meals stick in my mind as one of the first times I recognised the potential pitfalls of the food identity I had been constructing for myself. And, perhaps, the privilege that comes from not constantly straining to fit in culturally. Lots of my friends were raised on '90s-era convenience foods and a seasoning-averse British post-war canon. An okra stew, vividly green and slimy in texture, may well have struck them as intolerably weird and practically from another world. Yet there is something to be said for standing on firmer ground in terms of identity. My hunch is that one reason my white friends were emboldened to embrace a little more culinary adventurousness – whether in the form of a uselessly hot prawn madras, the calamari at a plate-smashing high-street taverna or irradiated sweet and sour pork from a Cantonese takeaway – was that they perhaps weren't second-guessing everything in the same way. My cautious pickiness was a timidity born from both familial programming and the fear of getting it wrong; of ostracisation through difference. Those late-night curries showed me that this approach was neither sustainable nor all that successful when it came to trying to blend in.

Thankfully, by this point, my cultural diet had actually started to become a little more varied than my culinary one. Or, at least, one key aspect of it was. One unfortunate side effect of the fact I'd stopped skateboarding was that I also lost my link to that particular movement's innate weirdness and countercultural tendencies; to the obscure rock songs I would hear on skate videos, the connection to streetwear brands and graffiti culture or experimental filmmakers like Harmony Korine. I had, in the space of just a few years, turned fully into one of the avowed 'normies' or 'Kevins' I would rail against. My atmosphere was, increasingly, the ambient chauvinism of postmillennial media, superclubs at the edge of Kentish retail parks and vast, beer-scented chain pubs, illegally showing 3 p.m. football matches on the big screen. 'I'd really expect you to be reading a proper newspaper, Jimi,' tut-tutted Mr Potts, my garrulous head of sixth form, one day, as he saw me flicking through an orphaned copy of the *Daily Star* in the common room. I was hardly a total grunting lummox. But I probably wasn't far off.

Still, if there was one important piece of counterprogramming that redressed the balance, then it was studying drama, first at GCSE and then at A level. As a fairly natural and unashamed show-off, acting had always been something that I both enjoyed and found, if not completely easy, then so innate that I never came to associate it with effort or stress. Here, I am sure that a therapist, armchair or otherwise, might point out that the daily performance of overlapping cultural identities acted as a kind of preparation. I don't doubt that it had an impact. But the thing that caused studying drama to spill out beyond something that was a kind of occasional parlour trick – a means to get attention and kudos while rattling off impressions during improv games in drama classes, or teasing the headmaster while in character as Fagin in a school production of *Oliver!* – was the presence of a completely life-changing and inspirational teacher.

Miss Rae hit BS like a reverberating tremor from a different cultural universe. Where, previously, the school drama department's approach had been a shonky, jazz-handsing populism – an attitude neatly encapsulated by a production of *Charlie and the Chocolate Factory* where the gushing majesty of Wonka's chocolate river was conjured by two Year 7s half-heartedly flapping a length of brown fabric – her arrival (alongside that of another great drama teacher called Mr Henry) instituted a time of creativity, experimentation and sudden, exhilarating weirdness; a time where we closed-minded, teenage suburbanites were challenged both academically and socially. Northern, radical and palpably liberal but with the funny-boned, mick-taking instinct of a natural clown (encouraging a cohort of us to go for bracing early-morning dips on a department trip to Greece, she memorably dubbed our band of dawn swimmers 'Freaks of the Sea'), she encouraged open-mindedness and a more principled engagement with the world without ever making a big deal about it.

Suddenly, alongside my usual, lulling atmosphere of Nigerian family gatherings at the weekend, strawpedoed Blue WKDs in a Yates's Wine Lodge, and hungover shifts under bright shopping-centre lighting, there were new disruptions that were as daunting as they were enlivening. We performed in Tarantino-inspired Shakespeare productions and experimentally Brechtian Lorca adaptations. We journeyed to the National and the Royal Court to watch inscrutable physical theatre performances or confronting, grisly Sarah Kane plays where the only common theme seemed to be a prolonged, gratuitous look at a middle-aged actor's penis. I lay on the cool, sprung floor of the department's main building, committedly trying to channel a leaf or a baby or a sea anemone or whatever, as my lairy friends from the football team banged on the windows and hooted, practically wetting themselves. (There was that tension between personas and identities, again.) The self-seriousness we all brought to productions – approaching a devised theatre module at AS level with the brooding intensity of an RSC performer preparing for *Hamlet* – would have, I'm sure, seemed completely ridiculous to everyone else. Yet I don't remember ever really caring. Leisa Rae – who in later years would become a friend who I was permitted to address, with some hesitancy, by her first name – cracked open all our worlds and genuinely changed my life and outlook.

What's more, when it came to food, she was also indirectly responsible for introducing me to a restaurant that was just about the most sophisticated thing that my relatively sheltered, seventeen-year-old brain could imagine: the Bexleyheath branch of Pizza Express – a place that just happened to be the traditional site of our celebratory meals after the last night of a school production. And, look, I know. From the vantage point of an abundant and infinitely varied modern food landscape, it is difficult to think of this high-street chain – which has more than three hundred branches in the UK – as anything other than the quintessence of all that is basic, everyday and inescapable; a perfunctory, public canteen of service-station dough balls, toddler crayons and discount code sloppy giuseppes that is so pervasive and everyday that it almost qualifies as gastronomic hold music.

Picky

All of this is true now. But in the context of a not especially adventurous outer London town in the early 2000s,
there really was something about the experience beyond
Pizza Express's fully glazed exterior that felt joltingly urbane,
cultured and adult. There was the flicker of candlelight and
jazz wafting from the stereo speakers. People nibbled at
olives and drank, not squash or Mountain Dew, but green
bottles of expensive fizzy water. The pizzas themselves were
crackly and thin, served on proper plates, and generally
eaten with knives and forks. It was food that I recognised,
served in the sort of sanitised chain environment I felt
comfortable with. And yet it was not McDonald's or Wimpy
or even Pizza Hut, where we would occasionally spend a
few hours abusing the generosity of lunchtime all-you-can-
eat offers, availing ourselves of the ice-cream factory and
concocting buffet 'salads' that were almost entirely
comprised of tortilla chips and bacon bits. It was not the
flashing quiz machines, ersatz signboards and immolated
mixed grill at our favoured high-street Wetherspoons.
Ridiculous as it sounds, this outpost of an expanding hospitality brand – still, at that point, bearing some of the hall-
marks of the Anglo-Italian food revolution that it was part of
when it emerged as a single Soho restaurant in 1965 – gave
me a fleeting glimpse of an enticing future interaction with
restaurants that sat outside the kid-centric, big brands I'd
been so effectively weaned on. Part of the appeal of Miss
Rae, and the other teachers in the drama department, was

that they almost treated us like grown-ups and peers. Unembarrassed engagement with a craft, and with profane, twisted and explicit art, bred a kind of reciprocal maturity.

Those Pizza Express dinners, where the teachers would drink wine and engage us in a gossipy post-mortem of the play, felt like an extension of this. It was an alluring collective fantasy; an extended performance wherein, rather than being secondary school students a few doors down from a Ladbrokes, we were West End veterans tying one on in Joe Allen or Broadway performers piling into Sardi's. Striped T-shirted pizzaioli worked in the kitchen; a knife went through a steaming American Hot. It was just the right level of adventurousness for my small-town sensibilities. A tantalising, distant transmission from the world of Italian delis, wee hours Ronnie Scott's gigs and continental hospitality culture. And, just as at the post-club curry house, it felt like a slightly less inhibited culinary life was calling out to me.

6

A Feast for the Fun Time Boys

When I think of the freighted, precipice period before my departure for university, I think, perhaps unexpectedly, of Ikea hot dogs. This was the autumn of 2002; a month or so before my nineteenth birthday and a few weeks out from the point when I was due to begin an English and Drama degree at Royal Holloway, University of London: a solidly regarded, Victorian-era institution nestled out beyond London's suburban south-west, roughly between Feltham prison and Windsor Castle, and arrayed around the Hogwartsian grandeur of a red-brick, neo-Renaissance main building known as Founder's.

I would be living alone for the first time in my life. Taking up an unnecessarily high-ceilinged halls of residence room within the ornate, chiselled splendour of that very same main building. For this I would require not just furnishings, crockery and other essential items but interiors flourishes that, in a more intangible way, would demarcate my freshly independent new identity. Ray, ever responsible, ever available, and with a precise sense of style that I had long been a watchful student of, offered to take me out to the vast Ikea across the river and in one of the industrialised retail parks that orbited Lakeside shopping centre.

And so off we went: into the vast, overloading dazzle of a consumerist behemoth where it seemed that every single detail – the bewildering proliferation of inexpensive, Scandi-named products; the winding, meatball-scented maze of the layout; the couples engaged in terse, whispered arguments near the paper tape measures – contributed to the feeling of having passed through into a different world entirely. Having made the short drive there in Ray's beloved Golf, the two of us walked through the regimented human highways of display futons, bedrooms, dining areas and office spaces, looking for elusive vestiges of personality as well as specifics like desk lamps, bed-sheets and uselessly slender squiggly mirrors.

The choices I made to project an air of debonair, style-conscious maturity are, in retrospect, hilariously teenage and of-their-time. There was a thin blue-on-white rug, a scraggy, doomed dwarf palm houseplant, and a hollow lime-green plastic armchair, like an overgrown potty for a gigantic toddler, with a matching side table. I cannot isolate the precise rationale behind any of these interiors decisions. But what I do remember, with a heavy vividness, is the feeling of thrumming excitement as Ray and I pushed a swaying trolley beyond the tills and out towards the food kiosk that is both a glittering oasis for frazzled shoppers and a confident acknowledgement of the fact that trips to Ikea are generally so prolonged they traverse multiple mealtimes.

Ikea founder Ingvar Kamprad's 1980s decision to make dining options a more central part of the megastore's event-ised offering has been so effective that it doesn't really register as particularly revolutionary. Still, we should never forget that it was once extremely unusual to commence the act of making purchases with an unhurried meal of gravy-drenched meatballs, splodged lingonberry jam, golden cascades of cafeteria fries and a climactic, fridge-compressed slice of Daim bar cake. This feasting approach, taken before or midway through the actual shopping, is, in the eyes of many, as intrinsic to the Ikea experience as tiny pencils, crumpled yellow cargo bags and marital disharmony.

But I have always thought that it is the snack bar that abuts the exits that is the purest and most potent expression of food at Ikea. This is the place where the available options – hot dogs, fries, and self-service ice-cream machines where the thunked insertion of a token brings forth juddering sound and a crazed, drooping quiff of Mr Whippy – do not really cohere into any clearly defined meal category; the emotional crash mat where the cheap functionality of a Billy bookcase is carried over into fast food; the place where they correctly understand that the very best hot dogs are modestly proportioned vessels for condiments, warm, sweet-bunned and small enough to be gulped down in multiples of two. That was the consoling experience that Ray and I indulged in, as we puzzled over the physics of how we would manage to get everything into the car. An Ikea hot dog is always the breasted tape of the finish line; the taste of hard-won victory and impending emancipation. And, as I thought about the thrilling and terrifying possibilities of the next three years, that feeling had never been more apparent or potent.

It is fair to say that, by that point, I was extremely ready for the liberated promise of higher education and a world beyond Bexleyheath and the A2 corridor towns where I'd spent most of my life. Partly this was the hormonal teenager's natural hunger for independence, privacy and adventure; the tantalising prospect of university's sprawled galaxy of potential parties, friendships and stimulating lectures conducted by maverick professors with statement frames and elbow-patched blazers. Alongside that, there was another important piece of motivation that had heavily seasoned my last year or so in sixth form and formed the emotional backdrop to how I approached higher education. Bluntly, I had experienced that most life-altering of adolescent milestones: a first, sour taste of heartbreak.

Round about the time that I was intensely focused on school theatre productions and glorying in the boundless sophistication of a provincial Pizza Express, I had (after a prolonged, almost Victorian courtship) started going out with a girl called Leah. Diminutive, fair and button-cute in a sort of wholesome, inscrutable way, she was, at the age of seventeen, my first proper girlfriend. To be clear, there had been romantic relationships before – most notably an intense, mostly epistolary interlude with one of the Hertfordshire girls we met on that drama trip to Greece (the one that inaugurated the 'Freaks of the Sea'). But most of these situations had been too short-lived or strange to really meet the established criteria; hurried trysts, a fortnight of dutiful hand-holding, ungainly spin-cycle snogs at underage discos and fumbling hands as Boyz II Men played and the house lights came up.

Leah represented the first time I had attempted one of the moony, unsmilingly self-serious and passionate long-term relationships that were all the rage among Bexleyheath's hail of teenage pregnancies and impulse-bought Argos engagement rings. It was the first time I had done the very un-Nigerian thing of introducing a girlfriend (and a white English one at that) to my mum; the first time I had professed love for someone and felt it as a heavy, sick-making ache. Did everyone have a period of their youth when they perhaps put too much onus on the idea of being romantically desired? A time when reciprocated attraction was overly bundled up with feelings and ideas related to acceptance, status, self-worth? Well, I think, given some of my anxieties around identity and the ever-lurking fear of being ostracised, othered or simply ignored among a sea of floppy-curtained boy band types, I definitely felt this. Wanting to be wanted had an undue prominence in my early life. And so, while I was also making a conscious attempt to be less of an alco-pop-crazed liability, those months locked in a quite chaste, very emotionally intense relationship with Leah gave me a feeling of radiating contentedness; of having finally become a grown-up with grown-up concerns.

Or, at least, that was the case until we broke up – a couple of days into an extremely noughties trip that saw almost the entirety of the upper sixth decamp to Faliraki for a misguidedly lengthy two-week package holiday. Though the split was officially mutual (and perhaps shaped by unspoken awareness of the approaching iceberg of university), it felt like this was similar to when it is 'mutually' agreed by a dissatisfied board that an unfancied football manager will tender his resignation. Though I sensed it was probably for the best in the long run, it affected me more than I perhaps realised. Back home, I ate my feelings in the form of hot sub sandwiches, primed with a bubbled layer of melted cheese, from the Quiznos concession in Bluewater; my friend Anoop knowingly side-eyed the yearning Al Green tracks I'd put on to mix CDs that we played in his hatchback. There is a photo of me, back in Faliraki in the days immediately after the break-up, stripped down to my pants in the street, wild-eyed and visibly feeling the effects of my slurped share of a lethally strong fish-bowl cocktail. The definitional image, I think we can all agree, of a young man handling things extremely well.

My response to this fairly typical moment of youthful heartsickness and romantic disappointment was to privately make some sizeable decisions about future conduct. The lovelorn, puppyish persona I had adopted for much of my last year of sixth form was shrugged off, like a jacket I no longer liked the look of. Wounded by having exhibited emotional vulnerability, I resolved to never leave myself open to it again; pivoted self-consciously towards detachment and a kind of gregarious, fun-loving self-interest. The project of affecting a mode of sombre, financially prudent maturity – exemplified by the fact I'd saved my Saturday job money and solely paid off the instalments for Faliraki without once having to petition my mum for a loan – was mostly abandoned in favour of wild spending, irresponsible early-hours misbehaviour and the indulgent daytime kebabs I'd buy after going to the barbershop. What's more, the lingering wound of my dad's abandonment felt like further evidence to support an unassailable fact. Heartbreak was a cruel inevitability. All relationships were probably doomed to fail and wreak all manner of collateral damage for others in the long run. Yes, better to remain withdrawn and controlled than feel the whipping sting of rejection. I returned to the WKD-drenched bars and garage clubs of Bexleyheath with this self-preservationist instinct and pronouncedly juvenile sense of moral righteousness. In terms of food, the low reserves of inquisitiveness I had built up probably dipped into the red zone. This was the broad period when enjoyment of the Christmas spread that my mum would prepare – not just turkey, jollof rice, stew, and enough trimmings to pacify a ravenous rugby team, but miniature, diagonal-cut bacon sandwiches for late breakfast – would be severely hampered by a stinking sambuca hangover. The focus was selfish revelry for revelry's sake; the aim a kind of emotional invulnerability. That ill-suited jacket was replaced by a kind of cold protective armour.

It was not an especially original response to the end of a meaningful relationship. But this was the invisible baggage that I heaved up the stairs into Founder's, alongside the boxes of CDs and DVDs, appliances, gleaming new Ikea products, and a freshly acquired *The Simpsons* poster that I proudly tacked above the bed. Mum and Ray had driven me around the perimeter of the M25 to Egham, the sleepy speck of a Surrey town that spread out at the base of the university's elevated hilltop site. I think I would have almost certainly had to clamp my eyes shut as Mum led us in some prayer to mark the momentous occasion. Yet my memory of it is that my family did not linger long and that, soon, I was fussing around in my vast first-floor room – with its strange basin in the corner and ornate wardrobe – hearing the parental chatter and rattling suitcase wheels of other arrivals in the corridor and feeling, with a flutter of nervous excitement, that this was the moment it all began.

Now, I know that the fretful first instance of attempting to make friends in university halls can be fraught for a lot of people. I have heard those stories of parents who impress on their kids that an ice-breaker – in the form of a kettle to make tea, or a packet of milk chocolate Hobnobs – is the way to go. I have also spoken to people who, driven by desperation and convenience, fell in with ill-matched socio-paths and didn't find their tribe until weeks or months later. But, through either an enormous fluke or my possibly almost manic determination to make connections and wring the higher education experience dry of everything it had to offer, I pretty much met the core of my university friendship group that afternoon and evening.

There was Pete: a loping, six foot seven, fellow English student from down the corridor who hailed from Leamington Spa, had a blackly comic, ever-whirring supercomputer for a brain, and wore some of the oversize streetwear brands I remembered from my skateboarding days. Craig, a buzz-cut north Londoner with an anarchic streak, a seemingly perma-nent nose blockage he was always trying to clear, and a shambling charm. And then there was Dan: a hilarious, irre-pressible, neurotic Essex boy and former chef who was twenty-two years old and duly treated, without irony, as if he was some sort of fascinating, doddering pensioner. Other friends, acquaintances and flings would continue to reveal themselves throughout the next few years; what felt like an infinite scroll of personalities to bump up against in lecture halls, student union bars, and the manicured lawns of the quad that sat at the centre of Founder's. However, the bulk of these relationships, forged through a shared sense of outsiderdom and piss-taking as love language, stood the test of time.

It was food that enabled and solidified a lot of those connections. I arrived at university with an eating identity that was still the same mass of contradictions; still the same muddle of jollof-appreciation, vegetable-avoidance, Americanised chain restaurant obsession and, at a low flicker, a growing desire to shake off some of the youthful pickiness that had given me such narrow culinary horizons. In keeping with this last instinct, something new and significant had recently made its way into the mix. During my last few years at BS, in the twilight of my teens, my active addiction to television had created an unexpected on-ramp into another world and nascent obsession: cooking shows. Keith Floyd cradling a sloshing glass of Beaujolais. Gary Rhodes with his gel-spiked hair and jazzy chequerboard trousers. Jamie Oliver leaning out to yank sprigs of fresh coriander from an unkempt window box. These chefs, with their calm explanations and enthusiasm for Mediterranean exotica, were my hungover salve as I slumped on the armchair at Mum's. The impression that cooking was achievable and glamorous, a vessel for a little more adventurousness around food, took hold. I had, by that point, started experimenting with recipes that, although laughably simple – sea bass, dressed and steamed in a neatly folded foil parcel; a one-pan fry-up that was a deft lesson in divergent cooking times – were important, tentative stepping stones on the route to a more varied and exploratory relationship with food. Tucked away within the possessions I'd hauled into my room at Founder's, there was a student cookbook and a somewhat dog-eared copy of *The Naked Chef* with an eighteenth birthday inscription from my mum. What better way to forge robust social relationships than with aspirational plates of carbonara and caprese salad and none-more-noughties chicken breasts wrapped in Parma ham?

If you are even slightly familiar with halls of residence facilities and the disposition of first-year university students, then you will be able to anticipate the slight flaw in this plan. Frothed, bruise-coloured pints of snakebite and blackcurrant stood in for meals. The spartan, grimly municipal shared kitchenette was essentially a kettle, a fridge and a microwave (plus, for literal weeks, a mislaid pair of pants pinned to a noticeboard). Appetite found its shape from unchecked quantities of alcohol, marijuana and time, afforded to young people whose collective understanding of restraint and self-control was, like their frontal lobes, still forming.

The result was that meals devolved to a kind of feral, ravenous chaos; a self-perpetuating performance where it felt, even at the time, that we were both winking at a dirtbag, undergraduate stereotype while unironically glorying in it. That an activity was a parody of maladjusted student grottiness did not actually count against it. Lunch would be a pre-packaged cheese sandwich on white bread, plus a layer of salt and vinegar Squares, scrunched down beneath stacked palms. Pot Noodles, Hunger Breaks' Full Monty breakfast in a can (complete with bean-juiced pustules of gristly, warmed Scotch egg), and those cat-foody, pepper-flecked foil trays of John West 'tuna mix' featured heavily. I have a repeated vision of myself, sitting at a sticky bar table, extracting hot, deliquesced slices of tomato from a cheese panini striped in ersatz grill marks.

Arrival at Royal Holloway heralded an opening up of my inwardly suburbanite universe; it thrust me into contact with students from all around the country and the world, enabling contact with a multitude of people across interwoven lines of class, race, gender, faith and culture. There were Kosovans and East Asians and Canadians and a shower-averse Greek guy who always seemed to be ferrying a giant delivery pizza back to the ripe heat of his room. But I think it's also fair to say that given the stubbornly picky, pleasure-forward tendencies of my appetite, that first year probably represented something of a step back. It was like a turbocharged form of the transition from the wholesomeness of the primary school dinner hall to the junky possibilities of secondary school. Encouraged by similarly inclined, largely working-class friends, away from the nourishing ballast of my mum's cooking, and with flaccid, heavily subsidised pints of Carling quickly presenting themselves as my most vital and financially ring-fenced form of caloric input, my eating slipped into an unapologetically childish dysfunction.

At one point, a proudly Cornish girl in our block felt so personally affronted by our love of Ginsters – not just the crimped, fridge-cold purses of knackered steak and swede, but the deeply weird, coleslaw-filled 'Buffet Bar' sausage logs that were a staple in the 2000s – that she asked her mum to send a special consignment of proper, homemade pasties back in order to lure us away from the mass-produced dark side. 'Well?' she asked, expectantly, as a group of us bit down into our sandstone hulks of crumbling pastry and thick cuts of very salty meat. 'Yeah, not bad,' I lied, quietly pining for the reliably unobtrusive, refrigerated blandness of a Ginsters. Separately, there was a period when the most consistent part of our diet was dry fistfuls of chocolate Frosties from mini boxes that would be hurled, through the fog of a hot-boxed bedroom, into grateful palms at 3 a.m. (we had so many of these because a friend had seen two boxes of complimentary samples beside a 'Please Take One' sign and simply carried the lot off to his halls).

The horrifying derangement of the undergraduate diet is a tale as old as time. Yet, to my mind, there was something acute about dropping my particular sensibility into Royal Holloway's social environment. Egham's inability to offer much in the way of a university town's usual distractions turned the sprawled campus into a concentrated universe unto itself. Raised walkways and leisure-industry-style food concessions. Toytown simulacrums of sports bars, tat-clogged Irish pubs, night clubs and launderettes, predomi-nantly run by disinterested near-teenagers in ill-fitting uniforms. Themed areas all spilling out from the postcard spires of a building that looked like a literal fairy-tale castle. University felt more like an explorable theme park than real life. It was a place of learning that struck me as funda-mentally unserious and free of much in the way of discern-ible jeopardy. And so I drank, ate and generally behaved accordingly.

If there was a semblance of stability during this period then it came from the canteen. Housed in a majestic, triple-height hall on the first floor of Founder's (there was an alter-native, modern facility, amid grey featureless halls of resi-dence, in the remote foothills of the campus's outer perimeter), Royal Holloway's main cafeteria comforted even as it confounded. Gleaming basins of yellow chips and flop-ping, regimentally cuboid carrot batons; hotel-style buffet breakfasts with pink folds of bacon that had been baked to chewy softness rather than fried; thin, grey cuts of 'minute steak', bean quesadillas edged in lethally brittle tortilla, and chicken burgers with a mulched clump of warmed lettuce at their heart. Compared to the academic food provision I had previously experienced, there was palpable ambition here, even if there didn't ever seem to be the skill or enthu-siasm to actually realise it.

Still, canteen was where I knew that I could use my faded charge card (a kind of culinary Oyster that could be topped up and used in select businesses on campus) to get myself a plate of chips and baked beans that I knew would only cost me 49p. It was the place where, for little over a pound, I could create an egg and bacon weekend breakfast sandwich, complete with pale, warm-breath toast slices and the additional carby hit of two hash browns, nuzzled beside each other and adhered to the bread with a sachet squirt of ketchup. Part of canteen's appeal was the ready availability of these dishes – cheap, cooked sustenance that, though hardly anything like balanced or buccaneering, was at least not completely nutritionally bankrupt.

This idea of inexpensiveness brings me on to the other significant facet of that university canteen. I remember looking up one day, bearing my tray of recessional lunchtime chips and beans, and noting one of my friends nonchalantly swerving the approaching bank of tills and walking his own food straight out of a fire exit, whistling as he went. There's every chance this wasn't the first time I had seen someone I knew get around financial constraints by just refusing to pay for things. In the mists of my memory, I have visions of emerging from the college shop and boggling, a little innocently, as pals magicked purloined bottles of Tropicana, Sure roll-ons and chocolate bars from jacket sleeves and clown car jeans pockets.

Yet it is that ambling confidence-trickster theft in the canteen that is most firmly fixed in my mind. Few images better encapsulate the reflexive mischief and disregard for rules of that first year; few scenes are more usefully illustrative of the fact that my social group viewed Royal Holloway as a corruptible, consequenceless fantasy land, only tangentially related to the real world beyond the campus perimeter. Even amid the rampant kleptomania of Bexleyheath, I had always been too much of an obedient scaredy-cat to ever shoplift (the one exception to this is a birthday card for one of my brothers that I swiped from a Crayford newsagents – an act of theft that feels like its own tangled morality play). At university, though, from within the wet clay of my reconfigured identity, I was open to new possibilities and the corrupting influence of friends. I was more inclined to see our little hustles related to food – blithely pocketing the sandwiches that were left in the unmanned, buzzing fridge of a student bar, say, or disappearing through that canteen fire exit with a cup of unpurchased milk for tea and cereal – as not just victimless crimes but barely crimes at all. This aversion to paying for things filtered out as well. By the second term of that first year I was working behind the bar at Crosslands: a swirly-carpeted, sticky-tabled approximation of a bright-lit pub that had a jukebox, attracted a faintly bookish, crumple-shirted clientele of outcasts (people banned from the official student union bars for fights or vomit-based transgressions were still allowed to drink in Crosslands), and stood in contrast to the foam parties, bellowing rugby players, and two-for-one shot deals that characterised other campus venues. I pulled pints and poured out slopping measures of tequila. I changed the barrel. I clamped inexplicably popular from-frozen paninis into a grubby toastie maker. These were my official roles and yet, soon, my job there came to be dominated by a complex system of doling out heavy discounts or free rounds to people I wanted to ingratiate myself with. Before long, as Crosslands' colleagues were working their own individual hustles, this accelerated into stray bits of stock (bottles of Becks, rustling bags of crisps, soft-edged Mars bars) finding their way into plastic bags at closing time, ahead of some after-hours party in my room. It was youthful exuberance, really. Light-fingeredness around food and drink was hardly a marker of my descent towards Al Capone-level, felonious villainy. But it was a period that signalled, in this newfound willingness to transgress and my latent tendency to emulate behaviours around me without much in the way of questioning, a significant shift in personality and moral core.

There was something else that was key, too. These adventures in petty theft (by and large a product of lax security that tended to assume undergraduates would abide by a kind of honesty bar system of payment) also shone a light on what would come to be a defining interplay between money, class and behaviour at university. Again, whether through pure luck or a form of magnetic recognition, lots of my firmest friends in that first term came from broadly similar backgrounds. Striving middle class. Less-than-flush rural middle

class. First-in-the-bloodline-to-actually-go-to-university working class. Though levels of privilege and financial safety net
diverged, we were among those who frittered away loans at
the maximum borrowing threshold, had credit card debt and
overdrafts, and occasionally bought pints with a pre-counted
stack of low-denomination coins. Royal Holloway, despite
grand appearances, was not a monolithically posh, wealthy
and old-fashioned environment; among a relatively multicultural student cohort, the quintessential undergraduate
was probably a solidly middle-class management student and
second-hand Fiat owner from the Home Counties. But
university was also the first time I experienced some of the
old-school hierarchical orthodoxies and upper-crust sneering of fee-paying schools. The first time I experienced the
performative Bullingdonian debasement and curdled 'dirty
pints' of sports team initiations; the first time I had been
somewhere where the notion of dressing up in counterfeit
Burberry for a student union 'Chav Night' was regarded as
light-hearted fun rather than the kind of grotesque embarrassment that would rightly get you chinned. Though we
were slave to all imaginable appetites and also active partici-
pants in the rolling performance of uni life (another group of
committed stoners who were our perpetual frenemies chris-
tened us 'The Fun Time Boys' with palpable scorn but inarguable accuracy), we also set ourselves up in opposition to it.
And so we didn't pay for everything we ate because we
couldn't afford to, but also because it became part of the way

we petulantly kicked against Royal Holloway's litany of rules and socially rewarded behaviours. That we were skint outsiders, doomed to live on our wits and stolen sandwiches, was both an incontrovertible fact and a tightly gripped, spiritual identity.

You may well have noticed that the glaring absence in this panorama of early university life is, well, much in the way of actual engagement with academia. It is, I think, quite a telling omission. That I was offered a place at Royal Holloway with a couple of A* grades at A level was the source of genuine pride and a radiating sense of achievement. To have sprung from Bexleyheath into a prestigious, important-sounding institution was the hard-won reward after late-night revision and homework sessions coupled with a life of quite nerdily committed study. Despite those occasional moments of youthful waywardness, I approached school with seriousness and discipline. Not just because of the smog of duty and parental expectation (and, let us be honest, fear) that hovers thickly over most second-generation immigrant kids. But also because it was something that lit me up and sparked my imagination. When it came to learning, as evinced by all that unsmiling commitment to David Mamet as interpreted by squeaky-voiced GCSE students, I was a credulous, unapologetic true believer.

Lots of that fell away at Royal Holloway. Just as university's limitless buffet of independence and liberty caused a degree of culinary regression, it also dampened what had long felt like a defining appetite for education for education's sake. English textbooks and modules struck me as dense and impenetrable. Other drama students, with their flashing zeal for performing, somehow seemed far more into it than me. Lectures very quickly became something that I blundered into late; rigour around all the reams of sign-up forms, essay assignments and course reading felt like something I was barely capable of, even as I strove to keep up and try harder. I think, really, it was quite a common instance of a shift in academic status and specialness. The creeping sense, experienced by many an overachieving state-school kid at a grand university, of no longer feeling like quite such an intellectual and cultural big fish in a relatively small pond.

Regardless of this, I remember that the actual study began to feel like a bit of a nuisance. I ignored vital admin and hurriedly skimmed books as a form of protection against a growing suspicion that I was massively out of my depth and, maybe, not all that smart after all. This was the other conscious part of my reconfigured, emotionally invulnerable persona. Work was hammered out at the last minute. Lectures and seminars were endured through a film of snakebite sweat. I slipped, imperceptibly, from someone capable of A* grades to a solid, unexceptional student in the hinterland between a 2:2 and a lower range 2:1. I was still far too much of a fearful goody-goody to completely disengage, but another major part of my self-conscious transformation in those first months was to essentially deprioritise almost everything at university that wasn't related to a kind of anarchic pleasure-seeking. Even now, the repeated scenes of that first term – a pub table strewn with plastic pint pots, cigarette dog-ends, and spent crisp packets, tightly folded into glinting triangles; a Finley Quaye CD trilling out through the smoke and laughter of a halls room; short-lived relationships and clumsy hookups that were their own sort of guileless, semi-ironic performance – feel like one rolling party. Albeit a party very occasionally punctuated by a dutiful trudge to the library to write 2,000 stilted words about a Chaucer passage I hadn't fully read or understood.

As the end of my first year at university approached, I would have been subsisting on 49p chips and beans, self-soothing with chained DVD episodes of *Futurama*, and carrying bin bags of stolen beers, crisps and chocolate bars to my room after a shift at Crosslands. Though I was having fun, I was limited by my lack of money and had the sense I had slightly slipped the moorings of myself. Some of the openness and optimism of that Ikea snack bar had evaporated. It would be a pressing need for funds, and the unexpected social collisions of higher education, that would bring about an even bigger change in the person I was becoming. And, beyond that, only further complicate the tangled, tricky business of food, finances and trying to fit in.

7

LAGOS II
Funeral Suya in the Fatherland

In the end, it was one woman's demise and another's new beginning that got me back to Nigeria. I had already explored other countries at that point: chip-stuffed gyros in Greece, late-night hot dogs in Reykjavik, puffy, hotel breakfast frittatas in Croatia. But by the spring of 2010, Mum had relocated to Lagos and a potential, mostly hypothetical trip to go out and visit her gained urgent solidity thanks to the passing of a beloved aunty. Mama-mi – so nicknamed because of her high, matriarchal status within the wider family – was Mum's eldest sibling and a relative I regarded with an abstract but intense fondness. Tiny, twinkly and with the signature buck-toothed grin of the Oyeyinkas, her status as Mum's proxy parent made her a kind of auxiliary grandma; a bustling, robust force who hummed the fond, half-remembered lullabies of my infancy and always radiated the kind of tactile affection that transcended the fact we sometimes struggled to understand each other.

Now, at the age of sixty-seven, she had died suddenly. And so it was set: my girlfriend, Madeleine, and I would head out, with apprehensive excitement, for a week of seeing Mum, visiting other relatives and attending the packed programme of funeral events that served to highlight the Yoruba people's inability to do anything by halves. Departures. Arrivals. Unions. To not mark them with vigour and expansiveness is to dishonour life's precious value. At twenty-six, following almost two decades of dogged avoidance, I was finally going to return to my ancestral home for an emotionally demanding, enormously significant trip that was seemingly going to be made on the hardest possible difficulty setting.

This was apparent right from the start. Not yet accustomed to the enervating scrum that begins at Lagos's Murtala Muhammed Airport – a place where tradition dictates that your first interaction with Nigerian culture will be via a bribe-hunting customs official asking, with a smile, 'So what have you brought for me?' – the next few days were so hazardous and unusual that there was barely space to register the supposed momentousness of this long-postponed homecoming. Here was the honking, juddering chaos of the roads, the swaying crates of purchasable mineral water on a column of street sellers' heads. Here were unfamiliar almost-relatives, appraising me with wistful regret and noting that my complexion was darker than it used to be when I was little. Here, in the car park beside the cemetery that would be my aunty's final resting place, was a horde of desperate beggars, thrusting amputated limbs at the glass as our driver edged us away, practically yawning at the ordinariness of the swarming bodies. Here was my Uncle Jibola, a gentle bear of a man and Mama-mi's second youngest brother, screaming, wailing and pleading, utterly inconsolable as we stood by the graveside.

Don't get me wrong. There was the joy and thrill of being back in Nigeria, too; the happy, nameless sense of belonging and the odd, bone-deep comfort of seeing innumerable other black faces either piling into battered *danfo* or beaming out from advertising billboards. Of realising that my blackness – a physical characteristic that shaped so much of how I moved through Britain – was, suddenly, just about the most ordinary and unexceptional thing in the world. (I will say here, though, that it was quite confronting to spot that the only other person I saw with their hair in messy twists like mine was a shoeless itinerant guy who seemed to live in a ditch beside the road.) Separately, there was joy and ballast to be found in the food. Steamed, chalky planks of yam with a softly spiced, pliable fold of omelette, thick with peppers and onions. Grey, faintly marbled balls of *eba*, or whipped cassava flour, carrying a familiar, slightly sour domestic musk. Shared trays of warm, freshly made *chin-chin*: the crunchable, deep-fried pastry pellets that have a craveable deliciousness despite the lingering sense-memory of dog biscuits appropriated for humans. Even if I wasn't partaking in the bone-clogged stews or hardcore swallows that would materialise on a table at my Aunty Toyin's house, their presence was comforting. A link to my deeper culture, but also the familiar smells, sounds and tactile sensations of our little patch of Lagos in Greater London.

However, despite these blasts of familiarity, the novel aspects of the trip – the grief, the alien environment, the act of introducing a white English partner to my many, many extremely Nigerian relatives – gave everything a heightened, blurring effect. Part of this is the passage of time and fading memory. Yet the defining feeling, at any given moment, was of not really knowing where I was being taken to or exactly what was due to happen next. Everywhere we went, heat bore down from grey, clouded skies, handkerchiefs were swiped uselessly across foreheads, and the emotional volume seemed to be cranked up to an unbearable level.

Which, I think, goes some way to explaining how unprepared I was for the moment when I had an unexpected encounter with my father. There had, I think, been some chatter about whether I might make plans to see him while I was in the country; entreaties from well-meaning uncles who were still friendly with him and didn't see anything all that peculiar about the painful scar of his estrangement or especially unusual about the fact I hadn't had any sort of meaningful contact with him for more than a decade. To me, he was still just a disembodied voice at the end of a phone line; the spectral force responsible for my brothers' private bindles of grievance and my mother's years of confusion, sadness and lone toil. Yet, to these uncles, as I gathered, he was a likeable and roguish hail fellow well met. A card and a laugh. So my response had been to bite my tongue and politely demur. But then, as the family and invited guests all gathered at Mama-mi's house for the wake-keeping – a practice where not just relatives and friends but the entire neighbourhood convene to pray and pay their open-casket respects to the deceased – this decision, like others related to interaction with the man known to most as Olumide Famurewa, was taken out of my hands.

I can picture a crowd of us, smartly dressed and damp-browed, making our way from muttered prayers in Mama-mi's darkened house and out into the brightness of a semi-rural street beyond an access barrier. The sight of my aunty's body, restful and poised but robbed of its igniting essence, had overloaded me somewhat. But there was relief to be moving on to the next phase of proceedings, whatever it entailed. Outside, there was another crush of bodies. The sense we were all being hustled on to some other defined phase of the week of mourning; Madeleine, Mum and my brother Ray were close by my side. And then, like the scene in a high-school movie where two adversaries encounter each other in the cafeteria, the kettling crowd around us parted slightly and another group broke in.

Very suddenly, there he was. A man who, like Nigeria itself, was the unseen force looming over almost every aspect of our lives in London. The person I think I had probably once ached to see but who, more recently, I only regarded with dimly recalled resentment. A human receptacle for conflicting currents of anger, pain, love, duty and maternal protectiveness. My chest constricted, I met the gaze beyond his sunglasses, and it all came back like a buried piece of source code. The swaggering demeanour. The thick moustache. The open, soft features and broad proboscis that people always said found their mirror in my own face. And the smile too; the devilish smirk at the perpetual joke of life. A smile I knew from photos and could just about discern as a fuzzy, flickering outline in the untrammelled depths of my brain's hard drive.

'Look who it is,' said Ray, with a measuredness and calm that I was already sure I wouldn't be able to muster. Mum must have said something too, but I have no memory of any exact words beyond her glare, the jostling motion of bodies around us, and the wordlessly agreed sense that, whatever this was, it would not be a prolonged encounter. Madeleine, either through the obvious physical resemblance or something Mum or Ray said, understood who this was and gripped me tightly from the side. Dad flashed that deflecting smile at Ray's words and then turned to me. He looked a little older; greyed, softened and plumper at the edges, in his traditional *agbada* robes and snug *fila* cap. The signature smile showed that he was now missing a tooth. But, beyond that, it was as if no time had passed from those faintly recalled days when he was a Toblerone-clutching, occasional presence rather than an abstract idea. 'Ah-ah, is this JJ?' he said, turning to address me, his voice the same gravelled, teasing burr. Madeleine held on; I forced myself to hold his tinted gaze. 'Or you don't remember me,' he said, after a beat. Now he turned, laughing, to address the watching chorus of onlookers. 'See, he doesn't remember me.' I took a breath and the bodies swirling around in the heat outside Mama-mi's house seemed to slow. 'No,' I said, through a tight jaw. 'I know who you are.'

And, with that, he was gone. Or, rather, we were. Mum, Madeleine, Ray and I hustled off into a waiting car and on to a celebration-of-life meal reserved for the closest family. Dad carried on with his retinue, off into Mama-mi's house to pay his respects, before disappearing into the mysterious ether from whence he sprang. Neither of us looked back.

Even describing this moment now, I slightly recoil at the soapy portentousness and drama of it. It feels embarrassing and overwrought. Though even that minimising instinct is a kind of parental inheritance. For all that Mum could occasionally be a woman of short temper, lacerating wit and volcanic, unstoppered reactiveness, she also stressed the importance of emotional control. Especially when we were in view of an audience that may judge us for a lack of stoicism, we were never to be flustered or rattled. Through life's trials and challenges – delayed trains, disobliging shop staff, the time we absentmindedly left bags of my cousin Tenne's newly bought clothes beneath our table in the McDonald's on The Strand – we were encouraged to never make a scene or forget the need to keep up appearances. The worst thing we could ever lose was our cool.

I think, beyond the obvious significance of it, that it is this maternal modelling and allergy to public showdowns that made the abortive reunion with my father so strange and discombobulating. Did he really think that I might not know who he was? Should I have challenged him in a more direct way, or prolonged the interaction? Pushed him for answers? Did it matter that I didn't especially want to do any of these things? So much that is related to my dad – his absence from my life, and the cultural context of it – feels abstract, hypothetical and difficult to grasp. These were the questions that buzzed about my head as we got into the car, my heart rate slowed, and Mum scathingly noted the disrespect of turning up to a wake-keeping in sunglasses.

Soon, we arrived outside the house of another sort-of relative (by then, it had become basically impossible to keep track of the blurred departures and arrivals) to drink and eat to my aunty's memory. My image, dulled by the tumult of having seen my father, is of intermingled browns as the sun came down on a gated compound edged in a perimeter wall spiked in broken glass; crowds spilling out on to a rust-coloured, untarred road, Afrobeats coming out of over-loaded speakers, and uncles sploshing ominous measures of cognac into plastic cups. Then, as if by magic, there was suddenly an ad-hoc suya stand: a rudimentary grill was set up on a verge beside the road, hauled into place by two unknown men. Smoking coals sent a dark, billowing plume up into the close, overcast atmosphere; glistening, sinuous pieces of marinated meat were pulled from a cool box and threaded on to dampened wooden skewers; there was the Wotsit-orange tub of *yaji* spice plus the customary accompaniment of roughly chopped red onion and tomatoes that always seemed soft enough to serve as ammunition at a set of medieval stocks.

It wasn't the slickly run, large-scale operation you'd find at one of Lagos's more storied suya spots. More likely, a cousin or uncle had engineered it with the haggled price and currency exchange that is the lubricating force that moves and motivates this megacity of more than 28 million. Yet its presence signalled the shift in tone and atmosphere following the morning's moments of final farewell and unscheduled reacquaintance. The wake-keeping and burial had been events to jointly endure. A chance to pay respects and deliver prayers; to look without blinking at the sadness of it, set Mama-mi dancing off to the perfect peace of heaven, and then cross over ourselves to a point of hard-won, red-eyed understanding.

But the arrival of the suya stand and the gathering beside it felt a lot more jubilant, party-ish and unapologetically celebratory. I had always been aware, from naming ceremonies, weddings and hall parties, that food was a source of both succour and meaning during important occasions. However, as this was only the second funeral I'd been to – and the very first Yoruba one I'd attended – I had, amid the emotional whiplash of my return, a building realisation of how Nigerians used ritualised eating as a joyful means to process bereavement. Not just that, in fact, but the intimate connectedness between life and death, between wailing, animalistic pain and the hedonistic release of party music, barbecue and a dwindling bottle of Rémy Martin at the *owambe* parties that are practically an intangible piece of cultural heritage. This is true of lots of cultures, of course. And particularly non-English ones. Nonetheless, there is an animating ritual and centrality to Nigerian funeral food that I suddenly appreciated and recognised as starkly different to the sombre respectfulness of cling-filmed sandwiches and gathered crowds around a tea urn in a carpeted suburban function room.

Given the overload of feeling that accompanied my long-postponed return to Nigeria, I appreciated the mirrored sense of bountiful intensity to be found in the funeral feasts that spilled out from my aunty's burial. And so it was that both Mama-mi's death and the destabilising encounter with my dad would come to be associated with the paper-swaddled spoils of that pop-up suya stand. *I know who you are.* Those words turned over and over in my mind, as we all stood and picked with spice-tinted fingers at warm, wobbling lobes of seared meat, gulped more cognac and cold Gulder beer from dusty, oversized bottles, and discussed the possibility of going, later on, to a club in Lagos. The exchange with my father had been perhaps fittingly inconclusive and unsatisfying; two very different, relative strangers sharing a halting, half interaction beside a dirt road. What I didn't realise at the time, as we scooped up peppered meat and onions in the dwindling West African sun, was that those would end up being the very last words I spoke to him.

There is a patch of central London where the impact of my father's absence all comes surging back. Just along from Leicester Square's noisy distractions, on the intersection of Haymarket and Piccadilly, there is a sculptural fountain set into the base of an office building: a lipped marble edge, the frothing spray of water, and four carved bronzes of horses, rearing up in the manufactured surf.

Officially called *The Horses of Helios*, it is one of those bland, minor landmarks that most Londoners would barely give a second glance; a touristy picture opportunity in the same broad continuum as the dilapidated red phone boxes that may well be the world's most dutifully photographed public latrines. All the same, this fountain is the site of a photo that was taken with my father during a rare early moment of safety, fun and contentedness that I can just about still discern. Me on his lap, perhaps, and my brothers and my mum either side of him as we sit and smile beneath the galloping steeds. Today, when I whizz by it on my bike or distractedly hustle past on my way to Soho, I either avert my gaze or stare it down, giving in to its throbbing psycho-geographic power.

It is a reminder of the fact that Olumide Famurewa did, despite it all, provide me with one or two potent memories that have the dull glow of positivity and happiness. Of course, the other aspect of the fountain's significance, the dim trace of that lost Kodak moment and the fact I have spent the intervening years ransacking it for meaning, is that it shows how scant my recollections of my father are. From the age of around six – and the period that, barring my birth in London, my family decided to settle in the UK for the long term – his permanent residence, his home, has never been the same as mine. This is an early, mist-shrouded period of life. Accented, here and there, by some of his returns in the half decade or so afterwards when he would still occasionally come to see us in London. To concentrate really hard on some of the things that I do actually remember about my father – his love of Phil Collins, an apparent carjacking in Lagos that left him with an angry, inflamed wound on the heel of his foot, a photograph of him looking bemused as he emerges from the bathroom in Sydney Road, a towel clamped around the solid drum of his belly – is to open a ravaged box of stray Lego pieces. There is not much, and it is difficult to discern if any of it connects into any sort of coherent structure.

This is the context that helps explain my particular experience of and attitude to Dad's fitful presence and prolonged absence from all our lives. Especially in relation to my older brothers, my mum, and other members of the wider family who had a very different relationship with him. What's more, it also gives a sense of why one of the strongest memories that I do have of him has cast such a long shadow.

One day when we were in the house on Littledale, and I was around nine or ten years old, I happened to be messing around with a brand-new box of cook's matches. Maybe I was merely meant to be putting them away after a trip to the supermarket. Maybe I'd been told to fetch them for a grown-up. Whatever the specifics, my memory is of fiddling with the cardboard drawer of the box, having perhaps been warned not to, and then looking on with horror as the whole thing gaped open and the entire payload of matches went tumbling all over the floor. Dad, who was back from Lagos, sharply told me that I needed to pick them all up. The impossible futility of the task ahead of me and the burning shame of having erred overwhelmed me and my lip wobbled. 'Ah, are you crying? Are you a baby?' he said, firmly but with an amused smile. It was too much. Instant hot tears came snivelling from my face as I picked up each of the fallen matches and pleaded with no one in particular, cursing my existence.

And do you know what my dad did, at that point? As I blubbed and pleaded? Well, he chuckled, teasingly, at how wet and dramatic I was being, and then went off to get a camera so he could memorialise my ridiculousness; to make a show of it.

Let us pause for a moment here. I think, regardless of particular cultural designation, this will be a form of cheerfully blundering and thoughtless 1980s and 1990s parenting that plenty of people will recognise. This, after all, was an era in which it was quite normal for children to be teased and smacked or snapped at in the sort of gently traumatising way that would be the future concern of a mental health professional. Not through cruelty for cruelty's sake. But, rather, through a sense of the importance of discipline, a desire to toughen children up, and a very human frustration with filial behaviours you could not comprehend or adequately control. What's more, show me a parent who hasn't miscalculated or overreached when it comes to the particular sensitivities of their children, who hasn't, however momentarily, forgotten that though they are descended from you they are very much their own people, and I will show you someone who is either a liar or delusional.

What's significant, I think, is that my memories of my dad are so limited that this bit of teasing with the matches has an undue prominence when it comes to my sense of him. When I try to focus on the man who is the spectre at the feast of my life, when I try to really lock in on the person whose presence I missed out on, I think of the moustachioed smile and the camera flash and my embarrassed tears.

'Oh, that was just Olumide,' said my mum, with a rueful smile, when I told her about this story years later. And that was it, as well. The match box incident was two misaligned personalities in conflict with each other. It was my dad trying to counteract my catastrophising English softness with what I gather was his signature Nigerian brand of tough, needling insult comedy. He was showing me who he was and hoping to nudge me down that behavioural path.

So what sort of man was he? Though much of his life and his long, complicated relationship with my mum is either unknown to me or shrouded in a fog of mystery, it is a question worth asking. There is also the fact that the particulars of lots of this biography stretch beyond the bounds of that which it is my business to know or share. But here is what I am aware of, in relation to the broader context of how my father and I ended up having that clenched exchange outside Mama-mi's house. Born in 1947 and raised in Ilesha, a city in the Yoruba heartland of Nigeria's south-west, Dad first met Mum, an upper-middle-class Lagosian princess, at university in the early 1970s.

In 1975 they were married; by 1976 my eldest brother, Folarin, had been born and within seven years both Ray and I would arrive. Yet the early context of my parents' relationship – namely, Dad's sense of class inferiority and the feeling they were somewhat mismatched in terms of temperament and culture – would set the texture of the rest of their lives and ours. Though, notably, these foundational fractures would not grow into full destabilising fissures for years to come.

In the infancy of our family's life in Lagos, there was happiness, the neat, conformist balance of a nuclear family and a boom-time abundance that Folarin especially got to enjoy and romanticise. This period has a folkloric, magical hue, when it is discussed in the family. And I cannot help but think that there was a continuation of this magic – a kind of collective suspension of disbelief that we all continued to engage in even as we moved to London and the separateness of Dad's existence became more obviously apparent. That paternal void was the hole in the boat; a fact that we were all jointly engaged in denying even as we baled out freezing, ankle-deep water.

Throughout this period of unpredictable but semi-consistent contact, Dad's presence in our lives would be marked by food as much as anything else. Not just the airport Toblerones that would herald his return, but the trays prepared by Mum – the creamy mound of *amala* or pounded yam swallow; the richly carmine stew, hazardously clogged with delicate fish bones; the shallow bowl of warm water for his fingers – that were delivered to him in his upholstered throne and signalled his status as both head of the household and honoured, occasional guest.

However, meals marked his absence too. Food was everything in our family. Yet, even if I scour the deepest, cobwebbed recesses of my mind, there is not, save for that duty-free chocolate, a single memory of being fed by him or even eating alongside him during this period. A patterned plate of softened, white-fleshed sweet potato and slurried corned-beef stew. The wonder of an egg perfectly steam-boiled in the sharply clamped folds of a Breville toastie maker. All of us gathered around the wafting fryer smell and condensation-beaded bucket of a Friday night KFC. Dad is not in any of these formative, oft-repeated scenes, a sure sign that his active role in our lives was very much open to interpretation and a further, complicating snag in the mechanics of our relationship. Eating and drinking was how we marked our time and negotiated life trials and triumphs. To not know how we ate, to not know the shared pleasure we took from the warm heel of fresh-baked super-market baguette devoured in the Big Sainsbury's car park, was to not know us at all.

And yet, on and on the fantasy went. I looked at friends who had divorced parents, stepdads and somewhat errant biological fathers, and saw no parallel between our lives. Mum notes that, on hearing that my childminder's daughter was growing up without any sort of contact with her dad, I expressed the kind of clucking, judgemental disbelief a convent Mother Superior would have been proud of. The fiction around my father's role in our lives was that strong; a trotted-out explanatory line that I knew off by heart. Oh, my dad? Yeah, the only reason we don't all live in the same house is that his engineering business is based in Lagos.

He's always coming back to see us, and he's actually going to move here permanently soon.

This was the protective fantasy and rhetoric. Never mind that, as the 1990s edged forward, landmark birthdays and achievements ticked by, and milestones were passed, he wasn't there. Never mind that, by the early 2000s, whatever financial support he was meant to be providing had evaporated to the point that Mum needed a second job. Never mind that basic contact let alone visits were simply no longer a thing. The falsehood that we were part of an unbroken, two-parent home was like a wilful lie we had been telling for so long that it no longer registered as untrue.

What's more, there were cultural forces insulating men like my father from too much questioning or judgement. This applied in the sense of a broad societal moment – a post-war age where the expectation was that the man of the house would be an emotionally and physically distant provider, a loving tyrant who sat in the armchair with a newspaper, doled out discipline, and disappeared to pubs and betting shops or out on other mysterious assignations. Free from judgement as long as he put food on the table; head of a family he was often only peripherally a part of.

But, for my dad, there was also the intensifying influence of his Yoruba heritage. Gender roles always seemed especially complex and contradictory within our culture. Though mothers, grandmothers and aunties (related or otherwise) were the visible, highly influential figureheads of our sprawled family units, it was men who were afforded deference and a kind of behavioural impunity. Relatedly, the norms of traditional village life, where it was the right of every paterfamilias to have multiple wives and many children, persisted even in modern metropolises like Lagos and London. Then you have the fact that to live separately from your children – liberated from the more tiresome aspects of childcare in order to focus on work and making money – was a kind of memetic, self-perpetuating fashion among Nigerian men especially. We neither sought nor expected a rationalising apology for Dad's estrangement. It was hand-waved away as an enshrined fact of culture and a mark of his unwillingness to assimilate; as unshakeable and immutable as his fondness for whipped tubers, robustly seasoned stews and the cold bitter gulp of stout. To wish him to live with us in London permanently was to wish him into being a different person.

Years later, I can look at this with some measuredness and the softening lens of cultural context. But back then? As the new millennium hit and I crossed over from adolescence into young adulthood? My feelings generally formed into a low resentment, steadily simmering at the heart of my being. By the early 2000s, the fiction of Dad's active connection to the family had been irreparably shattered. He had, as far as we knew, not actually come to London for approaching a decade and, though he and my mum still had conversations on the phone – often hostile and accusatory, occasionally teasing and loving, always in an overproof-strength Yoruba that it was difficult for me to completely follow – any contact or engagement I had with him was minimal. Those scant memories of him had begun to fade and my feelings were shifting from the specifics related to a person and more a shadowed absence; a lost or denied idea rather than a particular parental sensibility or consciousness that I was pining for.

In this period, my rare conversations with him felt, in truth, like a tiresome obligation. 'Folajimi,' came the low, rumbling voice over the phone. 'Do you know who this is?' From there it would be the kind of courteous, boiler-plate questions – *How is school? Are you being a good boy?* – that betrayed a lack of familiarity with any aspects of my life, personality or interests. In fact, more than that, they hinted at the arrested nature of our relationship. He had missed so much that his image of me was frozen at the point of that small child, squirming on his lap before a fountain or blubbering amid a carpet of spilled matches. It was like he was peering through a telescope at the past form of a distant planet. And so he went on, trying half-heartedly to engage the little boy he had known. Never realising that the seventeen-year-old on the other side of the line saw the conversation as an interminable distraction from his paused *Pro Evolution Soccer* game and mid-afternoon bowl of Frosties.

Soon, this more neutral approach to what basically amounted to parental abandonment proved insufficient. My feelings were activated into something more pronounced and burning. An emotional shift that was shaped, mostly, by a deeper appreciation of the impact Dad's absence had inevitably had on Mum's life and circumstances; to the obvious connection between his denial of all forms of support and her palpable struggle to keep the expensive, enervating show of solely raising three children on the road. To be clear, this was 'struggle' only in the superhumanly durable sense that someone of Kofo Famurewa's natural disposition would ever countenance it. Even at a young and especially self-obsessed age, I tended to stand back in awe and grateful, disbelieving appreciation whenever I was reminded of Mum's inextinguishable fire, unrivalled toughness and bottomless reservoir of generous selflessness. Her stubborn creativity and resourcefulness when it came to cooking translated to everything else, and life was a kind of Buckaroo game that alighted on how much this little woman could single-handedly heap on to her shoulders without collapsing.

Taking in nieces, nephews and the offspring of close friends, for prolonged, indeterminate periods? Cooking a late-night meal, propped up only by force of will and a microwaved mug of Gold Blend, despite the fact her fourteen-hour workday had begun with a 4 a.m. cleaning shift at a Dartford office building? Providing academic, moral and financial support to three occasionally erratic young men who always seemed to have their hands out for a cadged tenner? Mum took all this on with the loving, determined pugnaciousness of someone who saw no other available alternative. As with Dad, and his inalienable right to be an absent Yoruba patriarch, answerable to no one, this was Mum's cultural coding. She was one of countless West African single mothers by proxy, lent indomitability by both nature and nurture. Onions, peppers and plopping cans of plum tomatoes were blitzed for stew; sweetcorn was nuked in the working microwave beneath the broken one. And, in the kitchen as in life, Mum leant into the surrounding chaos and emerged, against the odds, with something quietly extraordinary.

This is an oft-repeated rhetoric about Nigerian mothers, immigrant mothers, and single mothers of all stripes more generally. But it would be remiss to gloss this period as one where Dad's absence never led to visible signs that Mum was feeling the strain. For all the garrulous chatter and passionate invective of our house, there was still a lot to do with family issues that remained unaddressed and unexpressed; a veiled secrecy and obfuscation that covered everything from Mum and Dad's separation to all sorts of matters related to sex, drugs or any of the adult world's other manifold temptations. Nonetheless, even in the depths of my teenage self-centredness I picked up on things.

Mum, on the phone to Dad, her voice raised and desperate after some latest broken promise or period of uncontactable disappearance. Mum, tearful, exhausted and wrung

out, trying to forcibly keep Folarin in the house and physically reprimand him during a particularly wayward period
in his early twenties. Mum, after a last-roll-of-the-dice return
to Lagos in the mid-2000s, matter-of-factly revealing to us
that she'd just discovered a new, world-shaking betrayal that,
without wanting to stray fully into family secrets that aren't
solely mine to tell, hinted that we were not his only depend-
ents and that those airport Toblerones were perhaps being
bought in bulk. For all Mum's unfazed determination and
sharp-tongued humour, the years of bearing so much alone
inevitably left a mark. One day, sent to fetch some paracetamol from her handbag, I found a new, hardly touched pack
of cigarettes – bought, she would later confide, as part of a
one-time experiment to see if lighting up could provide a
salve for her shredded nerves.

For me, the feeling of finding these was akin to seeing a
bottle of Glen's vodka and a crack pipe tumble out of Santa's
pocket. But I got it. Here was a woman who justifiably craved
some relief from the pressure; here were the swan legs frantically kicking beneath my contented, happy passage
through life. Kofo Oyeyinka, the prideful, spiky, smart girl
from Surulere who spurned Olumide Famurewa's initial
advances, was still in there. And she knew she deserved
better than the terms of a life and a marriage changed without her say-so. This was the backdrop to that encounter in
2010 and the years that followed it – a sense of profound
gratitude and sadness on my mum's behalf and, for my dad,

a steady closing off of emotion. If there had been a low, flickering pilot light of curiosity or affection for him then this
was the moment that it was completely extinguished.

So it's fair to say that when Mum called, in 2014, to tell us
that Dad had died, there was no obvious shape to my feelings. Even now, the particulars of the news and how it was
disseminated are a little hazy. I have an image of long iPhone
messages from Mum and my siblings, peppered with both
rote, mournful prayers and harsher, more accusatory
language. There was, amid second-hand mutterings about a
prolonged illness and typically Nigerian aversion to medical
specificity, no clear cause of death given. The nested questions and deceptions of Dad's time on this earth followed
him into the afterlife. His bequeathal to those that survived
him was a tangled, tense communication network of semi-
estranged relatives sharing information between Britain,
Nigeria and America.

Everyone was passing on solemn apologies and best
wishes, when it wasn't immediately clear what they were for.
The regret felt formless and general. How do you go about
mourning a dad who you didn't know in any meaningful
way? With all of this swirling, it is not all that surprising that
those first few days after the news had hit only come back to
me as an ill-defined, unsteadying blur.

What I absolutely do remember, however, is the day when
my brothers and I went back to Mum's for a planned

conference call to discuss the particulars of the funeral. She was still at the Crayford house so it felt, fittingly, almost like an act of time travel. Ray, Folarin and I pushing in from biting April cold to sink deep into the reclinable corner sofa. The low murmur of Sky Sports News and the close, cluttered warmth of the living room, with its Palm Sunday crosses and grinning gallery of family pictures. Mum bustling in now and again to set down food – a wibbly serving of spiced eggs, sausages split down the middle and pushed into the pan to cook quicker – variously expressing sadness at the closed chapter represented by my father's passing and a kind of appalled wonder at the broken wickedness of his spirit. 'Ah, Olumide,' she would occasionally proclaim, from the midst of a breathless, teeth-kissing monologue from the kitchen. She was mournful regret and enlivening, defiant rage in conflict with each other; a twitching, kinetic mass of contradictory feelings, theories and additional, unsavoury revelations about Dad that she had been privy to in the last few days.

And then, once we had eaten, we gathered around the bed in the murk of Mum's bedroom while one of Dad's brothers put his case forward through the loudspeaker of a phone in the middle of the bed. It was my Uncle Joseph – a man I had scarcely seen nor spoken to since those long, endless summers in Michigan. Images flickered of the wedding garter, the smushed cake, a basketball hitting the backboard and bouncing out onto a driveway. Uncle Joseph spoke, with the slick measuredness of someone used to defusing corporate conflict, of his deep regret and sorrow. At Dad's absence from our lives. At the hovering toxic cloud of his apparent other indiscretions. And at the lamentable cold war that this behaviour had precipitated between the Oyeyinka and Famurewa sides of the family. Mum stood, paced and forcibly delivered some home truths; Folarin and Ray – asserting that they were no longer boys, but adults and fathers themselves – passionately said their piece, and I did too.

As with the standoff four years previously, outside Mamami's house, it all felt like a moment of such uncharacteristic melodrama and confrontation that it was like it was happening to someone else. After a few minutes of spiking tension – where it seemed increasingly obvious that my uncle was as in the dark as many of us about the particulars of his brother's life and recent wilderness years – talk turned to the existence of an online memorial and plans for a funeral in Lagos. 'What is done is done but he was your father,' said my uncle, in a sorrowful mid-Atlantic voice. 'And so I hope that you guys can head out for the burial.'

He was your father. The notion of feeling 'gaslit' is an overused piece of comparative rhetoric. Yet it is hard to think of a better means of describing what years of this pretence around my father had done to me and, by extension, my mum and my brothers. The more challenging and traumatic aspects of our collective experience had been given a kind of cultural cover by the idea that there was nothing unusual about it; that life was complicated, marriage was hard, and my dad was just another fallible Yoruba patriarch intensely committed to business interests in the country. All fair. But, given I was in the first idealistic flush of parenthood myself, I had a building sense that to merely use Nigerianness as an excuse – for both parental neglect and, also, an unquestioning sense of filial loyalty – felt off, and in some way inadequate.

Fatherhood felt to me like it was something earned through consistent, active participation rather than declared because of biology and cultural convention. Awaking to the challenge of it and being present anyway was the point. And so I spoke up, and told my uncle, as respectfully as I could, that I had no desire to go to Dad's funeral to honour the memory of someone I didn't know. 'My loyalty is to Mum,' I said, voice clear and unwavering, though I sensed what a transgressive act it seemed to deny the wishes of elders. I felt resolute. Or, at least, I thought I was. There was more conversation on the phone between my uncle and my brothers, who were either less firm in their stance (Ray) or very keen to be there, despite it all (Folarin). I remember looking over at Mum and, though her grief still wore a scowling mask of anger, there was a faint smile on her face, and a hint of something that looked like pride.

8

Down and Out in
Egham and London

Beyond the shock of the unforeseen encounter with my dad, one of the hidden comforts of that 2010 return to Lagos was how broadly similar it was to other childhood holidays I had experienced. I would be in domestic environments that were generally familiar; there would be relatives on hand to provide a degree of consistency and security. In fact, you could say that up until the last days of my teens, summers had generally come in two distinct flavours. Some years it would be south-east London, cage football, stray cousins, and blowing out a dusty N64 cartridge as if it were a harmonica. Others it would be the shivering chill of condo air-conditioning, Steve Urkel on the television, the rank back note of Hershey's Kisses and those long, sweltering interregnums in America.

But the July of 2004 brought the jolt of something new in terms of both cuisine and culture. As our second year at Royal Holloway sputtered to a close and summer yawned before us, my friend Dan and I somehow formulated a plan to combine both a holiday and temporary employment. Arabella – a mate of Dan's who wore her cartoonish poshness with amiable good humour – let slip that her mum was in need of some handymen to perform a few menial painting jobs on the grand, dishevelled home she had recently bought in France's rural south-east. Dan, ever alive to ways that he could turn the social inequities at Royal Holloway to his advantage, suggested that he and I could do it. That Arabella, as I remember it, was open to some form of romantic escalation in her and Dan's friendship probably only helped our cause.

I do not recall the particulars of putting it all together or exactly how Dan and I – who were always united in being either perennially skint or briefly and incontinently flush with loan money – managed to pay for the necessary flights and car hire. Somehow, motivated by adventure and financial necessity, we pulled it off. And soon we were in the high-summer swelter of a tiny little village near Avignon in Provence preparing for a week of work (followed by a pleasure-seeking trip to the western Mediterranean coast), and broadly enacting what felt like a sexually charged arthouse movie about class tension, beautiful coastal vistas and practical ineptitude. Think Y *Tu Mamá También* remade by the Chuckle Brothers.

The week comes back to me as a series of sun-bleached, hyperreal scenes, thick with both triumph and calamity. The creaking, haunted gloom of Arabella's mother's cobwebbed home, in a former village schoolhouse. Dan and I, hunched over paint pots and removed window shutters in the pummelling sunshine of the yard, as Arabella lazed nearby, reading a paperback in a bikini. The whooshing sight of French countryside through the hire-car windows, as we cranked a Kings of Leon CD and scream-sang gibberish lyrics at the top of our lungs. It was only ten days or so away. Yet it felt like a crash course in experiencing the possibilities of a fascinating, inscrutable and ruggedly picturesque environment; a fleeting taste of the kind of free-wheeling gap-year adventure that, through both cultural expectation and my own impatience to move on to the next staging post of life, never really seemed like a viable option. Throw in the simmering situation with Dan and Arabella – a dynamic that meant it was never clear whether my presence was blocking a potential union or opening up the tantalising possibility of a temporary throuple – and I think you have an even greater sense of why it is all still so vivid, so charged. Though occurring outside term time, it was a piece of education every bit as significant as what was taking place in the overheated lecture halls and seminar rooms of my first two years at Royal Holloway.

Naturally, this acquiring of new forms of knowledge very much applied to food. To be clear: some of this was the strangeness and scarcity of experiencing a slow-paced Provencal backwater through the prism of our status as both invited guests and hired staff. As a child of chain restaurants, corporate standardisation and big-city abundance, this was the first time I had encountered a 'restaurant' like the lone establishment in the village: a shadowed, menu-less micro-bistro that opened for a handful of haphazard hours every day, served only an indeterminate brown stew and frothed halves of draught beer, and was peopled by scowling locals who frowned as Dan and I sidled in. Separately, Arabella's mother, small, fluttery and not especially warm or sociable, could occasionally be heard muttering to her daughter about our work schedule there ('I just want to make sure they're justifying their time here,' she said, at one point, as Dan and I lurked in some unseen corridor, widening our eyes in horror) and became the person we relied upon for at least one meal a day.

To say that these dishes were not bountiful expressions of love and butter-laden indulgence is to be far too coy about it. One evening after a day of committed toil in the sunshine, there was just a shallow puddle of thin, cabbage-choked broth for the day's main meal. Needless to say, it became the stuff of furious legend. 'Soup for dinner!' repeated Dan, later, with spluttering disbelief, as we took a pacing constitutional around the village on our lunch break. My memory is that my hunger overrode any of my pickiness when we were faced by these bizarre staff meals. Yet I can still feel, in my bones, the awkward, creeping strangeness of those few days in the musty Havisham-ish halls of that old schoolhouse; the sense that, in trying to engineer a hustle whereupon we were essentially paid to be on holiday, we had fallen into the trap of second-class citizenship and wilful servitude (that there were other, posher friends of Arabella's arriving later in the summer for what sounded like a more straightforward vacation did not help matters).

Thankfully, as work had ended for that week, and Arabella's mum handed over the sheaf of euros that would be our payment, our culinary education became less inhibited and loaded. There was a trip to a farmers' market in another village, where local cheese stalls had the thick, honking ripeness of a sun-warmed nappy bin. There were tiny, thrumming boulangeries serving cracked, featherlight baguettes, formed into an irregular well-fired point, that were light years beyond the supermarket batons I knew and loved. There was a gleaming, futuristic service station – complete with the decidedly French presence of self-service red wine and coarse-cut steak haché, drowned in a butter-glossed au poivre sauce – that was genuinely better than about 80 per cent of the actual restaurants I had been to. In Perpignan, after billowy omelettes, frites and absinthe, we went tearing into the moonlit waves in just our underwear.

Obviously, those archival cooking-show clips on *Saturday Kitchen*, and the ambient reverence of the culture at large, had given me a sense of French dining's importance and offhand brilliance. I affected the unfazed demeanour and experimental spirit that I had taken with me to Royal Holloway. But to experience some of the languor and ceremony of the French approach to eating, to eat in an environment where great produce was boringly commonplace and lunch was an enshrined moment of pause, was truly revelatory. Faced with the newness of this, I was similarly encouraged to be new. Midway through our road trip, we joined the swarm of tourists within Carcassonne's walled medieval citadel for the local delicacy that every other person was ordering: brimming terracotta dishes of cassoulet, clogged with white beans, burnished pieces of pork and game, and ornamented by a ravishing, fragrant broth solidifying, here and there, into a kind of jelly.

Yes, it was basically a slightly naff piece of mass-produced theme park dining not all that dissimilar from those giant Disney World turkey legs. True, it also fitted my general eating credo of stodgy, salty, vegetable-light brownness above all. Nonetheless, that cassoulet, and my greedy appreciation of its ever-shifting, succulent heft, felt like a pivotal stop-off on my journey towards a more inquisitive and trusting approach to food and to life. Here was the benefit of exposure to new people, new experiences. Here, in contrast to that nervous boy, fearfully looking for the most inoffensive thing on a curry house menu, was someone open to letting new discoveries shift his culinary identity. For a set-in-his-ways British-Nigerian kid, visiting mainland Europe for basically the first time, it was a small but significant step. Later on, after Carcassonne and the cassoulet, Arabella, Dan and I sat in a frothing hotel hot tub, sipping supermarché cava as the sun went down over a twinkling harbour. I was three months from my twenty-first birthday, weeks ahead of the shadowed unknowns of my final year at uni, and still as poor as ever. Even so, the world rippled anew with delicious possibility.

The impact of France was almost certainly amplified by a sharp contrast with what had generally preceded it. First year ended. Those idiosyncratic halls of residence rooms were swapped for rented three-beds and four-beds in the surrounding area. We officially handed over the sticky baton of fresher status to a brand-new batch of over-excited, pot-plant-clutching inebriates. All the same, this supposed progression, a non-negotiable step away from the bubble of campus and out into a preparatory approximation of the real world, only seemed to yield newly discovered sublevels of chaotic immaturity.

Dan, Pete, Craig and I all moved from our burrows in Founder's into a shared semi-detached house in a place called Englefield Green – a fairly insalubrious residential area that lay about a twenty-minute walk from campus and had an impoverished edginess that reminded me of home – and it was like we had wordlessly agreed to fill out an entirely new bingo card of student clichés. This began with the house itself. Set on a long, curving road of family proper-ties appropriated for students by opportunistic landlords, ours was a fairly spacious three-bed (with a cannily subdivided extra bedroom), rigged with its own design quirks and bent out of all shape by our anarchic attitude and general indolence. Not long after we moved in, an especially riotous house party yielded a hole in the living-room wall (caused by a flung George Foreman grill) and a mysterious wisp of white fungus that grew out from a kitchen worktop. The main toilet, thanks to an inept piece of planning from a spatially challenged plumber, had a half porthole carved into its door, all the better for mischievous housemates to reach a terrifying hand through. Late on in the year, a leaking radiator near the front door turned a stretch of carpet into a fetid entrance swamp that, rather than try to fix or call the landlord about, we simply asked girlfriends, potential paramours and other visitors to vault over. Then there were our next-door neighbours: a family of scowling locals who embodied the occasionally violent 'town and gown' wars that proliferated in the area, and would spend what felt like every waking moment percussively booting a football at our front door.

And, oh, the smells! Craig's dank troll hole beneath the stairs seemed to emanate the drifting scent of fried onions; Pete's room, in Dan's deathless coinage, had a low funk that was suggestive of an unlicensed elephant enclosure. It's a measure of the partial commitment to order and cleanliness I had grown up around (not to mention my capacity for compartmentalisation of all categories) that I always made sure my room was a relative sanctuary – all low lighting, proudly displayed DVD collection and mood-setting R&B CDs, judiciously locked and guarded whenever there were house parties. Yet there was rarely a day when I came home and didn't find some new, deposit-endangering piece of damage; some part of the house that was freshly out of bounds thanks to a shooting range of ash-flecked beer cans or an overstuffed bin bag left to weep in the middle of a room. Again, none of this is especially novel in the context of student housing. We were not the first undergraduates to plumb new depths of slatternly debasement while living under the same roof. But there seemed to be a particularly stark volatility and derangement to putting the id of all our personalities together, away from the policing and structure of campus. As other friends in Englefield Green started to have concertedly grown-up dinner parties, we seemed to be lashing out a little at the spectre of adult seriousness and laughing from within the wreckage.

This, of course, brings us to what the second year did to my culinary life and still-forming eating identity. Surely, I hear you say, finally having access to an actual kitchen meant that I could crack the spines of those cookbooks and start to throw together the things I saw TV chefs knocking up under the glare of studio lighting? Not quite. There was rarely a moment in that house when the kitchen hadn't been turned into the kind of toxic blast zone that required surgical gloves and a protective cordon of biohazard tape. A lettuce head that someone had bought to make a salad sat on one of the counters for literal weeks, turning to mulch. There was an unexplained, fine dusting of Bisto all over the other surfaces and sections of the floor. One day, we came home to find Craig, asleep, as the oven plumed black smoke from the 'cottage pie' (unseasoned mince, a whole onion and giant hunks of quartered, unwashed potato) he had decided to cook one afternoon. Here was that *Jackass*-level atmosphere of pranks, impulsiveness and occasional idiocy that we all revelled in, translated to food. A world in which behaviour seemed to work backwards from how amusing the eventual anecdote would be.

True, we did decamp to the flat section of roof outside Pete's room once, on a sweltering heatwave day towards the end of term, for an unexpectedly competent barbecue of burgers, hot dogs and those flavourless corn cobs that come in beslimed, shrink-wrapped packaging. But I seem also to remember that we frisbeed most of the rubbish we had into the overgrown back garden, nestling beer bottles and paper plates in the undergrowth to join so many discarded pizza boxes and flicked roaches. My wimpy squeamishness around decomposition and food mess caused an inevitable retreat. My memory of those days is that I had a growing number of opinions about cuisine but, living in an inhospitable domestic environment and largely focused on the whirl of university's social distractions, I had neither the real knowledge nor inclination to further explore any of them.

That said, my sensibilities and understanding around food did continue to shift. As exemplified by the trip to France, the last two years of university really did represent a pivotal period in the reconfiguring of my appetite and its relationship to self. It was just that a lot of these revelations tended to occur not in any sort of domestic space, but in places where food was paid for. Naturally, lots of this continued the running theme of grimy student cliché. I remember that, for a time, every night out ended with the moment when we would all slump on sofas in the living room (beneath the George Foreman-created crater), posting molten slices of pepperoni and jalapeño Tops Pizza into our mouths. Punctuation to all the oceans of snakebite and Smirnoff Ice-spiked 'turbo shandies' came from pub fry-ups, consoling trays of curly fries in the midst of a student union club night, and Rustlers burgers in rubbery, microwaved buns. A trash-forward diet that ensured my graduation photo, rather than a snapshot of a youthful twenty-one-year-old on the precipice of adulthood, instead depicts a beer-puffed man-child tipping merrily towards his damp-browed, Vegas Elvis era.

However, this was an epoch rich with other, less predictable instances of culinary initiation. Somehow, this period at Royal Holloway was also the first time my dining vernacular expanded to include quite a diverse range of restaurants. Which, I suppose, is another way of saying this: for a gang of impoverished culinary dunces, we seemed to spend an awful lot of our time eating out.

In that second year especially, we would all hop on a train to the Outback Steakhouse – a short-lived, quasi-Australian grill chain with all the cultural nuance of a Foster's advert – in nearby Staines for the bloomin' onion: an intricately cut and petalled whole allium, dredged in a narcotically addictive spiced batter and deep-fried to a golden, cragged crisp. There were regular trips to Don Beni, a clamorous, cluttered Englefield Green trattoria where, a world away from the Pizza Express years, I had my first tentative experiences with cream-laden salmon pastas, lobster, and wine that wasn't syrupy-sweet Liebfraumilch. On Sundays, we routinely piled into a friend's moss-furred hatchback to head to the closest Toby Carvery for ribboned slices of lamb, great drenchings of mint sauce and a cloud of gravy so thick you practically had to hack through it.

And then there was the mid-noughties novelty of a Nando's. At once primally familiar and in possession of a wholly novel slick efficiency, the Staines branch of the soon-to-be inescapable South African barbecue behemoth became our most abiding treat and ritual. Gathered cutlery, bottles of 'wild herb' sauce and a thunking hailstorm of self-service ice. Counterfeiting cockerel stamps on our loyalty cards. Pulling liberally sauced shreds of chicken meat from the bone to the strains of twangy, faintly lusophone pop, followed by a stroll to the neighbouring Odeon for a mindless blockbuster. 'Nando's-cinema?' Dan would occasionally say, running the words together to cement the sense we were all speaking a strange private language of consumerist, retail park escapism. We had always been a social group especially prone to intense fixations, whether it was a prolonged White Russian phase inspired by *The Big Lebowski* or a brief, intense obsession with marathon poker games in the third year. This period of Carvery yorkies, pasta al salmone and peri-salted chips was no different. It was just that the role we seemed to be playing was that of cash-rich suburbanite gourmets, in active retreat from the realities of undergraduate life.

If you are wondering how we actually went about funding this restaurant habit then the answer is more than a little complicated. Throughout my last two years at uni, there was an occasional income from part-time jobs. Not just Crosslands (where, perhaps unsurprisingly, I was eventually denied regular shifts because of my slackness with bar stock and fripperies like actually cashing out properly). But also: short-lived stints taking bets at Royal Ascot racecourse nearby and, in another period, working the luggage concession in the Staines branch of Debenhams (this last job mainly involved sleeping off hangovers in the stock room). This work meant that, alongside my loan instalments and occasional cash injections from my mum, there was a flow of money coming into my account to support some of this dining habit.

Yet the simplest way to explain how we afforded all these meals at local trattorias and chain restaurants is to say that we didn't always actually pay for them. Not initially, at least.

At some point in our second year, Dan and I realised that there'd often be a lag between our actual, cratering bank balances and the ability our debit cards had to pay for things. Dubbed 'Magicard', this phenomenon became a kind of mystical force to us; the benevolent hand of fate that would intervene whenever we handed our Visa Electrons over to waiters, cashiers and bar staff, who probably wondered why we looked on the verge of grateful, flooding tears when they told us that, yes, the cashback we had requested had gone through. Never mind that we were, in a financial sense, robbing Peter to pay an especially sadistic, knuckle-cracking Paul. Never mind that the payment lag would mean the terrifying heart-sink of a negative balance on a monthly statement, crippling fees that would prove to be a drain for years to come, and a poverty so desperate that the only thing I could do was bunk the train from Egham to Waterloo (often, for added glamour, hiding from ticket inspectors in the rattling stink chamber of the toilet), before making my way to my mum's for a hot meal and whatever cash she could spare. To spend money that I didn't have on unnecessarily lavish dinners made total sense as part of the extended delusion of university's fantasy world and my own, newly constructed persona. It was, as with the revelations of that trip to France, an investment in a different sort of gastrocultural education.

And so, what did the gluttonous chaos of that second-year house share and the flagrant Magicard years teach me?

Whether through the natural process of getting older, the instinct to emulate behaviour around me, or some combination of the two, some of my pickier tendencies fell away. By my third year I was back in Founder's and shuffling down to the dining hall, yet my choice had evolved beyond the monolithically beige to involve side servings of green beans, clattered with as much flavour-boosting salt and pepper as possible. A girl I knew loudly exhorted that 'tea is a savoury drink', and so duly shamed me out of my long-held belief that every brew was just a milky delivery system for biscuit residue and three heaped teaspoons of sugar. A Turkish-heritage friend called Deniz dragged us to a tandoori house and put my curry-wimp days firmly in the past by introducing me to the glory of saag aloo and swirled, buttery pats of paratha. All this, and countless other little opinions and modelled behaviours, lastingly altered my culinary world-view, like lapping waves remoulding a rock formation.

But another function of this unusual eating education was that it underscored the significance, and hidden value, of my own home and existing beliefs. 'You're not getting breast meat?' Dan would query, with a disbelieving eyebrow waggle, whenever I went for chicken legs, wings and thighs at whichever Nando's, KFC or Carvery-coded Sunday roast venue we'd landed in that particular day. 'You know that's the cheapest bit of the chicken, right?' I did not necessarily have the language back then to explain why I always stridently made this choice; I couldn't fully articulate that, as a

diaspora kid, I had an understanding of the superior flavour-
ful succulence of dark poultry meat that predated any
conscious sense of having acquired that nugget of knowledge. And yet, what I remember is holding firm, rather than
acquiescing as I normally would when afforded other opportunities to assimilate socially.

Separately, I remember a drama seminar where my insistence that fresh seafood stalls were a mainstay outside pubs
– a regular fixture among Bexleyheath's cockles- and whelks-
mad East End diaspora – was met with mocking derision by
classmates who didn't hail from London's Estuary borders.
Palate and taste is formed through exposure to new things.
It also, I think, emerges through a kind of stress-testing of
opinions – adding what appeals, binning what doesn't – and
how these outside forces reconfigure existing values, kinks
and culinary proclivities into something new. Royal
Holloway gave me an occasionally confused abundance of
this. Those antic days of pilfered cheese sandwiches, junk-
food feasts amid a trash-heaped house share, Gascon stew
within a medieval citadel, and financially negligent restau-
rant-hopping had a dual function: it was both intensely
novel and formative, and it cast the eating life that had come
before in a striking new light.

But if revelations about my food identity were accompanied by an odd, creeping placelessness, then that transferred
into other aspects of my twilight at university. By the time I
was deep into my third year, ensconced in a jammily

acquired split-level room that was wedged into one of Founder's ornate turrets, the pogoing, study-averse energy I had brought to uni had settled somewhat. Shifts at Debenhams brought relative stability to the whirring blender of my monthly finances. My friendship group had swelled and diversified a touch to encompass budding rappers, thoughtful red-wine drinkers who dragged me along to Royal Court plays, and droll, R&B-loving second years who I'd met within the hedonistic mire of the university football team. I had felt a renewed spark for my degree, thanks to enlivening courses about Booker winners and African-American dramatists, and was huffing my way to the dizzy heights of a solid 2:1 BA classification.

Yes, OK. There was still also the matter of some inarguable emotional immaturity, a fairly craven aversion to awkward confrontations. Not to mention a stubbornly absent sense of perspective and priorities (here we flashback to all those times I splurged on gig tickets with money I didn't really have or wrote out ill-advised, rubber cheques to hire speakers for the live music night I was involved in organising). But when I remember that period, as the late winter of 2005 morphed into a cloistered spring of dissertations and exams, I mostly think of my building desire to be done with university. I think of myself, not for the first time, twitchily awaiting the next life stage as if it were a late-running bus.

I arrived at Royal Holloway hungry for adventures, independence, gently broadened cultural horizons, and the kind of soft personality reset that is probably on the itinerary of most undergraduates. Yet after three years of familiar rhythms within the bubble of Egham, both the shiny novelty of the place and the sense it was any kind of approximation of adulthood began to seem questionable. The dining hall breakfasts and discarded jacket potatoes on unbussed bar tables. The game of hormonal musical chairs that kept throwing up ever more implausible romantic combinations on campus. The loitering, developmentally arrested recent graduates who could still be seen haunting student bars like ghosts at the snakebite-fuelled feast. What had once seemed so grown-up and rich with possibility now struck me as inert and juvenile.

On top of that, whatever changes I had undergone since leaving home nudged me further into a sort of code-switch-ing limbo. In Egham I would have to listen to people point out, not completely inaccurately, that the suburban south-east wasn't 'real London'. Or make assumptions about what childhood must have been like as a black kid growing up in a legendarily white and intolerant community. 'God, that must have been tough,' said one girl, puffing out her cheeks sadly as if to imply that 90s Bexleyheath was basically the antebellum South.

Equally, when I was back home during holidays and read-ing weeks, I'd loudly rail against things I once blithely accepted. Why did we have to go home to put some ridicu-lous shirt and shiny loafers on before going out? Why

couldn't I wear a begrimed pair of battered Converse without running afoul of the neckless sadists among a nightclub's
security team? To come home with this kind of punchable
hauteur was its own tiresome cliché. All the same, I couldn't
help myself. And so the sense that neither environment
wholly fitted me started to grow.

There is a particularly revealing moment from that final
year that I remember, involving Jen, a fantastically ill-suited,
red-haired second-year girl who I had been seeing for a term
or two. Some of her friends – Cambridgeshire-based, gram-
mar-school educated, lightly posh – had come to the university for a weekend and had been keen to meet me. After they
scurried off, Jen came sauntering back into the bar and
reported, through a smile, the details of their verdict. 'Well?'
I asked, pecking at the thin, bubbled head on my pint of
Carling. She laughed to herself. 'They said, "We weren't
expecting that voice to come out of him".'

We can put a pin in the flagrant offensiveness and questionable choice of romantic partner for a moment. Yet there
it was again. That stalking sense that much of the world saw
the tangled mass of things that made me who I was – namely,
a British-Nigerian, lapsed drama nerd and pint-sinking
university footballer who spoke with a faint barrow-boy
twang – and struggled to reconcile it with any kind of available categorisation. As borne out by the jumbled nature of
my eating identity, the tension between inner desire and
outside expectation had never been so pronounced.

Those three years at Royal Holloway had enriched my character contradictions but had, equally, intensified my paranoia about them. The sure-footed, untouchable progression that I had envisioned never really materialised. This feeling, coupled with the fractious squabbles and obligatory zombie-march hedonism that characterised those last weeks of university, contributed to my impatient desire for the next phase, whatever it may be. And so I set about cultivating an unlikely exit route, out into the glare of the working world and a profession I knew very little about. The body may have been part of a horde of addled, demob-happy graduates, dancing on a bar as security tried to haul us down (an act that I'm pretty sure means I'm still banned from all student union venues to this date), but the spirit was elsewhere. It was, in this sense, a regurgitated form of the feelings I'd had at the end of secondary school. But, as I was about to discover, moving to the next designated life stage was not necessarily the same thing as true growth.

9

Desk Curry and the Lunchtime Breadline

The British men's magazine industry of the mid-2000s was a thrusting mass of contradictions. On the one hand, it was a predictable reflection of the times: a wildly successful manifestation of both post-Cool Britannia social optimism and irony-larded sexual and cultural permissiveness. On the other, it was a bizarre relic, an increasingly outmoded monument to a brand of gonzo capering and leering hypersexuality that would mystify future generations.

Functioning alcoholics in Hawaiian shirts entered a second decade of arch, Hunter S. Thompson-inspired adventuring. Weekly titles emerged, ratcheting up the nudity and dialling down the words (the latter a result of an infamous *Nuts* market research discovery that a quarter of British men were functionally illiterate). *FHM* magazine – at that point selling more than half a million copies a month – projected a blotchy, nude image of television presenter Gail Porter on to the Houses of Parliament. The justified, party's-over reckoning would come. So too the retrospective sense that, as the internet grew in prominence, this sector was a doomed apex predator, slowly bleeding out from an unseen mortal wound. But for then, it was expensive stunts and shamelessness and the pervading sense that none of it was to be taken seriously.

This, after three years of university, was the strange realm that I found myself in: a looking-glass tumbled through at the age of twenty-one, following the capture of a job at a monthly title called *Maxim*. It was, with some key differences of approach and sensibility, an atmosphere that fitted the lad mag expectations of feeling like one long, extended stag weekend. Lavish parties with open bars and first-class trips to report on Nevadan roadkill chefs or Japanese air guitar contests. Video games, TV series, gadgets and albums spirited to the office on expensively booked courier bikes, months before release. Meetings held in pubs and daily tea rounds that were decided with a raucous, office-wide darts game that got ever more prolonged and complex with each passing week. If I shut my eyes, I can still smell the odd, perfumed cocoa butter scent of a prosthetic masturbation aid that loitered near my desk for weeks. There was another stubborn odour as well. Almost every aspect of it reeked of a privilege and excess that wasn't always fairly meted out. But I do not know if any single image from this period feels quite as representative of the particularly strange, last-days-of-Rome decadence of that era as The Day of the Deskbound Curry House.

As I remember it, I was a few months into my time at *Maxim*, acclimatising to my surroundings and trying as best I could to live on a £15,000 annual salary that, even twenty years ago, was hilariously insufficient. It was lunchtime. I had returned to my desk bearing a budget-conscious, extremely sensible trousers meal-deal combo of an M&S tuna and sweetcorn sandwich, salt and vinegar crisps, and the great indulgence of pudding: a puck of light muffin sponge wedged in a bubbled moat of chocolate mousse. I looked around at the usual panorama of other colleagues idly tucking into their own desk-meals; the cling-filmed rolls from home, the steaming pots of soup, the doorstop chicken escalope sandwiches with floury, golden-brown hulls. And then that is when I saw it. Or, probably more likely, smelt it.

Simon, a particularly droll senior editor with a perched mop of brown ringlets, approached the central bank of desks with multiple brown paper bags, heralded by a waft of jasmine rice, cumin and ghee-simmered onions. He sat down opposite me and, as I nibbled down on damp, fridge-cold granary bread, commenced unpacking the most lavish and meticulous of Indian takeaway orders. A creamy, fragrant chicken curry of mottled browns and oranges. Turmeric-tinted mushroom rice and a tandoor-blistered naan. A chilled bottle of Cobra beer that was the size of a lava lamp.

In my mind, it could only have been more expansive and indulgent if he had set up a little lazy Susan of chutneys, or temporarily employed a waistcoated waiter to hurry over with some warm, lemon-scented flannels. But the image of it, and the fact that, beyond a few admiring comments, Simon's pop-up tandoori house barely caused a flicker of interest in the office, stayed with me. This was my first, penny-dropping appreciation of an environment where the lines between work and play were confusingly and wilfully blurred; my first sense of the gulf in status, wealth and cultural know-how between me and many of my new, much older colleagues. This was the beginning of another uncertain performance, another course of study into just how much my snakebite-pickled consciousness still had to absorb. Food, more often than not, was right on the frontline of this disorienting, thrilling new education.

We should rewind a little. It's fair to say that to have fallen straight into a job as a journalist was not part of any carefully concocted professional master plan. Having gone to university with no real sense of what my future vocational path would be, a desire to pursue writing in some form started to gain momentum midway through. In our second year (and in a rare burst of motivated focus), Pete and I had created Superbad: a fanzine-inspired, alternative student magazine filled with campus in-jokes and Sharpie-drawn cartoons, printed on to folded sheafs of white A4 and sold behind the bar at Crosslands at 50p a copy. Crudely produced in more than one sense, it was, for better or worse, a frenzied grab-bag of ideas – a lasting monument to the timeless youthful tendency towards creative fearlessness, cathartic sniping, and labouring under the misapprehension that you are far cleverer than you actually are (to keep me eternally humble, the final issue memorialises a time when I thought 'ownerism' was a fancy word for masturbation).

All the same, Superbad developed something of a cult following on campus throughout our two years or so of sporadic, haphazardly coherent output. More than that, it legitimised the idea that writing – something that I had loved fervently since primary school – might be a viable professional path. It lit a fire of determination and focus in me that I think even I was surprised by; and it gave me a memorable, if extremely specific, calling card to bundle up with the CVs I started sending off in response to the junior roles and newsroom apprenticeships I saw advertised in the *Guardian*'s media jobs pull-out.

So it was that, in the late summer of 2005, following a few bemused, early rejections from other places, I found myself with a glinting golden ticket beyond the wild imaginings of even the most optimistic graduate: an actual job as a junior staff writer on a national magazine. Never mind that I'd have probably been on similar money if I went back and worked full-time at H&M. From the moment I negotiated the glossy splendour of the magazine's glass-walled offices in Fitzrovia for my first interview (wearing a hurriedly bought BHS suit that was plainly unnecessary when set against an

office of people in jeans and faded band T-shirts), I had the
sense of having slipped into the kind of dream job where the
notion that work might actually be fun was more than a
transgressive daydream.

That said, dress code was not the only area where I needed
to make some dramatic social adjustments and recalibra-
tions. *Maxim*, at that time, was edited by Greg Gutfeld: a
gruff-voiced, American-born provocateur who looked a little
like a squat, gym-going Ben Stiller and was more interested
in cramming silly, subversive and highly cancellable jokes
into the magazine than he was into winning the titillating
arms race that, at that time, was becoming ever more defining among men's magazines. (That Greg would go on to
become a very famous Fox News host, Trump surrogate and
voracious metaphorical drinker of 'liberal tears' is both a
completely wild heel turn and, on reflection, not all that
surprising a development.)

This bit of moral judo from the magazine – that it would
feature scantily clad women while also mocking and subvert-
ing the ridiculousness of that as a value proposition – seemed
to seep into the team and the atmosphere. Everyone on the
writing staff at *Maxim* seemed devastatingly quick and
funny and fearless. Both sensitive and educated yet committed to a kind of cage-rattling darkness. They were, to my
mind, these prowling, leather-jacketed creatures of the night
who brimmed with arcane pop cultural knowledge, turned
in pyrotechnic, Wolfeian prose, and always seemed to be

sliding from some daring, personally embarrassing assign-
ment straight into after-work drinks at the pub. I didn't even
understand what most people were talking about (that 'copy'
meant the words in the magazine genuinely took me a few
days to privately piece together). And so, feeling as out of my
intellectual depth as I had done throughout periods of that
first year at university, I overcompensated and overcorrected.
I tried, while having never felt more like a naive kid from
Crayford who still lived in a box room at his mum's, to affect
some of the cool, black-hearted hedonism and disaffected-
ness that I encountered.

However, as behavioural performances went, it seemed
to be one where the parameters were ever shifting. I
committed to the role of being someone who could craft
copy with the signature brand of unhinged clever-silliness
that would get Greg emerging from his office with a sheaf
of proofs, cackling with satisfaction. To the idea that I was a
seen-it-all party animal, and gonzo adventurer, up for all
the outlandish, pointedly embarrassing story ideas that were
thrown my way, yet always judiciously blasé and sceptical
when it came to glamour model interviews and the job's
other, obviously laddy obligations. I tried, all at once, to be
both game and unfazed.

There was an early interview when I caused the assembled members of The Prodigy to sigh wearily in response to
a very involved question about biscuits. There was a trip to
Stockholm for a ridiculous, Benny-Hill-level music video

shoot where the entire point was that I would lurk in the frame of our photographer's photos of scantily clad models, like *Where's Wally* made flesh. I never missed a lunchtime or post-work trip to the pub if I could help it. Two other staffers and I experienced what it was like to be male strippers (complete, hauntingly, with spangly silver thongs and unconvincing firemen's uniforms) and I didn't even get to write up the story. My life was the sharp-tongued crackle and improvisatory 'yes-and' atmosphere of the office; the glimmering flop-sweat of a perpetual hangover and the strain of trying, desperately, to make my latest effortful performance look effortless.

But almost from the moment that I joined *Maxim*, there was growing anxiety about the magazine's dwindling readership. Wedged in a conceptually tricksy middle ground between the aspirational gloss of GQ and the weeklies' uncomplicated Lynx advert package of sport, bants, and girls-next-door who wafted through life in a state of perpetual sexual availability, we were under pressure to do something to arrest the slide. One solution, particularly pushed by a dominant new senior editor, was that those of us on the writing staff needed to do more of the swashbuckling, larger-than-life adventure stories that magazines like *Loaded* had used to invent the genre. 'We need to start getting you boys some stamps on your passports,' he would say, plainly agitating for writers who were more willing to engage wholeheartedly with the hell-raising dream of working on a men's mag.

Separately, it was said that neither I nor the other junior writer – a talented, daft, Essex-raised *Red Dwarf* aficionado called Nick – were 'proper lads'. That we were angsty, soft house cats that didn't know how lucky we were to be living the dream of every squaddie, junior data entry drone or electrician's apprentice who avidly read our articles. It was a fun office, but it could be a brutal one too; a merciless bear pit of elaborate pranks, needling running jokes and the hovering sense that we were all in constant competition with each other to earn the favour of our bosses. To take my existing hang-ups around identity into an environment where it was implied I was being the wrong sort of man was, well, more than a little disorienting.

Thankfully, the culinary education that came from swapping Egham and Staines for Fitzrovia and Soho was more straightforward. To wash up in that part of the capital, in that era, was to have serendipitously caught a long-tailed gastronomic revolution that seeped into all manner of places. Childhood had given me Nigerian foundations and a powerful ardour for processed foods; university had threaded in trattorias, a new universe of chains, and the pleasure-forward, junky chaos of having to feed myself without supervision. Yet those first months working near Goodge Street (a part of London I barely knew, given it did not feature on my teenage map of skateboarding spots) showed just how much there was I still had to learn in terms of food literacy.

Urbane colleagues spoke with authoritative certainty about curries at Gaylord (a forty-year-old celebrity magnet with a name that felt like an acute test for someone who grew up in 1990s Bexleyheath) and the secret handshake of an off-menu hamburger at Joe Allen; other, equally skint junior members of staff and I went to glitzy press launches at Sketch and knew to strategically position ourselves at the specific point where an ever-refreshed tray of miniature burgers would continually emerge.

And then there were the independent sandwich shops, delis and hot-food counters that used to proliferate around Tottenham Court Road and Oxford Street. Part of the same broad gastronomic tradition as famous Soho stalwarts like Bar Italia, Balans and Lina Stores, these businesses have, I think, an unheralded importance in the context of modern dining. Often wedged into a narrow corridor of a nicotine-yellow space, and dominated by a glass display counter bearing an undulating massif of cress-flecked egg mayonnaise and potato salad piles, the best examples seemed to marry a warm approachability with some of the care and creativity of a market-led bistro. Put simply, it was in these environments that a stubbornly restaurant-wary dilettante like me might be encouraged to explore and experiment with food.

In later years working as a journalist in this part of the capital, it would mean the generically named Cafe Soho, near Lexington Street, where a proprietary tuna mayonnaise mix, hopping with dill and paprika, would be pushed into the buttered cleft of a warm jacket potato. Then there was that white-fronted, short-lived cafe near Chancery Lane, where fish-finger sandwiches came on soft white bloomer and were primed with a shattering handful of thick-cut salt and vinegar crisps. Or Malletti, down towards Clerkenwell, for pizza a la metro and fiery, richly sauced arrabbiata paccheri, squidged tight into foil trays and fired to order. That first decade or so of West End lunches, punctuated by complex, spiced carrot soups trickled in olive oil and the textural drop-kick of generously stuffed banh mi, taught me about food in the kind of relaxed context where I was actually ready to receive the lessons.

But the most memorable haunt from those *Maxim* days was a place called the Squat and Gobble: a Fitzrovia cafe and takeaway spot with a hearty, hot specials programme that might alight on a rich chicken curry or sausages and onion gravy on a mustardy, transcendent mash studded with carrots and peas. I had, by this point, continued to be curious about a new range of food and all the culinary splendour that I was encountering through far more culturally experienced colleagues. But how do you make the gastronomic leap when you are hamstrung by finances, youth or both? How do you engage with a food landscape of lunches at The Ivy, The Eagle and St John, when your life is more about the waft of frying burger onions and a night bus back to Kent? Those fleeting, payday millionaire days when I could treat myself to a steaming tray from Squat and

Gobble or the like were both security blanket and lifeline; among the few times I felt I was experiencing some approximation of the glamorous new, dream-job life I was supposedly now living.

As evinced by Simon's desk-bound Indian, food was the ultimate marker of identity and status in an office like that one. Lean weeks for those of us lower down the staff pecking order would be marked by a pivot to foil-wrapped ham sandwiches or tinned soups slopped out into bowls in the confines of the kitchenette. I remember senior staff members, meanwhile, would avail themselves of steaming pies from the office local, vast trays of sushi or hangover-soothing orders from the chip shop, complete with a beckoning wisp of vinegar that would send the rest of the office flapping over like ravenous seagulls.

As with the smudged lines between work and play, the privilege of my job at *Maxim* was a stubborn tangle further complicated by the behaviour of those around me. In one sense, it was an atmosphere of limitless abundance, favour and spoilt-baby advantage; of movie premières, ever-flowing freebies (everything from tech products to limited-edition soft drinks, delivered to the office by rictus-grinned girls in hot pants or a bewildered-looking mariachi band) and servers forever appearing at your shoulder with trays of champagne. Of crashing on the plush Heal's sofas of early-thirties art designer colleagues who had already bought themselves fragrant studio flats in Islington townhouses.

But then, in another sense, this proximity to jet-set signifiers only served to underscore the absurdity of the basic things lots of us couldn't afford. I would regularly see a fellow writer striding down to a Tottenham Court bureau de change because he needed to exchange a rumpled $20 bill from some recent, glamorous press trip in order to actually buy lunch. A few years later, in similarly financially straitened times, my pre-payday penury was so bad that the only thing I could stretch to, after toddling out at lunchtime, was a single 19p roll from Sainsbury's. The literal breadline. I aimlessly paced the back streets near Oxford Circus, thwarted and depressed, and bumped into two colleagues. 'Are you just having a bread roll for lunch?' one of them asked, with a quizzical laugh. 'What?' I said, raising the cellophane bag as if I had just myself noticed it. 'Ha, no, no. I'm just going to . . . get a soup. From somewhere else.' It was not even slightly convincing but I shuffled off all the same, feeling both aching shame and, of course, palpable hunger.

This wasn't real, fully-out-of-options poverty, of course. It was more a result of lax budgeting that could be remedied if I swallowed my pride and asked my mum or my aunt to spot me £20 to keep me going (paid in cash, to escape the continued vortex of my overdrawn account, of course). But it further illustrated the contradictions of this new, supposedly fancy, gainfully employed existence. I was still living at my mum's and unable to realistically stretch to renting my own place. I was still missing my stop on the last train home and waking from a drunken stupor to find I now had to somehow get to Crayford from Gravesend. I still had no kitchen of my own in which to put some of this growing culinary curiosity into action. What was supposed to be a giant step towards an important and covetable form of adulthood was starting to look a lot like standing still. For all the promise and progression I had envisaged during my last years at university, I still had a foot stubbornly planted in the shrapnel-counting, round-dodging world of the undergraduate.

10

The No Credit Crunch

It's necessary for us to jump ahead a little bit here. Roughly three years after my life-altering arrival at *Maxim*, I found myself just off Goodge Street, averting my gaze from all the scampering ghosts making their way to the Squat and Gobble, the King and Queen pub, the Cleveland Street magazine offices and all the other old haunts of that former life. On that day, I no longer worked nearby. I was walking to have dinner with a girl and her parents at a south Indian restaurant where the giant, dimpled dosas hung over tray-plates like surplus rolls of carpet. That girl was called Madeleine. And to understand the phase of life that followed my entry into the professional world, and all that would follow, you need to know the story of her, and of us.

It is accurate to say that before Madeleine was my wife, or even officially my girlfriend, she was a fellow obsessive about food, appetite and the eternal conundrum of what the next meal might be. It was a bonding agent and point of debate right from the start. After our first meeting, among an unmanageably large group at a Bristol pub (an event that would end up being slightly edited out of our lore because it wasn't as significant as our second meeting), the main point of connection was a shared, 1 a.m. fervour for Magic Roll: a legendary tipping-out-time venue on the edge of the city's Clifton Triangle where fresh, vigorously herbed falafels and a proliferation of sauces, fixings and (seemingly) mysterious, crumbled narcotics were tightly twisted into soft flatbreads and turned into a warm, enlivening cosh of pure flavour. Every sane Bristolian, adoptive or otherwise, loved Magic Roll. All the same, I remember a privately shared intensity of delight, a mirrored feeling that this was almost certainly the best bit of the night, as we messily dispatched our wraps in the half-glow of street light.

Then there were the nettles. Weeks later, once we had entered that exciting though undefined early phase where mutual fondness could yet blossom into either a relationship or a mystifying ghosting, we spoke on the phone. She sounded, through the crackle of my pay-as-you-go Sony Ericsson, like she was somewhere open and wind-whipped. 'I'm actually just out with my friend Laurie,' came the bright voice, perched, as it forever was, on the edge of a trilling laugh. 'We're actually out foraging as he wants to make a nettle soup.' Can you imagine what my facial response to this news might have been? As a staunchly city-raised Nigerian, whose main associations with nettles involved dog piss, stung extremities in the summertime, and the frantic search for a remedying patch of dock leaves? Whatever I said next, I know it would have been accompanied by eyes widened in disbelief. Of course, buried within any sort of bewildered or scornful impulse, there was anxiety and worry around how much I still needed to learn about food; the cold fear of being rejected or left out and the feeling that I had missed some important meeting at which it was decided that, yes, of course park nettles could be soup now.

More generally, there was the food focus of mine and Madeleine's correspondence. I think to exhume these texts and MySpace messages would be unwise – the sort of thing that could cause a singularity of embarrassment so powerful it might instantly undo our entire relationship. But I remember, even now, that the gist of them, amid the fizzing, early excitement of personalities magnetising, was a kind of tennis match of degustational desire. 'Think I'm going to just make some pasta.' 'Oh god, I might get a kebab actually.' 'Hehe. Is it bad that I'm already thinking about lunch?' Madeleine was beautiful. Madeleine, at a worldly twenty-seven to my hapless twenty-three, had a car, and a gym membership, and a radiating aura of serene, unflustered maturity. Madeleine emitted a wry, mischievous sense of humour that crackled out at a frequency not audible to everyone. There was lots that mortared the building blocks of what was, at first, nothing more than reciprocated interest and desire for continued proximity. Yet the sense of having met someone else who thought about meals as much as I did at this point in life, who regarded them as an opportunity for some day-saving jolt of joy, was a big part of nurturing that feeling.

So, yes. It is true to say that food was a vital ingredient in the initial months of the relationship that would come to be maybe the most important in my life. But it is probably even truer to say that what really defined those early months of courtship was this: finding a way to enjoy and savour food together while overcoming the obstacle of my continued poverty. This was early 2007, on the fragrant shoulder of spring, and it had been almost a year since I had left *Maxim* and moved to Bath for work. A new city. A new life. A new job in journalism, away from the psychodrama of lad mags, that nudged my salary up to the nosebleed territory of £20,000 per annum.

The only problem was that, amid all this supposedly adult development, the financial convulsions of youth proved harder to shake off. It was a familiar pattern. The dog days of each month would bring the usual cash-strapped, slow crawl towards a brief interregnum of bill-paying and flush payday splurging; the usual declined card payments, nursed pints of pub cordial and housebound Friday nights having nothing but sleep and chained *Family Guy* episodes for dinner.

All survivable if you only need to worry about yourself and are content with being an occasional shut-in. But absolutely not ideal if, as I was, you are a single, twenty-something, tethered to a pre-Tinder dating world of pub meet-ups and strobe-lit assignations on grubby dance floors, and determined to present the best possible version of yourself to a prospective partner. Add in the background influence of growing up in the 1990s and early 2000s – a time when hit R&B songs placed great social emphasis on not being a bill-shirking 'scrub'– and it wouldn't do. Yes, there would occasionally be girls who would hand-wave my protestations of poverty and buy my pints all night, as if I were an especially pathetic young gigolo. Yes, by the time I'd met Madeleine, there was an excitement to seeing the little red envelope icon flash up on MySpace, to indicate a new message from her (I maintain that refreshing a computer or laptop until that envelope appeared remains the most pure and potent notifications high in internet history). However, there was shame and embarrassment, and it flowed from the fact my lack of phone credit meant we regularly needed to use fledgling social media platforms to communicate. Thankfully, it was the sort of stifling embarrassment from which creative solutions bloom.

In those early, formless throes of our first seeing each other, I cooked Madeleine a meal that would become particularly important in the history of our relationship. Cooking with a degree of confidence and prolonged enthusiasm had started to become a personality feature by that juncture. Having finally gained access to a kitchen that wasn't a) my mother's domain or b) a stereotypically studenty bacterial hellscape, I could at last experiment with some of the teachings absorbed from my steady diet of Jamie, Nigella, Gordon and the marathon episodes of *Saturday Kitchen* and *Sunday Brunch* (né *Something for the Weekend*) that would lap at my weekend hangovers like a soothing tide.

What sort of culinary output did this yield? Mostly it was the sort of foundational home-cooked canon that worked with the safety net of a jarred sauce or pre-bought paste; curries, noodle stir-fries with too many beansprouts, and slightly watery spaghetti bolognese where the flat featureless-ness of value tinned tomatoes hadn't quite been eradicated through patient cooking. That I was eating with a bit more nourishing variation, thanks to the incremental influence of outside forces, was significant. But, alongside that, this was also the point at which cooking's growing cachet and status within the wider culture started to have an impact on me. The point at which cheerful male incompetence in the kitchen ceased to be an option for a nascent generation of metrosexual, banister-sliding would-be Jamies. The point at which ambitious kitchen projects seemed not just achievable, but like a vital way for young, gastro-curious men like me to declare status, express themselves creatively, and, hopefully, engender desirability in those they wished to be desired by.

And so, that goes some way to explaining why, having been invited over to my place one Saturday night and prom-ised dinner (to be clear: this was because I couldn't afford to take her out), Madeleine arrived to find me, inspired by some recent recipe I'd seen on TV, making her battered cod and chips from scratch. I can still see it all now. The brown bottle of London Pride that I'd used to make a bubbled, thick batter; the messy dredging of white fish fillets and the noisy roil and spatter as they were lowered into oil; the sweet scent of frozen peas, which, just to affirm that this was the mid-noughties, would be combined with chopped mint and mashed up into a verdant, clumpy side dish. 'Oh my God,' said Madeleine, slowly, as she poked her head in on my intensely hunched figure and the steamy chip-shop atmosphere of the kitchen.

To say that, set against a field of Peperami-breathed twenty-something men who could barely cook toast, I had impressed her is to put it mildly. And, look, I know. I can't escape the fact that this is an elaborate bit of humblebragging (please hold in your minds that all this was only happening because I was such a budgeting-averse, financial nightmare). Nonetheless, it became a core memory and moment. Not just in my life but in the development of my eating identity and relationship with food. Here was an example of the power of food as both bonding agent and courtship dance; a light-bulb ping revelation that showed me the benefits of perceived good taste, culinary knowledge and diligence in the kitchen. Here too was a sign that maybe, just maybe, I had it within me to grow up, to change, and to create new memories and attitudes to food, based on my consciousness conjoined with that of others. But also, perhaps, an overconfidence and competitiveness in the kitchen that wasn't always wholly positive.

'I just remember that I couldn't quite believe you were making fish and chips from scratch,' is how Madeleine would often put it, in later years. 'I was just a bit like, "Who is this guy?"' *Who is this guy?* As it so happens, that was a question I had been prompted to ask myself a lot in the intervening year. And it all began with London, *Maxim*, and the first acrid taste of professional failure that had brought me to that happy, proud moment in the kitchen in Bath.

My first ever experience of a Christmas party at *Maxim* was memorable for all the wrong reasons. A true sentence, yes, but also a contradictory one, considering there are vast portions of the evening that I either do not remember or have spent the intervening two decades trying to actively suppress. You know that there is a time-honoured tradition at festive work gatherings, in Britain especially, of at least one employee torching all self-respect on the altar of crazed overindulgence? And you know that if you are a relatively new and low-status member of staff, then the imperative to not become the cringe-making story of the night is only heightened? Well, if you put these two considerations together and multiply the embarrassment level by at least ten, you will have a broad sense of the screeching, memory-holed horror that occurred on that night in early December 2005.

Right from the start, it was clear that my indiscriminate undergraduate thirst level was going to be incompatible with the social expectations of the evening. Pre-drinking among the carousing, smartly attired bodies at the office local, I have a clear memory of making the premature decision to crank my consumption – of beers, and shots, and who knows what else – up to eleven, while not quite registering that all the seasoned, cirrhotic grown-ups around me were easing themselves into the night's excesses. Soon, we were piling into taxis, bound for a company-wide event at a fancy hotel, and things dissolved into a fragmented haze, pieced together after the fact via my own dim recollections and the gleefully horrified eyewitness accounts of my colleagues.

The feeling, if I had to describe it, was of having floated up from my body to the point where my actions were a distant, partially glimpsed horror movie I had no control over. Oh look, that kid who looks a lot like me is stumbling around the dance floor, crashing tables of drinks on to the floor and screaming Arctic Monkeys lyrics into the ears of any people not nimble enough to slip his grasp. Oh look, now he has accidentally headbutted a woman from a different department, David Brent-style, and he is being manfully bundled into a cab. Oh look, now he is at his kind, patient friend Martin's flat, walking into wardrobes in his pants, refusing to sleep and yanking a loo-roll holder off the wall.

Excitable twenty-two-year-old gets carried away at office party is hardly a unique and unexpected outcome. And I did my best, throughout the subsequent days of head-in-hands shame and profuse apology, to laugh at myself and lean into the ridiculousness of it. But I think that even then I sensed that this was a telling moment of slippage – a betraying sign that, somewhere within the flailing performance of trying to keep up at *Maxim*, I had slightly lost the run of myself. I fell asleep at after-parties; tried, with limited success, to hit the opaque moving target of the magazine's tone, commissioning approach and office politicking. I was, as evidenced by the Christmas party fiasco, capable of being a liability in the acute way that only a twenty-something with minimal impulse control can. But I look back at that somewhat inept, impressionable version of myself and see someone who just needed a bit of clear guidance and nurturing.

It would not arrive. By March of 2006, plummeting circulation had led to Greg's departure as editor (in his official departure statement he joked, true to form, that if he had to look at another scantily clad picture of unit-shifting noughties soap star Jennifer Ellison, he would 'have a seizure'); there was whispered talk of other firings and, one nothing afternoon, I was summoned into one of the glass-walled offices to be met by a tight-jawed male publisher and a woman from HR I had never seen before. 'I'm sorry to say that we're going to have to terminate your contract,' said the publisher, with the consoling head-tilt of a visiting oncologist. The person from HR gave some reasoning and detailed the terms of my dismissal. My face got unbearably hot. And then I was out, across the office floor and close to tears, before I exited down an echoey stairwell, texting friends to let them know what had happened. I truly felt that I had completely blown it and that this was the end of my mayfly journalism career; that through negligence, hubris or some combination of both, I had taken this golden ticket and mistakenly run it through a washing machine. Much later that evening, I sat in a West End chain pub with my friend Austin, picking miserably at a splayed packet of salt and vinegar Nobby's Nuts as a Champions League game played from a TV in the corner. I felt, with total certainty, that my almost-year at *Maxim* would be something I told disbelieving colleagues about when I was folding T-shirts on some shop floor in Bluewater.

Of course, this wasn't quite the case. Thanks to commiserative colleagues vouching for me with other editors they knew, I soon landed a few freelance shifts at the men's weeklies that *Maxim* was now looking to stylistically emulate. The work was untaxing; the lunch options by its offices near the South Bank (especially warm bow ties of giant farfalle in a richly piquant tomato sauce, sacrilegiously blobbed with pesto) fittingly in keeping with my project of recuperative healing. My summer settled into a new, steady rhythm, and there was even a short-lived relationship with a girl called Anya: a fellow journalist who lived in Dalston (right at the edge of my known universe of London), and had mature, studiedly unimpressed friends who drank white wine and ate aioli-dolloped giant chips in gastropubs. It was the stability and nudge towards a less chaotic existence that I needed. Yet, the fact I was still living at my mum's, the fact that I was still emotionally and physically proximate to the smouldering crash site of my time at *Maxim*, made it feel a lot like stasis.

And so, when I was offered a job at a new entertainment website in Bath (having negotiated the usual obstacle course of application, writing sample and interview), it felt a little like a sign from the universe. From the moment my family came back to the UK to settle permanently, most of my life had been lived within the magnetic field of the M25. Childhood. Education. Work. Friends. All of it was bundled up in a familiar little nucleus, memories and history overlaid invisibly on to the same rooms, streets, trains and buses. The adventurous things that friends at university had already experienced or were about to experience – travelling to south-east Asia; enrolment at a Parisian drama school; working at an American performing arts camp – only affirmed how little I had seen of the world or done myself; how wedded I was to London's safety net of familiarity and emergency support systems. OK, moving to a genteel spa town, a place that was under three hours by train away from my mum's, was hardly a lost summer of inter-railing or a remote, Tasmanian farm stay. But it was a start.

I arrived in Bath in the autumn of 2006 with little prior knowledge of it as a place, or appreciable sense of what I had signed up for. I did not know about the thigh-burning inclines of the city's terrain or the West Country's ceaseless, veiling haze of sideways rain; I did not know that it was customary to say 'Cheers, drives' (never 'driver') as you disembarked a bus, or that all that grand Georgian architecture was just as likely to contain a branch of Vodka Revolution as it was a Jane Austen museum or a neoclassical spa facility. I had not really thought about moving away from everyone I knew, the specifics of my new job or what it would be like to share a house with relative strangers. It was a pretty heedless, impulsive leap. And, for better or worse, this sense of unmoored unfamiliarity would go on to shape what would come to be a defining part of my development as both a person and an eater.

The year or so I spent in Bath can probably be split up into two distinct parts. There was the back half, in early 2007, that contained Magic Roll, meeting Madeleine and those homemade fish and chips; a period of picturesque, blue-skied ease, social bounty and raucous indie nights on swaying boats moored up in Bristol. It was a time of occasional poverty, yes, but also one where I had interesting friends, a promising new relationship, an untaxing job (essentially churning out programme summaries and short, tonally arid features for the beta phase of a digital TV provider's eternally delayed official website) and, for the first time, access to a space where I could consistently start cooking for myself, developing skills and preferences with each scantly marinated piece of griddled chicken or slightly greying, over-boiled egg.

In contrast, the half of my Bath era that preceded this, running from autumn to the depths of winter in early 2007, was marked by isolated drift, alienation and a sense of profound, stabbing homesickness. It wasn't just that I had completely underestimated the magnitude of the move – a shift that saw me transition from the abundance of London, which teemed with friends, family and familiarity, to the kind of social destitution that meant every relationship was hard-won and tightly gripped. I made plenty of friends in that first month and there were people in the area that I knew (notably, my university friend Laura, who was in Bristol on the same postgrad course as Madeleine, and so ended up introducing us). All the same, I had to acclimatise to a new behavioural tenor; to being less picky socially, clinging limpet-like to a group of pub acquaintances who I barely had anything in common with, and to being the guy who asks colleagues out for a pint with a tremulous note of desperation in his voice.

So, yes, all of that was an adjustment. But one of the aspects of those early months in Bath that proved most chal-lenging was that it was the first time I'd been acquainted with something that is a rite of passage for most young professionals. Namely, the fascinatingly awful housemate.

From the moment I first met him to discuss the prospect of taking one of the vacant rooms in a swish, conveniently located mews house up towards the town centre's north-eastern edge, Tristan had possessed a uniquely befuddling energy. Ringlet-haired, stubble-jawed and recently landed in a plum graduate-scheme job at a local design agency, he spoke with a roaming, quasi-Irish accent and trafficked in a brand of gently bullying, small-town alpha-dom. Initially, I was grateful to him for welcoming me into his fold of vaguely rugby-coded, hard-drinking friends. But then, in active conflict with my desperate desire for people to hang out with, there came the obstacle of his many weird, controlling traits.

Lots of these applied to food – whether it was passive-aggressively chiding me for only washing the kitchen utensils and crockery I'd used, forcing me to partake in the claggy refried beans that he would plop out of a tin on 'fajita night', or making off-colour cracks about the pickle-heavy meals that Luba, the Lithuanian girl we lived with, would make. I remember him objecting to the fact I wanted to put a microwave – a vitally important appliance in the context of my Nigerian household and childhood – in the kitchen. 'Yeah, we don't really believe in using them, dude,' he said, as if I wanted to heat my baked beans with a raging indoor tyre fire. 'Your housemate then,' began my friend Mark, after he had come down for the weekend and suffered through Tristan talking over both of us and ordering breakfasts on our behalf before we'd even had a chance to appraise the menu. 'Bit of a bell end.' And all this is before we get on to his stressfully tempestuous relationship – with Jen, a scowling Cumbrian girl who religiously watched every soap and had a pet rabbit that she would occasionally let loose from its cage, as if the living-room carpet were a rolling meadow – and the fact he'd occasionally blunder into my room in a drunken stupor, mistaking it for the loo.

The upshot was that once I had met Madeleine, and also had a steady roster of good friends, I consciously had as little contact as possible with Tristan. When I didn't eat out – most thrillingly, at a creaking, ancient pub called The Raven, where stupendously good, gravy-drenched venison pies shimmered in the flickering candlelight – meals were prepared in the kitchen and then hurriedly taken up to my room. Tristan, for his part, made constant attempts to invite me out – a development that seemed less about craving my company or including me so much as a prideful inability to comprehend that someone might not want to hang out with him.

My last contact with him of any sort came months later, when his mum called, in the manner of a kneecapping, Home Counties debt-collector, to brightly remind me that I still owed her son some outstanding money towards bills. But when I think of those days of cohabitation in Bath, I regard it with a kind of character-building gratitude. I was finally in a position where I was nudging towards a degree of emotional maturity, gaining confidence in the kitchen and ready, perhaps, to return to London. I had been given a tantalising taste of what a non-student house-share could be like. And now, thanks to Tristan, Jen, and that ridiculous, lolloping bunny, I had a blueprint for precisely what I didn't want.

11

Requiem for a Spurned Goujon

If you happened to be walking down New Cross Road in the brisk, bundled-up winter of early 2011, then there's every chance you would have heard it. A roar, clamour and clatter, punching out through the open first-floor windows of an unremarkable corner pub in the midst of refurbishment. At street level, gathered crowds in tiny, jauntily perched beanies looked down at phones and then back up at the building with puzzlement. The international symbol that something of consequence was happening nearby.

And then, behind the building and up an unsteady metal staircase, there lurked the source of all the commotion and mystery: a candlelit dining room turned into a raging furnace of noise, heat and enthralling controlled chaos. Grinning hordes made their way through the tight maze of mismatched tables and chairs, ferrying paper plates of burgers, mac and cheese and glistening stacks of onion rings through the crowd. Cranked stereo speakers jostled with dozens of voices all talking over each other. Behind the bar, ice was being noisily chipped from the edge of a giant, slow-melting block, as if a troupe of polar explorers were in the midst of cocktail hour.

This, as those with memories not irreparably damaged by house-grog consumption will attest, was MEATeasy: a short-lived, south-east London burger residency that was the springboard for the all-conquering MEATliquor chain, a pure, glinting encapsulation of a very 2010s collective mania for both authentic street food and ephemeral, internet-fuelled pop-ups, and (thanks to multiple glowing notices in the national press) one of the most exciting restaurant openings in the country that year. For those in the London food scene who went, its three-month existence has attained a kind of folkloric glow and reverberative afterlife. Whether you were actually there or not, the sense is that you should probably just imply that you were. It is the Sex Pistols at the Lesser Free Trade Hall for people who have a lot of very involved opinions about craft beer, Martin's Potato Rolls and Buffalo wing crispness.

For me, the lasting impact was perhaps even greater. Nestled in the anarchic gloom one February night, thrilling at the squat-rave atmosphere, the extraordinarily lucid flavours and textures, and the heavy curtain of griddled beef scent, I had the feeling of having reached a point of biographical resolution and meaningful breakthrough. Here, in my native, oft-ignored corner of south-east London, was a dining story making national waves. Here was the grease-laden, edible Americana of my youth – the lacy, golden mounds of triple-cooked fries, the hot dogs pinned down by slow-cooked chilli, the ersatz Big Macs, cooked to a dripping medium-rare – rendered and regarded with high culinary seriousness. Here was an electrifying, youthful manifestation of the wider restaurant landscape that actually felt accessible. Every one of my trips to MEATEasy (for there were repeat visits throughout its short run) was like a Tetris block sliding neatly into place. It was both full-circle moment and gateway drug into a new world of gastronomic obsessiveness.

In this sense, it was broadly in step with my return to London and the four years or so that had preceded it. My time in Bath ended with the no-hard-feelings shrug of a happy yet fundamentally incompatible relationship between me and the city. By the early summer of 2007, having grown increasingly disillusioned by the professional side of my otherwise cushy life in the West Country, I'd got a job as an entertainment writer at *Zoo*, the more verbose and trench-ant of the still-dominant men's weeklies (to be clear, the delivery system for the jokes, band interviews and pop-culture puns was still acres and acres of female flesh). To be returning to the city of my birth and the lad mag firmament could have felt like a backward step. Yet it was a rare oppor-tunity to write about film, TV, music and video games, alongside a wildly talented, laceratingly self-aware team, for a hugely successful publication ('entertainment writer', blessedly, was not a euphemism for morally dicey glamour model interviews). And with Madeleine following me to London, and into a Hackney flatshare – where she lived for around eighteen months before joining me in New Cross – it meant London life would have a different shape.

More pressingly, the fact I was now earning a decent-ish wage, coupled with the faintly scarring house-share experience in Bath, meant that I was determined to get my own rented flat rather than return to a Crayford box room haunted by the ghost of GCSE revision and furtive Eurotrash-watching. Enter Chris Austin (always just 'Austin', thanks to a surfeit of secondary-school Chrises): a strapping, ursine softie who had been one of my best friends since the age of twelve and who, with a well-paid, commission-incentivised job in the sales department at a newspaper publisher, found that he was also looking to make the leap and finally move out of home. Maybe there is an alternate timeline where I end up living with someone who just isn't that fussed about food. Maybe that ambivalence would have permanently altered the trajectory of my own obsessiveness. In any event, Austin and I were on such similar paths of knitted-browed culinary discovery – sticky cookbook pages, bookmarked BBC recipes, and haphazardly chopped herbs, dropped from a great height – that living together worked as a kind of intensifier. The moment in summer 2007 when we moved into a top-floor, two-bedroom flat in New Cross (paying a scarcely believable, combined £750 a month between us) would mark the definitive moment, aided by a sense of both collaboration and friendly competition, that my youthful dining enthusiasms met an adult rigour and commitment. After all those years of fearful avoidance, I was finally ready to properly learn and discover.

Lots of this, as with MEATEasy, applied to eating out. This was a time of orange-hued sizzler platters in glass-fronted, BYOB curry houses; of melting away a Friday night hangover with an infernal pad krapow at the Walpole, a vast, musty sports bar with a passable Thai kitchen, near New Cross station. It was a time of the Royal Albert: the Deptford local that practically became an extension of our living room and served a stellar, eclectic menu covering everything from hot-sauce-daubed fried plantain to a whole chicken Sunday roast platter that came with a carving knife, innumerable fixings, and a rustling cascade of house-made parsnip crisps. Elsewhere, there were the other restaurants and food pilgrimages – down into the flickering darkness of Andrew Edmunds, over to Franco Manca's shoebox first pizzeria in Brixton Village, into Carnaby Street's Cha Cha Moon, a strange, pan-Asian Wagamama spin-off where a half-price soft-launch offer seemed to last for the entirety of its existence – that I was more open to and (just about) able to afford.

Going to a range of restaurants exposes you to a range of different culinary ideas. Golden, butter-fried girolle mush-rooms on toast at Rivington in Greenwich, say, or the snaf-fleable little snacking cubes of complimentary Parmesan that encapsulate the old-school largesse of Bloomsbury's Ciao Bella. My eating identity still expressed itself through low-level kinks and pleasures – through the heavy, vinegar-doused paper bouquet of a chip butty that would be my stomach-lining ritual before work nights out – but it felt a little like I was making up for lost restaurant-going time.

Still, if there was a place where mine and Austin's fixations around food and cooking were most apparent, then it was at home. It was a time when chefs had moved even further to the centre of the culture, a time when Heston Blumenthal popped up on chat shows and Gordon Ramsay would be clapping his hands together and swearing from within a Friday night magazine show format, and we allowed ourselves to be swept along with it. When I think of that first New Cross flat, I think of its parties – the orphaned cans of six-for-£5 Foster's, entwined bodies in the cramped darkness of the living room, Roots Manuva cranked to obnoxious volume and a laissez-faire attitude to indoor smoking that meant we might as well have withdrawn every penny of our deposit money and set fire to it. But I also think of the delight we took in the specifics of what we ate and its surrounding context. I think of the expeditions to Deptford Market for fresh loaves of Percy Ingles granary bread, oven-warm and thickly swarmed with fragrant seeds; the habit we had of creating a kind of stereo effect through eating our dinner in front of a Rick Stein travelogue; the collaborative weekend fry-ups, mustard-smeared steak sandwiches and shared ardour for a one-pan sausage and bean stew, garnished with twigs of fresh thyme.

It was not always smooth sailing. This period, more than anything, represents culinary trial and error, and the full emergence of my slight tendency towards impulsive, faintly chaotic overconfidence in the kitchen. (If I ever want to shudder with the sort of embarrassed force that might cause a muscle injury, I need only remember a fascinatingly unappetising blancmange of 'corned-beef hash', or the time I bought some pre-mixed eggnog for a US-themed Christmas drinks and, for reasons unknown, served it goppingly warm, with a congealed skin on top.) However, from this broad seedbed – of *MasterChef* marathons, mind-expanding restaurant visits, and a surrounding culture that put increasing value on a kind of informed gourmandism – a new mode of genuine culinary openness and curiosity finally emerged.

I have a vision of a particular benchmark meal cooked for Madeleine's sister, Bridget: an open sandwich of warm, dill-flecked potato salad, pan-fried mackerel and a beetroot purée that was my lone, augmentative flourish to an existing recipe. Green things? Unapologetically 'fishy' fish? Actual beetroot, the lurgy-carrying purple menace of my youth? I do not want to oversimplify this progression. By the time Austin (amicably) moved out of the flat so Madeleine could move in, around 2009, I was still very much a twenty-six-year-old media professional with a perennially overdrawn bank account, a voracious Jäger-bomb thirst, and the gherkin-y scent of complimentary mini burgers forever on my breath; I was still the person who, on a lavish press trip to Los Angeles for a video game expo, had drunkenly plummeted from the banister of a fancy hotel straight into the lobby area's knee-deep marble fountain. Yet, almost imperceptibly, I was shedding much of my pickiness and tipping towards something like the balanced nutritious attitude of adulthood.

I remember running a half marathon in Greenwich, in the same year as all those clamorous MEATEasy meals. Madeleine and my mum had both come to watch and, following lots of complex text message logistics, I hobbled from the O2 to meet them at a lay-by not far from the permanently clogged road down towards the Blackwall Tunnel. There were hugs and hellos as I arrived at Madeleine's royal-blue Toyota Yaris; hearty congratulations as I got in the passenger side and pulled the seat belt across a body still damp with sweat. As Madeleine eased the car out, I surfed the dissipating endorphin surge and idly unpeeled a banana. Mum yelped as if a tarantula had just come scuttling out of the air-conditioning vent. 'So you're eating bananas now?' she said, with a mix of amusement, surprise and clucking disbelief. 'I never thought I'd see the day.' Whether spoken or not, there was the hanging sentiment that this was Madeleine's influence. That other forces were shaping my personhood and palate. When it came to food, I had changed so steadily and stealthily that even I hadn't noticed. But there was a new phase of this cycle coming over the horizon. And the biggest change and greatest challenge of adulthood was about to come screaming into my life.

People often forget that the national mood before the 2012 Olympics was, generally speaking, that of a country bracing for an unmitigated disaster. Hailed in retrospect as the golden last gasp of a more hopeful and unified age, the London games were as much a victory for subverted expectations as anything else. With the ruthless efficiency and dizzying spectacle of Beijing 2008 fresh in the mind, British culture fell into something like a protective crouch of inferiority complex and pre-emptive complaining.

It would be comparatively underwhelming. It would be ruinously expensive. It would be so laughably disorganised as to become a national disgrace. In 2010, while still working at Zoo, I sat upstairs in a pub near Wimbledon as the character comedian Al Murray prompted the assembled crowd to gleefully shout: 'London 2012 – it's gonna be a bit shit.' Part of the joy of getting swept up in the strange, feverish magic of that summer – the parachuting monarch, the postboxes spray-painted gold, the slightly gawky Olympians, biting down on newly won medals – was that it felt so unfamiliar. It was like a rabidly infectious strain of patriotic earnestness and collectivism, gripping even the members of the public who had long thought they were naturally immune. Maybe . . . not everything was destined to be a bit shit?

This giddiness and positivity was on the sweltering air as Madeleine and I sat, miserable and tense, in a waiting room at St Thomas' hospital in Westminster. This was a weekday lunchtime in August; the early pregnancy unit that is discreetly set down a scrubbed, detergent-scented corridor on the eighth floor. That location means that, as well as stacks of ragged lifestyle magazines and the chatty burr of a small flatscreen television, visiting outpatients can distract themselves with what lies beyond the vast windows: a sweeping half-panorama of the city, and the sunlit ripple of the Thames, shrunk down to a whirring miniature. On that August day, I remember looking out towards the river, as Olympic cyclists hared down a Surrey hillside on the TV, and almost cowering at its majesty. It was a living screensaver that could yet come to signify either boundless joy or painful dejection.

It was a room and a view that Madeleine and I were all too familiar with. Just two months earlier we had been back there, hoping for reassurance that complications related to a very, very new, seven-week-old pregnancy were, in fact, nothing to worry about. That first trip comes back to me in fragmented snatches. Madeleine's stirruped legs and her hand gripping mine; the flatulent report of cold gel squirted on to a smooth white probe; the detectable shift in the sonographer's bright, positive demeanour as she divined something from the hissing sound and monochromatic swirls on the screen to her left; the sad, vacant little anteroom where we were told, with regret, that the pregnancy was not viable and that we now needed to manage a miscarriage that was already underway.

At that point I was twenty-eight and Madeleine was thirty-three. We had been together for five years and it had felt like we'd moved through each designated relationship stage – me in 2010 proposing on Clifton Suspension Bridge (yes, I now know it is a notorious suicide spot); our wedding in a Deptford church and lively reception in a Thames-side function room where the sound system kept cutting out; buying our first home, on the ground floor of a Victorian terrace in New Cross, getting a rescue cat (a crazed, white-and-brindled serial home invader we called Tango) and deciding to start a family – with a breezy, unpressurised sense of readiness. We were very firmly in that turnstile phase between gently feral youth and grudging adulthood; a reality that descended with each passing hen and stag WhatsApp group, each remote wedding or pub summons to peer into a Bugaboo at someone's snoozing progeny.

But when I am moved to open the strongbox of grief related to this moment (and when I think, also, about the fact it came just a year or so after the death of Madeleine's dad), I always think about how comparatively young and unprepared for it we were. Madeleine wept, dissolved into my arms, and somehow we made it home. If consolation came through the next few days of convalescence, it involved episodes of *30 Rock*, the curled heft of a snoring cat, and orange-tinged, enliveningly greasy onion bhajis from our favoured local takeaway.

And so, as we sat in that same eighth-floor eyrie for a second time – with Madeleine having once again fallen pregnant and felt the same physical complications and traumatised sense of dread – it was like we had been cursed to relive the same nightmare, only this time with additional close-ups of Bradley Wiggins' sideburns in the background. We sat in the same room of muttering prospective mothers and suited partners; heard our name called and trudged nervously back into the exact same room that we had walked into a few weeks earlier. I gripped Madeleine's hand, fixed my eyes on some indeterminate spot in the corner of the darkened room, and braced for the inevitable, ears flooded with the staticky whoosh of the ultrasound. I could not look up. I wondered how we might possibly overcome more grief; more disappointment and fear.

'And that . . .' said the sonographer, a smile in her voice, as she whirred and clicked at buttons, '. . . is baby's heartbeat.' She indicated something on the screen as a sound like the rhythmic beating of wings grew louder. A steady, barely detectable strobing in the darkness; radar blipping with a faint sign of life. We both looked at the screen and I can remember that we laughed and smiled and cooed a little goofily as a potent mixed draught of adrenalised relief, elation and terror washed over us. Soon, we were sent off with important details (a viable pregnancy between seven and eight weeks; all progressing as it should; come back closer to twelve weeks for another scan) and walking, with a kind of drunken exhaustion, down the South Bank and suddenly feeling ravenous.

We wafted towards Gourmet Pizza Company: a barnacled, decades-old tourist trap in a gigantic ersatz beach shack between the Oxo Tower and the National Theatre. There was the usual thick flow of tourists, puffing, mid-afternoon joggers, and skateboarders clattering down towards the undercroft. 'Here?' I said, in the way that you do when decision paralysis has set in and you are ready to wave the white flag. It is one of those places that isn't even visible to most Londoners; a solid, stalwart purveyor of those oddly pale, stone-baked specimens that lack the blackened, bubbled leopard-spotting of a rapidly fired Neapolitan pie. I have a vision of the solidified yolk of an egg adorning Madeleine's Florentine-inspired one and an unnecessary carpet of bagged rocket covering my choice. Nonetheless, we ate with a shattered, happy fervour and replayed the entire scene in the ultrasound room over and over again, making it feel real through repetition.

This would not be the last time that parenthood, food, and intense emotional exhaustion would intertwine for us. That first pregnancy ended joyfully but, also, almost as dramatically as it had begun. My lasting memory of Madeleine finally going into a long-delayed labour that following spring – beyond an attritional battle with an uncooperative TENS machine – is of her slumping exhaustedly over the side of a hospital birthing pool to throw up the tortellini she had eaten that afternoon.

She would not be able to even look at those little ricotta-and-spinach-filled parcels for literal years after; that she happened to be wearing a freebie T-shirt I'd been sent as part of the promotional campaign for a mythological blockbuster called *Clash of the Titans* – giant tagline on the front: 'Release the Kraken!' – is also indelibly fixed in my mind. I remember being ejected from the maternity ward later that night – after Dylan, a fine-featured, snoozing doll with a shock of matted black hair, was at last born by caesarean section – at a moment of near-overwhelming hunger. I sat in the quiet of our living room, messily communing with a liberally sauced, mixed doner kebab. Exhausted and relieved and conscious, also, that its memorable deliciousness was at least partially drawn from the fact I had temporarily escaped this terrifying new responsibility.

Then there would be the birth of Remi, our youngest. An intensely challenging, flaming obstacle course of emotional hazards and a period perhaps best subtitled 'Survival Through Remoulade'. There was the pain of two more early miscarriages, which made us wonder just how much more our hearts could take. There was the edgy battery of eventual pregnancy complications – a knotty, months-long matrix of hospital visits, daily medications, tense, throat-tightening ultrasounds, and interrelated renal issues that

Madeleine negotiated with superhuman strength and posi-tivity – that would ultimately mean admittance to hospital, for an indeterminate period of effective bed rest, only thirty weeks into the pregnancy. Then there was the eventual birth, two months early, in an operating theatre I was not permitted to enter; my lonely pacing down a darkened corri-dor, a gripped plastic cup in my hand, as desperate, plead-ing tears threatened to surface and I pictured a slow-flipping coin of fate. Reading Winnie-the-Pooh stories to the tiny figure, swamped by tubes, monitoring devices and intuba-tion apparatus, in the bleeping incubator that Dylan matter-of-factly called 'the tank'.

If this period, the first two hospital-bound weeks of Remi's prematurely commenced and miraculously sustained life, had a physical texture then it was a kind of determined fugue state: a sleepless, repeated blur of motion that took me back and forth between our house, the hospital, the playground and Dylan's pre-school, focused and frantic as I squashed down the worry and self-pity I didn't have time to feel. If it had a taste, meanwhile, then it was the lunch from a deli near Lewisham hospital that I would buy with ritual-ised regularity: a slice of leek and bacon quiche, set within an especially short, buttery crust, and served beside a pale, sharp tangle of celeriac remoulade.

Through the howling psychological tempest of that fort-night, through a brief period when I was visiting Madeleine and Remi on different floors of the hospital, this was our ballast and firmly gripped life buoy. The rich, salty jab of oven-warmed quiche; the contrasting, creamy chill of the remoulade. It was a reliable constant at a time when everything seemed to be in an undefined and destabilising flux. A culinary salve where Madeleine's consistent delight at something that hit so many of her personal pleasure points (vegetables, cheese, rich, luxuriant, faintly sweet creaminess) only amplified mine. Then would come all the comforts and confounding realities of those years of early parenthood: the pouches of spaghetti bolognese squirted on to plastic weaning spoons; the potty shamefully placed under the table in a busy cafe; croissant flakes on a snoozing head in a baby carrier; the garden peas bobbing in the grim, slurried reservoir of a plastic bib taken off after dinner time.

But, at that point on the South Bank, all of this was unlived and unknown. At that point, there was just the precious, fragile possibility of that high-summer day at Gourmet Pizza Company. If everything went to plan, this would be the first of many lunches where it wasn't just two of us at the table. On the one hand, it was serviceable pizza in the midst of a hysterical Olympian summer. On the other, it was the first meal of an entirely new existence.

The mess was unfathomable; the smell intense. Standing up in the little kitchen of our New Cross flat, hunched over a bubbling pan of oil and surveying the splatted, floury ruin of the worktop, I had the clear, damp-browed sense that I had taken on more than I could handle. Dylan was a one-year-old at that point. Fully in the early, exploratory foothills of eating life and a particular fan of crunched carrot sticks, plainest plain tuna mayonnaise on gently smooshed jacket potato, and apples, slowly gnawed from the raisin-strewn seat of a pram.

By this point I was working at *ShortList*, an upmarket men's magazine, and had continued to raise my culinary and social game accordingly. There had been Dishoom bacon naan and freebie weekends at Michelin-starred tasting menu restaurants. There was a sauce-spattered copy of Yotam Ottolenghi's *Plenty* on the shelves and the granite heft of a pestle and mortar beside the toaster. In other words, at the age of thirty-one, I was high enough on the supply of my own gastronomic capabilities to have decided to dutifully follow a child-friendly recipe for plaice goujons. It would be, like the battered fish dish that I had made for Madeleine all those years ago, the kind of nourishing, impressive act of love that would bond our little family together. Or that was the initial plan. Midway through a lengthier than anticipated process, and with the strict, 5 p.m. buzzer of toddler teatime approaching, I was starting to have the kind of doubts that all moderately ambitious home cooks will be familiar with. Should the smell of fish really have been that pronounced? Was the batter supposed to be that thick? And should the recipe really have yielded a whole shoal of around forty, puffy misshapen fish strips, as if I were genuinely starting a takeaway rather than just trying to feed one very tiny human? I put these questions out of my mind and told myself that it would all be worth it when I saw the contented look on Dylan's face; the joy as he happily gobbled one after another. Because if I knew anything about cooking, it was that putting in a good amount of effort is almost always richly rewarded.

Anyone who has cooked for a child will not be surprised by what happened next. Dylan did not like the goujons or particularly appreciate the extra, cooked-from-scratch effort I had put in. In fact, what Dylan did, as an encouraging parental face looked on, was raise one of the misshapen, pallidly fried plaice fingers, sniff it distastefully, and then swipe it off the tray-table before loudly wailing. If this was an early introduction to the karmic inevitability of a former fussy eater ending up having especially picky children then it would not be my last one.

From this salutary lesson onwards and through Remi's arrival, mealtimes would be a continued education in the dwindling iceberg of things that they would both still happily eat. Dylan liked sausages and chicken and fruit but would not countenance soft potatoes of any kind (mash, jackets) or vegetables that had been cooked; Remi liked porridge and plain rice and bread and pasta, but could not bear any greens apart from frozen peas and literally had to leave the room if someone unpeeled a banana nearby. Plates of fried rice would cause gasping tears and anguish if there was a visible shred of onion. Pieces of fusilli would be rejected because they were 'touching' the unutterable horror of a very bland, cheesy butternut squash sauce. Crunchy peanut butter would be spurned because it was, somehow, too crunchy.

Naturally, this can induce a kind of madness. The challenges of mealtimes – trying to gently promote a diet that you know will be nutritionally beneficial while also being sensitive to the emotions of your offspring – are emblematic of the broader challenges of modern parenthood. If children are an extension of self that cannot always be controlled, if they remind you of a lifelong vulnerability and the end of what was likely a long phase of concerted selfishness and self-interest, then that is especially pronounced in the culinary sphere. Adults raised in atmospheres of late bedtimes, lax screen-time policing and scant vegetable consumption find themselves trying to right the generational ship. And the fact that Madeleine and I were now tethered to these picky eaters meant that we absorbed that anxiety; that we felt especially embarrassed to send a pre-play-date primer featuring the short list of mostly processed things our kids would eat; that being at a dinner party with those children who happily wolfed down hearty stews and ate broccoli florets like they were Tangfastics, while our spawn sullenly nibbled on a bread roll, was to feel both jealous and judged.

This is where my own personal experience with picky eating helped. To focus on the things that the children didn't eat was to not appreciate the things that they did, or the joy that we still found in mealtimes. One aspect of this was that – in the image of the pleasure-forward dining environment that I grew up in – we made a point of leaning into the faintly nutritious things Dylan and Remi liked, and tried to not make the dinner table a place of stress, punishment or misguidedly labour-intensive fish goujons. The extreme example of this was the outrageous pandering that my mum would practise on the Tuesdays that she watched the kids in the phase before they were both in school; a glorious, wild interlude where I would come home from work to the candied scent of fried plantain, a pick and mix of three or four separate, laboriously prepared dinners on the table, and the happy, soul-lifting feeling that the home I grew up in and the one that I was making had momentarily converged.

Instead, we tended to deal in something that was a sweet spot between this and the stricter approach that encourages children to try things that they have decided they do not like. It is, I suppose, a picky tea in more ways than one. There is normally something that is more weighted towards what Madeleine and I are craving, a crossover carb dish that everyone enjoys, and a few of the vegetables and cut fruit pieces that we know they will eat. Gastronomic cohesion is slightly put to one side. One of them will inevitably clamber up to the cupboard to get a bottle of the ketchup we go through so quickly that it might as well be plumbed. And that too is OK.

Phone credit is not as much of an issue these days. Yet just as when I was cooking for Madeleine in that Bath house-share, food remains my favourite means of looking after someone and expressing the inexpressible. Stacks of fluffy weekend pancakes that elicit wide grins and little pleasure-groans; making Madeleine boiled egg and toast soldiers with the little, rubbled salt and pepper pile that I first saw her put on a plate years ago; takeaway, sharply crisped cheese toast-ies, pressed into palms as they leave the door for swimming lessons. So much of my life up to university and immedi-ately afterwards was about the eternal question of my own identity. The joy of loving and being loved, of having our own little cultivated universe of four, is of creating a shared culinary identity that is both distinct from mine and Madeleine's and an extension of it.

And that applies to the things the kids have inherited, not from me, but from a mother who is much more in touch with foraging and the messy reality of where food comes from. Almost two decades after that phone call about nettle soup, Madeleine was away for the weekend and, by the Saturday afternoon, the kids were screen-drunk and deliri-ous. Ambling back from a sunset stroll, we made our way down a neighbouring road bordered by the unkempt hedge-row of a hilltop park. Noodling at my phone, I suddenly looked to my right to see that the kids were no longer there. And then I looked back and saw them: side by side and jointly engaged in pulling ripe blackberries from the brambles and straight into their grinning gobs. It is something that I can't imagine having ever done at their age. But this is the joy of appetite formed through both inheritance and individuality. They are picky like their dad. But they are picky in their own beautifully incomprehensible and irrational ways too.

12

Critical Mass

To understand how I stumbled into restaurant criticism, you first have to understand how I made a purposeful stride into the world of newspapers. By 2015, I had been working at *ShortList* for almost five years and had latterly become the freely distributed men's magazine's features editor; a frantic but rewarding quarterbacking role that involved commissioning writers, occasionally interviewing an eclectic cadre of genuine idols (Liam Gallagher! Martin Amis! Leonardo DiCaprio!), and careful mediation between journalists and senior editors.

It was perhaps the first time I had approached a job with a mixture of enthusiasm, diligence and fully-in-the-bag devotion to the broader mission of the enterprise (which, in this case, was a successful men's magazine that didn't have a *Razzle*-level nipple count). There were lavish company parties, industry award nominations and memorably ravishing lunchtime porchetta rolls from a stall on Leather Lane; I even took an eighteen-month-old Dylan to Stockholm as part of a story exploring Scandinavian attitudes to shared parental leave. Nonetheless, I was once again eager for the next phase; agitating a little impatiently for a promotion or sign of career (and pay) progression that wasn't possible at *ShortList*. It is this state of mind that helps to explain why, after an unexpected approach and whirlwind interview process, I made the heedless leap into the role of Features Executive at what was then the London *Evening Standard*: a grand-sounding job that meant a very modest salary bump, a commute that would take me to Kensington rather than Holborn, and a whiplash readjustment when it came to professional environment.

This culture shock came in unrelenting waves. Where *ShortList* occupied a glass-walled open-plan building with meeting rooms named after hip, British youthquake films, and lad mag HQs tended towards a fratty chaos, the *Standard* lay within Northcliffe House: a vast, grandly corporate Death Star with the *Daily Mail* on its upper floors, protestors occasionally thronging the automated security doors, acres of gleaming marble, and the drifting aqueous scent of fountains and carp pools in a sparkling atrium lobby. Thanks to the fact that the print deadline for the paper was in the late morning, I would often have to leave our south-east London home in the pre-dawn darkness ('farmers' hours', as one editor cheerfully described it, with fittingly Cotswoldsian euphemism).

At magazines, I had grown accustomed to a certain casualness of creative approach and attire; to vibrantly furnished break-out areas, thoroughly mood-boarded concepts, meticulously curated playlists drifting from MP3 speakers, and familiar editorial staff in vintage T-shirts and turned-up selvedge denim. While I was still trying to adjust to the new commissioning and headline-writing duties of my new job (actually a more junior role than I realised), I also had to get used to the frenetic, hard-charging rigours of a newsroom environment where music was a no-no, most men wore suits, and there never seemed to be time or space for much in the way of deliberation.

No time to have a prolonged meeting about a proposed feature. No time to think about a headline beyond the lightning round of blurted puns a few moments before the page needed to go. No time for the sharply dressed colleague from the news desk to actually bother introducing himself before sternly passing on a message. The necessities of a breaking news environment meant everything happened at this adrenalised, highly caffeinated clip. And the fact that I came from a state-educated, non-newspaper background meant so many of the elusive codes and cues of the world – the name-dropped politicians, the *Tatler*-ish gossip about proto-nepo babies, what NFI meant (not fucking invited, apparently) – only added to the feeling of straining to keep up. If I visualise my time on the features desk there, then I see my frazzled figure, in a buttoned-up Uniqlo shirt and chinos, sprinting to the subs desk to catch some grievous clanger; I see the deep, deliberate breath out as we moved, almost immediately, from one day's edition to the next; I see the time that one of my editors invited me to a reception at 11 Downing Street because, it transpired, the event was themed around ethnic diversity and the South Asian colleague she'd intended to take along had been called away at the last minute. I see myself in the food hall of the adjacent Kensington High Street branch of Whole Foods, self-soothing during my truncated lunch hour with an odd, warm Mexican salad in a fried tortilla bowl. Professional stress seeps out in odd ways, and I also remember this period as one where my Friday nights out had a particular desperate intensity. I would meet friends in West End pubs and at street food markets, and be taken aback by just how vigorously I was pursuing not the respite of a few drinks, but a wild-eyed temporary oblivion.

This is not to say that my time on the features desk at the *Standard* was wholly unenjoyable. The colleagues in my immediate orbit at that time – people who matched caustic intelligence and humour with a scarcely believable speed of output and the unflustered nervelessness of field surgeons – were as infectious as the dopamine hit of working in such a knife-edge environment. There was also an incalculable thrill that came from being at the forefront of elections being fought, stories breaking, and huge, world-shaking ideas proliferating into the mainstream (I heard one of my editors mutter the word 'Brexit', after an ambassadorial reception, at least six months before it became a widely used term and ever-rumbling national psychodrama).

From learning about the inner workings of a serious news organisation to going along with colleagues to west London Lebanese institutions like Maroush for hugely enjoyable platters of kaleidoscopic mezze, that first year at the *Standard* was an invaluable education. It just became clearer and clearer, as I approached twelve months there, that both my skillset and my disposition were ill-suited to the demands and side effects of its breakneck pace. One day, I wandered back from the loo after all our pages had gone to press and watched one of the staff on the diary desk – a part of the paper that was especially hard-living and nocturnal – pour themself a large measure of post-deadline brandy with an unsteady hand. It was not a huge deal, in the context of a topsy-turvy work schedule where the quitting-time release that most people experienced at 5 p.m. happened to occur at 10.30 in the morning. This was all par for the course, and pretty mild in the world of newspapers. A hard drinking Fleet Street veteran, capable of spotting a dangling modifier even through a film of morning whisky, would probably scoff at my pearl-clutching. Yet it seemed to me a physical representation of the job's intense, nerve-jangling stresses and the desperate things people were doing to moderate. By the time I made it back to my desk, I knew that, somehow, I needed to hand in my notice and make the leap back into the wilds of self-employment.

*　　*　　*

Though I was only in that job a year, it was this period – plus a steady bridging phase of freelance commissions for the *Standard* – that meant I was a writer on the company's radar; a known quantity who left on decent terms and could be trusted with gig reviews, actor interviews, or trend pieces that put forward an enthusiastic if flimsy case for why, say, Penge was the new Hackney. All of this meant that, in the summer of 2018, when I was asked to write a one-off restaurant review for the *Standard*'s glossy supplement *ES Magazine* – as the latest guest columnist in a rotating series that had been underway for several months – I did not think much of it.

I was excited and honoured, of course. Yet I was so oblivious to the idea that it might be some sort of test run to take over the role permanently (with the position having been vacant for so long, I assumed the magazine would spin the mystery diner wheel every week for the foreseeable) that I approached it with gusto but without any sense of pressure. I suppose it's likely that some of this confident nonchalance made its way into that very first review of a mostly very forgettable pan-Asian place in a prime, glass-fronted site near Carnaby Street.

Whatever it was, and at the risk of retrofitting narrative inevitability on to something that could have gone either way, the experience of that first write-up gave me a strange, flow-state feeling of rare professional certainty. A puzzle piece slotting into place; a light going on; a wall being punched through to reveal an immaculately appointed room that had always been lurking there. Restaurant writing took so many of my lifelong fixations as a writer and a person – fascination with culture and identity, intense specificity around food, a particular kink for detailed descriptions of atmosphere – and drew them together into one complex, indulgently full-fat gumbo. As someone who had read restaurant reviews with analytical interest, my particular approach to it, the voice and the register, seemed instantly clear. Beyond that, to just have the opportunity (extended after the editor of *ES Magazine* immediately asked me to write another guest review) was exhilarating. I do not want to overplay the Cinderella bit; I had, at that point, been working as a moderately successful journalist for thirteen years and always felt I had ability on the page. It was just that I never got the sense, right from the earliest *Maxim* days, that I was ever viewed as star writer or columnist material. That shifted when, a few days before a family holiday to the molten black sands and nerve-jangling mountain roads of the Canary Islands, I was asked to become the magazine's next full-time restaurant critic. It felt a little like I was a dependable journalistic piano carrier, finally afforded the chance to play.

That first year or so of the job was a honeyed blur of slightly blundering excitement. I frequently over-ordered and made reams of unnecessarily thorough notes. I pseudonymously booked tables and then, like a terrible spy, completely forgot this when the restaurant called my phone number and asked if they were speaking to 'Andy'. I slowly let all that early exuberance and occasional righteous scorn (there was a dismayingly gritty, faecal blob of chocolate mousse that very nearly pushed me over the edge at a Richmond hotel restaurant) settle into something like trust in my own instincts and opinions.

Though I didn't fully appreciate it at the time, 2018 was a particular global inflection point for food media in the US and the UK especially. Three prominent restaurant writer posts at American newspapers had been filled by female writers of colour; sites like Eater and the megaphone of social media popularised a kind of gastrocultural vigilantism, if writers were ever guilty of any particularly egregious insensitivities or generalisations. There was a renewed movement to highlight smaller, scrappier food establishments of the kind famously championed by food writers like Jonathan Gold and Charles Campion. Where once restaurant columnists could cheerfully disparage entire eating cultures with impunity, suddenly, comments like that caused a prolonged and justified stink. There was, not for the first time but with a fresh vigour, an appreciation that the restaurant could be a locus for more nuanced conversations about regional specificity in food, culture and how migration changes cities.

As a rare black face in a historically white field, I was undoubtedly one of the beneficiaries of this broader shift.

But I was spurred on and inspired by it too. Having initially found some of the hospitality industry focus on my race a little bewildering, I was soon proudly leaning into my particular perspective as a lapsed picky eater, elder millennial and suburbanite British-Nigerian. There is a great deal of performance and stricture to the job of a restaurant critic; lots of people could probably do a passable karaoke impression of the form even before the rollout of generative AI.

But what was my version of restaurant criticism, pushed through the required filter and expectations of the genre? What was my take on the role? Yes, a fair bit of my reviewing output included fresh pasta counters, Michelin-starred waterside icons and risible Mayfair 'clubstaurants'. However, emboldened by the exciting things that were happening in food writing and London more generally, that first year at *ES Magazine* featured 805: a Nigerian institution and post-church filling station on Old Kent Road. It featured Island Social Club, a raucous, short-lived residency that spliced buttery Trinidadian roti and weapons-grade rum cocktails in a Dalston cafe. It featured an annual festive tradition where I took my mum along – pronouncedly Nigerian restaurant grumbling included – for a Christmassy lunch somewhere grand and old-fashioned. To write about my mum and, implicitly, Yoruba culture in this sort of environment felt like a small but meaningful act.

Which is not to say that there wouldn't occasionally be reminders of how conspicuously different I was, set alongside most restaurant writers. A few years into my life as a critic, I took both my mum and my Aunty Toyin to Rules in Covent Garden – a creaking, widely celebrated more than two-hundred-year-old establishment widely held to be one of London's oldest restaurants – and had the meal thoroughly ruined by the presence of a grotesquely racist, somewhat golliwog-ish carving that adorns an ancient piece of furniture near the entrance. I wrote about the experience of encountering this and the inherent thoughtlessness of the fact the restaurant has seemingly ignored repeated requests to have the carving removed or at least covered. (It has since been adapted and repainted.) I detailed, as best I could, just how dehumanising, enraging and saddening something like this was; about what it says about the respect and welcome afforded to black patrons of one of the country's most famous restaurants. And then, in the days after my words had been published, I received an email from an unknown address.

'I find extremely offensive the myriad emails from Nigerians claiming I can benefit from lottery wins / wills / etc. but I don't suggest that you should all be repatriated. Get over yourself.'

There it was. My punishment for having had the temerity to calmly explain why I had found something so hurtful. The other, darker aspect of this idea of the assumed characteristics and behavioural expectations that people tend to saddle restaurant critics with. Of the idea that they ought to look and behave in a certain way. And the sense, beyond that, that my palate, perspective and persona didn't fit the mould and wasn't welcome. It felt, right from the start, like I was making my way through a professional world that hadn't necessarily been built for me. And if I wanted some more supporting evidence, well, I only needed to look back at the birth of the whole waistband-straining enterprise.

Restaurant criticism may have been born in France but, like thinly chipped potatoes dunked in hot fryer oil, it was very much perfected in America. History has it that one of the very first was Alexandre-Balthazar-Laurent Grimod de La Reynière: a floridly named Parisian aristocrat who, from the early 1800s, published a pioneering guidebook to the French capital's eateries and household chefs called the *Gourmand's Almanac*.

By the early twentieth century, Michelin had put out its first hotel and restaurant guide – a marketing wheeze to sell new tyres through both advertising and the wear and tear occasioned by far-flung culinary pilgrimages – and in the decades around a boomerist, mid-century peak, more and more guidebooks (on both sides of the Atlantic) sprang from the primordial ooze of Grimod de La Reynière's initial breakthrough. *Adventures in Good Eating*, founded by a travelling salesman called Duncan Hines, mapped America; *The Good Food Guide* did the same in Britain. Minimalist in form, arid in tone and often the work of an unbylined author operating beneath a famous figurehead or brand, these guides were, generally, straightforwardly informative exercises in consumer journalism and canny entrepreneurship. The soup was good; the ribs were worth the trip; the waitstaff could be more attentive. There was no sense of a consistent consciousness behind the pronouncements, and the clipped style made the average Yelp or TripAdvisor reviewer sound like a Joycean high stylist.

But then came Craig Claiborne. Named the inaugural food editor of the *New York Times* in 1957, Claiborne was a trained chef, Korean war veteran and half-moon-spectacled bon viveur who wrote economic, incisive prose and grandly set down a code of conduct – reviews would be done anonymously, based on at least three separate visits, rated in accordance with a four-star system and always paid for by the newspaper, with no wiggle room for freebies – that would pretty much become the industry standard for the next sixty years and counting. His antecedents, New Yorkers like Gael Greene, Mimi Sheraton and Ruth Reichl, plus voracious, Angeleno Pulitzer prize-winner Jonathan Gold, arrived a few decades later to add the dramatic flair, lush verbiage and opinionated pyrotechnics that would become the genre's signature.

The processional journey from starters to desserts; the acerbic asides; the precise, stately meter and luxuriant abundance. It is all there, passed through the ages by memetic transfer. To read a quality restaurant column now from the

'90s, '80s or even the '60s is to be taken aback by how modern it feels. As I took up the mantle in the late 2010s, pronouncing self-importantly on burratas and orders of smacked cucumbers, I was flagrantly ripping off the likes of Claiborne, Reichl and Gold without even really knowing it. All restaurant writing, like a loaf containing a portion of a precious, centuries-old starter, carries the trace of what came before.

This was part of the gnawing challenge of those otherwise ridiculously privileged and enjoyable early years. Right from the start, it felt that the durable caricature of what a restaurant critic should act and look like – in essence, Anton Ego, the fearsome, improbably thin, animated antagonist from *Ratatouille* – weighed heavy. At the photo shoot that would accompany the announcement of my role at *ES Magazine*, the no-nonsense Spanish picture editor orchestrating the shots frowned at my overshirt. 'Would you maybe wear a blazer?' I politely demurred. Years later, writing about restaurants for a different editor, the smiling photograph above my words was suddenly replaced by a sterner one. 'The feeling here', explained a colleague over email, after I had asked what had happened, 'was that it would be good if you looked a bit less approachable.' Here, again, was that creeping feeling that I wasn't playing my ascribed role correctly.

And, look, I had no qualms about savaging terrible restaurants; a sharp sensitivity to why things worked and why they didn't – to muddled, unnecessarily high-concept menus, vibeless dining rooms or aioli with the telltale, bullying presence of too much raw garlic – was a useful lasting vestige of my childhood pickiness. But I was also conscious, as I heaved my Brompton bike into some new-wave izakaya or gastropub, that I hardly had the scarf-tossing hauteur of the classic restaurant critic. Striding confidently into The Ritz or raging about an insufficiently chilled Sancerre was not part of my cultural upbringing.

To be clear: Nigerians were absolutely not above complaining. But the hard-wired immigrant imperative to not make trouble, or draw attention to oneself, definitely meant that the scornful kabuki of some modern restaurant writing – with its exaggeratedly scatological similes and high-handed insistence that a slightly underpowered sauce was a travesty that warranted capital punishment – always felt both transgressive and ridiculous. From their Eisenhower-era birth, the first modern restaurant critics were avatars for their predominantly white, bourgeoisie readerships. Yes, they journeyed to places cooking cuisines that sat outside the European orthodoxy, but these were generally exotically designated as 'ethnic eating' (aren't French and Italian both ethnicities?). So how do you authentically impose your perspective when it diverges wildly from this template? How do you muster righteous scorn and entitlement when, culturally, you have been brought up to be a humble, discreet and grateful good immigrant?

Maybe it was this driving conundrum that made the pandemic such a professionally fascinating time. Don't get me wrong. Craig Claiborne could never have foreseen the full-scale epidemiological disaster that would afflict global hospitality. The heaped miseries of that period – covering everything from Covid deaths and prolonged isolation to the slow-moving poly-crisis across the restaurant industry – should never be forgotten or brushed aside. But in 2020, when *ES Magazine* was put on indefinite hiatus and then re-emerged into a world scuttling from one lockdown to the next, the puzzle of how to be a restaurant critic in a time of no restaurants was one that I found oddly thrilling.

Open to the possibilities of something that didn't necessarily fit the frame of traditional hospitality, I wrote about bougie park-drinking and squid sandwiches proffered out of London Fields hatches to restive Coachella-level crowds; I reported on the thrill of reopened restaurants, meal kit ennui and the highly sophisticated, family-specific jollof rice delivery service that my mum mobilised, her little face-masked figure retreating into the night like a septuagenarian superhero. By 2021 I had won three industry awards (the first things I had ever won, bar a Bud Ice-branded CD player at a university limbo competition); I had taken over from Fay Maschler – a genre-defining restaurant critic every bit as important in the UK as Claiborne, Greene and Gold were in the US – as restaurant critic of the *Evening Standard*. I had, with each passing review, continued to hone my voice and eating identity.

Slowly but surely, I finally felt like I was finding a way to reconcile the expectations of restaurant criticism, the cobwebbed cultural baggage of it, with an accurate and honest representation of who I actually was. I needed to find a way to be both. And not long into the seismic vocational shift of my food writing career, I was handed an opportunity to do this in just about the most widely viewed and potentially terrifying environment imaginable.

Picture any nervy, portentous walk you'd care to name – a solo trudge into a new secondary school class, the clip-clopping, echoey journey up to a lectern for a reading in church – and I will tell you it was more intense. In the late autumn of 2018, the automatic doors of a people carrier clunked and whooshed open before depositing me at a network of hangar-sized studios in London's East End. 'Jimi?' said a producer, before quickly hushing the walkie-talkie crackling on their hip. 'Let me take you to the green room.' I hefted my bag, took a deep, deliberate breath and followed down a maze of side doors and corridors until we pushed into a room where familiar chatter and guffawing could be heard.

'Oh, hello,' said one smartly dressed figure, as others in the cramped room either looked up briefly from conversations, glanced over from the mirrored perch of the hair and make-up chair, or worked through a scale of cooing that registered both wariness and surprise. I tried very hard to affect calm and unflustered smoothness. This was a room of maybe the most well-known and recognisable restaurant

critics in the country; people with years and years of experience holding forth about food on television and in national
newspapers. It was the very first time that I had been invited
along for a day of filming on *MasterChef*; a surreal, fever
dream moment for someone who owed their nascent career
in food media to a voracious youthful diet of cooking TV
shows. I shook hands, muttered greetings, and hoped that
the internal screaming wasn't too obvious.

Would it terminally compromise Grace Dent's glamorously formidable, acid-tongued reputation to say that she
was the first person to come over to me? As my pulse quick-
ened and I stress-slurped my third coffee of the morning, the
rest of the room returned to their conversations and she
sidled over. 'I absolutely love that you've just walked in,' she
said, conspiratorial and sincere. 'I was literally just thinking
to myself, "Jimi should be here".'

Was that true? In all honesty, there hadn't really been
much of an opportunity to consider it. When I was only a
month or two into the job at *ES Magazine*, members of
MasterChef's production team had approached me for a
meeting, amid the stressful, industrialist hubbub of a
Shoreditch coffee shop, to sound me out about the prospect of appearing on the show. Still a little dazed by the
whiplash speed of this new life in food media, I expressed
willingness without really thinking about it too deeply. My
sense of it was of the sink-or-swim approach that, since my
calamitous exit from *Maxim*, had got me any number of

freelance writing jobs and desk shifts on nothing more than the say-so of a professional contact who had decided to vouch for me. There were no promises or expectations. If I was comfortable and engaging on camera then maybe I would be asked back; if not, then my stilted, one-off performance would be forgotten but for a memorialising space in the eternal vastness of the iPlayer library. As with the entry to the world of restaurant writing, I took the plunge with zero expectations and a shrugging determination to not put too much stock in it.

Or, at least, that was my mindset during that coffee-shop meeting. By the time the other critics and I had been led from the green room through to the judging chamber and placed at a table beneath hot studio lighting and the glare of two cameras, the gravity of what I'd walked into finally descended. I do not remember a great deal about that first appearance. Furthermore, I think it's important to not let too much light in on the magic of how those shows come together (to be clear: the magic in this instance is several journalists gossiping like the unruly table at the wedding, cramming in multiple jus-trickled dishes to the point of uncomfortable distension, and then being practically rolled out of the double doors and into waiting taxis, like Veruca Salt in *Charlie and the Chocolate Factory*). But I do have an image of there being probably at least one or two too many of us at the table – as if a clerical error had led to an overstaffing issue. And I do recall that, putting aside a bit of tentativeness and the odd verboten glance directly at the camera, I acquitted myself well enough. Under the expectant gaze of colleagues who were much more experienced than me, I withstood the pressure and hopefully didn't quite channel the tense stiltedness of a hostage in a proof-of-life video.

What's more, as I was invited back to film on other occasions, I started to grow in confidence and comfort level. Started to realise, in fact, that the pressure of the show – to essentially freestyle a restaurant review with no safety net and the expectant glare of an entire film crew and other experts – was something I welcomed and thrived on. Here was an opportunity to discuss and deconstruct food and flavour; here was a chance to spark off other people and perform; here was the dialled-up, high-wire pressure and improvisatory element of those theatre productions I loved at school.

I was always conscious of the fact that this broadcast work was merely an extension of my work as a journalist; I reminded myself that the exhilarating ride of it could stop at any moment. However, as I made more and more appearances on other food shows, as I popped up on *Top Chef* and was a judge on a show alongside Jamie Oliver, I had another version of that slotted puzzle piece feeling. My lifelong, ever-growing obsession with food was, in many ways, an extension of my obsession with television. I was a living, breathing, gravy-slurping example of its democratising capabilities. And now, I was able to be a small part of the stories of food and culture that were being beamed into people's homes. Having perhaps fretted a little about my apparent ill-suitedness to the role of traditional restaurant critic, I started to see the virtue of a non-traditional perspective. One contestant made an Indo-Caribbean-inspired dish and I was able to talk knowledgeably about indentured Indian labourers and South Asian foodways in the West Indies; another made beef suya and, in between holding forth on its fiery moreishness, I could have wept at the overlapping of the personal and professional in my life. Authenticity can feel like a booby-trapped concept when you have been forged by different cultural forces. But under the unnatural dazzle of those studio lights, I found a way to truly feel like I was being myself.

In the summer of 2022, I finally lost what I would somewhat reluctantly call my Glastonbury virginity. A year before my fortieth birthday and four years into a newish life as a restaurant critic and occasional, gob-stuffing fixture on television, fate (in this instance, another journalist struck down with Covid) handed me a hurried commission from a newspaper arts desk and an eleventh hour press ticket to a festival I'd long ached to attend.

Cue three days of serendipitous, beginner's luck sunshine and the overloading sprawl of a bacchanalian city transposed to what seemed an infinite network of fields. Cue elbow-flinging circle pits, the commingled waft of pad Thai and smoke flares, bucket-hatted zoomers flagrantly jamming door keys into their nostrils, and trudging home through the wreckage of a double-rainbowed dawn. Cue the slow-dawning realisation – as I raced between sets, frantically wrote multiple articles and, at one point, had to finish a review on my phone after being thrown out of a press tent at 2 a.m. – that I should have perhaps checked the small print when it came to the amount of work I would need to do.

One consequence of this last point is that eating that weekend became a matter of chaotic, hurriedly grabbed necessity. Festivals are, of course, not traditionally regarded as hotbeds of gastronomic expressiveness and ambition. All the same, what I ate and drank while on Worthy Farm formed a discordant blur of mid-morning chana masalas, hastily scarfed cinnamon doughnuts and devil-may-care late-night coffees; it was an approach to consumption governed by whatever my lizard brain happened to be craving and whichever stall had the shortest queue. The real world and its attendant concerns and conventions had melted away.

Which all goes to explain why, through a haze of tired delirium, I found myself ambling along near The Other Stage bearing a tray of doner meat and chips. It was, even in the context of the kebab's unfairly stigmatised reputation, an especially grubby example: a great wodge of soggy fries, held down by strips of greyish, compound lamb, hectically striped in industrially produced chilli and garlic sauces. It was the kind of publicly shameful thing that needed to be eaten under cover of darkness. Or maybe even within the confines of a privacy hood. But I thought, because of hunger and the natural camouflage of a busy festival field, that I could chance it. So I started messily levering the gristly shavings of meat into my mouth as I staggered onward to the next stage. And that is when I felt the tap on my shoulder.

'Don't worry, Jimi,' said a woman in a playsuit, with a mischievous glint. 'I won't tell anyone.' I laughed, lowered the plastic fork and dabbed my mouth with a napkin. No rapid-fire retort came and so I settled on pantomiming a complicit, guilty-as-charged gesture, as she made her way off to join the criss-crossing junction of human traffic. I was, by that point, very slowly acclimatising to this odd new reality in which strangers recognised me. I was getting used to both the touching, delighted hellos and the more furtive instances of rubber-necking, friend-nudging and unsubtle pointing at a recently googled image on a phone screen. I was freshly familiar with the strange, surveilled self-consciousness that tended to follow these mostly very lovely (and still deeply surreal) encounters. But let us chalk it up: this was definitely the first time that I had been spotted as a publicly recognisable arbiter of good culinary taste while I was shovelling strips of lamb doner into my maw.

Why, alongside the fire-breathing spider structure at Arcadia and a man with a face inexplicably covered with dozens of clothes pegs, is this among the most unforgettable memories from my first time at the world's most famous music festival? Well, firstly, there's the fact that it is very funny in the way that only something mildly personally embarrassing can be. And the other is that it crystallised a couple of revelations that had been building over what, at that point, was my relatively short tenure as a working restaurant critic. The first was that there is a whole raft of things that nobody ever really tells you about the reality of belatedly entering a profession that contains both inherent, absurd privilege and an under-appreciated layer of complexity. The second was that the job came with expectations, a persona and a performance that existed independently of who I actually was. Never mind that I still saw myself as the same kebab-snaffling, decidedly ordinary bundle of culinary contradictions. The baggage, history and implicit power of the restaurant writer and TV gourmet – those snooty aesthetes, swilling a balloon of Armagnac and able to identify a split beurre blanc from the other side of a dining room – had its own weight and obligations. Or, to put it more simply: nothing weirds some people out like the presence of a restaurant critic.

Right from the start, I had ample opportunities to appreciate different forms of this. At a Marylebone restaurant, midway through a technically adept but tiresome riff on modern European cuisine, the chef emerged from the kitchen to practically stand over me as I ate, nodding a faintly threatening encouragement. Years later, a prolific restaurateur solicited my phone number after a (pretty favourable) review of his latest preposterous money-pit. 'So why was it only three stars rather than four,' he said, having called me almost instantly. My stuttered justifications were met with a laugh. 'I think you wanted to give it a four but you just thought, let me be left-wing, and give it a three.'

Dining rooms either lavished me with suspect levels of attention – add-ons from the kitchen, repeated offers to tour the private dining room, one Tamil proprietor who had to have it repeatedly explained to him that unless there was a bill, I couldn't ethically write my planned positive evaluation of the meal – or quaked at my arrival, to the imagined strains of The Imperial March. There was speculation and fuss and at least one well-meaning chef who engaged me at a party to issue a heartfelt, belated apology for a panna cotta I had completely forgot I'd eaten.

And, look, I know. There's not a violin microscopically small enough to play in honour of handsomely paid professional gluttons who sometimes . . . what . . . find it all a bit much? That doesn't really wash. Any restaurant critic who claims to not at least slightly enjoy the constant clamour, or the fuss, or the aura of power and respect that the role confers is lying to themselves. However, to fall into a job with so many ascribed characteristics and behaviours is strange. To still be a journalist in the same way you always have been and yet to learn, as an example, that identifying photographs of you are tacked on to the noticeboard in restaurant staff rooms all around the city is stranger still.

Given the volatile nature of my eating identity, the expectations of restaurant criticism had an impact on me well beyond my ability to eat doner shavings and chips in full view of passing strangers.

The clamour of a busy lunchtime service is dying down, the high whiff of richly roasted post-prandial coffee hangs in the air; and in the spartan, faintly industrial interior of a former Victorian warehouse near Borough Market, my pudding is set before me. This is Native: a sustainability-conscious British restaurant, with a playful sensibility and a New Nordic-level commitment to showcasing unusual, homegrown ingredients. In the past, this has meant pigeon kebabs and Solero-style ice lollies made with sea buckthorn; it has meant a squirrel lasagne that, very briefly, turned co-founders Ivan Tisdall-Downes and Imogen Davis into tabloid bêtes noires.

On that day, in 2019, the unusual menu item was ants: a generous handful of black, unmistakably insectoid bodies strewn on a pale flurry of buttermilk granita, hazelnut crumb and sweetened mushroom cremeux. They are, I am told, expertly foraged Kentish wood ants, supposedly possessed of a citric quality that appeals to new-wave kitchens not keen to use imported lemons or limes in any of their dishes. All plausible, especially in the context of credulous food-obsessives forever looking for shock factor, the haloing effect of a negligible environmental impact, and some new, button-pushing way of doing things.

But none of this really detracts from a lifetime of understandably negative associations related to insects in food. I think of the trooping column of ants that would occasionally be seen making their way towards the sugar bowl at our Crayford house; a cup of tea ruined by the presence of an arthropod corpse floating on the surface; the off-putting, chemical scent of recent Raid fumigation near the toaster. Conscious that I had come for lunch that day specifically to try that dessert (owing to the fact I was writing a longer, moderately silly piece about modern gastronomy's embrace of invertebrates), I fought to push these images out of my mind as a first, tentative spoon went in. Creamy earthiness, the crunch of nuts, and the undeniable mouthfeel of goo spurting from beaded little bodies; enlivening little jolts of sherbety lemon. I sat at my table for one, smiled at no one in particular, and went in for another spoonful.

Few moments, to my mind, encapsulate the dramatic turnaround in my culinary attitude like this one. Granted, an outré dessert garnished with an insect massacre is an extreme example. But my readiness to try it showed just how far I'd come from being a young person with a paralysing fear of fresh vegetables, the olfactory blast radius of an unpeeled banana and anything I deemed even remotely 'weird'. But by that point? And in the years that immediately preceded and followed my entry into the world of restaurant criticism? Well, the list of ostensibly adventurous (or just widely reviled) foodstuffs that I either didn't enjoy, or wouldn't make an active effort to get along with, was pretty small.

Wrinkled sweetbreads, gristly swatches of honeycomb tripe, skewered nubbins of chicken heart, or cuts of flash-fried liver with that faintly whiffy, ammonial quality. The intensely bitter crunch of radicchio, fistfuls of mushrooms and sprouts, broccoli or cauliflower hit with nothing but heat, oil and a little salt. Humming kimchi, Thai curries and sambals with a pungent undertow of shrimp paste or the murkily brown cuttlefish stew that occasionally makes an appearance at St John (these last two despite a mild allergy to molluscs and crustacea that means the occasional toll of enjoyment is a prophylactic antihistamine). If the younger me could travel forward in time and see the current me delighting at plates of pan-fried mushrooms, if he could see the joy I now derive from plugging the guttering of a celery stick with gobbets of honkingly ripe Tunworth cheese, then he would splutter out his cream soda, drop his bag of Wheat Crunchies, and wonder what the hell happened to us.

Again, lots of this is just basic growth. The project of looking around at other people eating the rainbow while you subsist on fifty shades of ultra-processed beige, and changing accordingly. But I think there are a few other defining factors at play too. The first is the simple business of professional obligation. Among all the many characteristics required of a halfway decent restaurant critic – writing ability, stamina, a kamikaze contempt for their cholesterol level

– one of the most important, I think, is a basic openness to and curiosity about food and cuisines of all kinds. This isn't always the case. Part of the confident pickiness of self-assured gourmets and traditional food writers was that they would profess a hatred of, say, aubergine or Portuguese food and comically double down on the idea that everyone else was wrong. The fact that my pickiness was mostly born of a lack of experience and an instinct to acclimatise meant that the rigours of the job became self-fulfilling. To convincingly play the role of someone with a voracious, indiscriminate appetite for cuisine was to go method and steadily, by degrees, become that person.

Relatedly, the second component of this was just that I finally got to experience food in its optimum state. Tomatoes that were actually lushly flavoursome, intensely perfumed and in season. Salad leaves that had been liberally seasoned and adroitly dressed. Christmas sprouts that had been flash-fried in butter rather than seemingly put on to a low simmer sometime in late November. Because I was so relatively inexperienced in the field of traditional restaurant culture, and things like seasonality, I took all of it on board with the evangelist zeal of the convert. And I realised that there was so much supposedly despised food that I just hadn't even tried a halfway decent version of.

And then, perhaps most lastingly, the final aspect of this was the freedom that comes from being around different groups of people; to hit reset on aspects of yourself and see what happens. As the baby of the family, I was accustomed to being regarded as a chronically lazy princeling who was uselessly inept when it came to DIY or anything practical. During school, I put a lot of energy into presenting as just another Bexleyheath boy. At uni, my persona was that of the emotionally unavailable, easily distracted Fun Time Boy. But what if I was none of these people? What if I was all of them?

Not long after I had first appeared on *MasterChef*, Joe, one of my oldest and closest friends, nudged me at the pub. 'You not doing your posh TV voice tonight?' It was a fond bit of needling; a signal that I was, in his view, not being true to the version of myself or performance that he knew. But it got to the heart of the code-switching, lifelong dance of different personas and identities and expectations that had been amplified by my entry into the world of food media. 'Ah,' I said, 'how do you know that that's not my real voice, and this isn't the one I'm putting on?'

For all the complexities of its ascribed roles and freighted history, restaurant criticism has had a transformational impact on my life, palate and openness. More than anything, it has given me a better understanding of my pickiness and taught me about the layered nature of identity. The job has given my sensitivities a life-changing new shape. It is not just that I now feel that I will forever be a restaurant critic. It is that, in a strange way, I think I probably always was one.

13

LAGOS III
Journey Mercies

It was the airport in Lagos, but not as I had previously known it. Trudging off the plane after a hemmed-in, six-hour flight, I felt tired, achy and as stale as the cabin air. Heavy plastic duty-free bags (full of the hastily grabbed biscuit tins and Baileys bottles that my mum had advised me to get) bit into my fingers and drooped concerningly; an ill-tempered queue formed ahead of passport control, corralled by a ragged group of uniformless young men wearing spurious laminate badges, and I braced for the usual shakedown at customs, the outstretched palms, insinuating smiles and reflexive extortion rackets that are their own form of culturally specific welcome. After that, it would be the thronged bodies and enervating gauntlet by the exits. I gripped my passport and steeled myself. It was late spring in 2024. I was back in Nigeria for the third time in my adult life and, for once, I knew what I was in for.

But on this occasion, the usual script wasn't followed. Once I had batted away a decidedly half-hearted attempt to elicit a bribe ('Famurewa is the same as my name, now. And you didn't bring anything for your brother?'), I was handed an immigration card and then hustled into a little sunken annexe. Tucked down a set of steps and mostly given over to a handful of unused, crudely divided cubicle offices, it was clearly a border control waiting room of sorts, but each component of it seemed more incongruous than the last. There was an unexplained deep pile of astroturf on the floor. A chirpy American-accented couple sat on sofas and chatted to one of the customs officers. Another officer sat behind a desk in a rumpled uniform, eating spaghetti out of a bagged takeaway container.

This would be the place where I would spend my first hour or so in the country; a holding zone for those without citizenship who, as I had, needed to be issued with a visa on arrival. My punishment for relinquishing the Nigerian part of myself was going to be an interminable wait and an inversion of the privilege I enjoyed, breezing through passport control at Heathrow or Gatwick. The symbolism could hardly have been more acute. Premier League highlights, backed by triumphal dance music, played on a television; the officer slurped noisily at his spaghetti. There might as well have been a sign on the wall reading: 'Bet You Wish You Had a Nigerian Passport Now, Don't You?'

If it was a starkly different arrival then that tracked with what promised to be a starkly different trip. It wasn't just that I was going to visit Lagos for the first time without the accompaniment of any immediate family – though that was of course a source of particular concern and worry for my mum. It was also that Lagos, rather than my final destination in the country, was going to act as a mere springboard for a leap into the unknown.

While I would be visiting family for the first couple of days, the main purpose of my visit was a work trip with a humanitarian organisation that was running a multitude of malnutrition programmes in the north. The specifics of the itinerary, which came bundled with a highly relaxing dossier of exhaustive security protocols for hostile environments, were trips up to the charity's projects in Abuja and Sokoto, a city near the border of Niger. The more intangible personal aim (beyond learning more about the issues the charity was working to combat) related to the promise I'd made myself five years ago, around the time of the Doomed Cow. Here was an opportunity to literally venture into uncharted territory when it came to Nigeria; here was a chance to cultivate my own interactions with the culture, people and cuisine without always experiencing it through the prism of a chaperoning relative. Here, really, was a way to push myself out of my comfort zone and finally grapple with the fears and negative associations that were the prime source of a lot of my pickiness. It all made sense. Yet, waiting for my visa, trading explanatory messages with Sunday, the driver my uncle had sent to pick me up that evening, I questioned the wisdom of this decision.

Things took on a more familiar shape beyond the walls of the airport. After finally being called to a cubicle office and issued with my visa, I managed to negotiate my way past at least two more layers of spuriously employed customs officials, striding out through baggage claim with just those duty-free bags and my small, carry-on case. (Even doing this felt like an act of ridiculous, *ajebota* rebellion and mark of my desire to meet my ancestral home on my own terms. I mean, who takes just a single, tiny suitcase and a backpack to Nigeria? When almost the entire point of travelling there is to get as many bursting, cellophane-wrapped suitcases and expanding holdalls – all filled with bulky items being muled for relatives – on to the plane as is humanly possible? One of the first things I saw upon arrival at Heathrow was an elated woman loudly praising Jesus because her laden baggage had come in under the weight allowance.)

The arrivals area presented another challenge of will and bloody-mindedness. A need to be robust and inconspicuous even as my western clothing signalled to all around me like a flashing, neon dollar sign. But following some coordination on the phone with Sunday – and a prolonged period where I paced the long, rag-tag hall of shuttered shops and tried to fend off the advances and pleading eyes of a man who appointed himself as my unrequested protector – I travelled out, through the ripe heat and edgy lawlessness of the car park, into a waiting Lincoln Navigator. The door thunked shut and the fetid clamour of outside shifted to a hushed, climate-controlled chill. Here was another reminder of the social privileges that, simply through a fluke of birth, completely alter and define my experience of Nigeria's daily challenges. 'Please . . . sah,' said my self-appointed body-guard, who had basically not done anything, holding out a hand for payment and shooting me a pleading, betrayed look through tinted glass as the car pulled away. Sunday laughed at the eternal joke of Lagos's chaotic hustle; welcomed me heartily and asked how my flight was. I had experienced my first test of this trip. It wasn't immediately clear whether I had passed or failed.

Socially and politically speaking, the country I was visiting was a dramatically different one to the one I had touched down in five years earlier for my uncle's seventieth birthday. Even set against the violent convulsions of its long and cheq-uered post-colonial history, Nigeria was, by all accounts, in an especially fractious and imperilled moment. The naira was cratering against the dollar. Post-Covid inflationary pressure plunged millions into poverty and sparked angry, violent protests. Ethnic and religious tensions compromised food production in the north. All the same, lots of this wasn't immediately obvious as I looked from the window on the way to the house in one of the city's purpose-built residential estates. There was the usual ever-flowing wave of bodies, making their way along darkened roads to a soundtrack of duelling car horns. The familiar dimly illuminated street

stalls, flagrant street urinators and low-slung, oblong build-
ings bounded by thin hedgerows of barbed wire. And then,
once we got to my aunt and uncle's place, there was the
usual lightly bruising affection and generosity. Even the fact
that everyone was in the midst of bracing for an imminent
programme of events – in this instance, not a birthday party
or a wedding, but the burial of my Uncle Layi's eldest
brother – felt of a piece with my memories of an environment that I only ever seemed to experience when it was in
the throes of a fraught bit of party-planning.

'JJ! You've put on weight,' said my Aunty Toyin, with buoy-
ant, matter-of-fact bluntness rather than any kind of intentional cruelty. Naturally, in almost the same breath, I was
directed towards the food that sat on the table within the
high-ceilinged dining area in the middle of the house's wood-
accented maze of mostly unoccupied rooms; to a couple of
swallows, a few different stews in lidded glass casseroles, and
a salad of shredded lettuce leaves, with finely diced peppers
turned into a kind of scantly lubricated dressing.

Despite the sting of my aunt's words, a literal and figurative
jab at a soft, tender part of me, my exhausted hunger won out.
The *amala* and *efo riro* on the table seemed to have a particular
magnetic field: a grey mass of soft-whipped, skin-on yam flour
and a hectic, concentrated swamp of greens cooked down
alongside a rich tomato stew. It is the kind of combination that
used to feel like the food of my elders or, more specifically, my
father; the starchy fug in the kitchen, Mum's industrious

humming, and a laden tray ferried out to the returned figure on the sofa. Now, as my uncle, my aunt, a distant cousin and I fill our plates and talk about my trip to Sokoto, I feel like it is something that I can claim as my own (thanks in part to the cultural currency these flavours now have in some of London's most celebrated contemporary restaurants).

The soothing, particular hum and unobtrusiveness of the *amala*. The deep, almost sour hit of the *efo riro*. As ever with Yoruba swallows and stews, to eat them as a diaspora kid is to be almost ambushed by the intense wave of pleasure and recognition. Soon, my mum appears on a video call that is dutifully passed around to everyone in the room. She thanks God for my safe arrival, expresses sadness that she isn't there as well, and radiates a visible pride that JJ – her perennially soft and fearful son with his decidedly un-Nigerian spirit and delicate constitution – is venturing so boldly into the unknown. And then she has an urgent final point before we say our goodbyes.

'Oh, and make sure you get some Imodium, son,' she says, the face beaming in from her Crayford living room fixed in an impression that conveys the serious likelihood that a week of Nigerian food will visit all manner of gastrointestinal calamities on me.

'Goodbye, Mother,' I say with a smile, before returning with renewed vigour to the richly spiced greys, greens and reds on my plate.

* * *

There is heat and then there is heat. I know the soporific swelter, Twister lollies and impulse-bought paddling pools of a London heatwave; I know the thick, tropical mugginess of Lagos and Miami, where bathwater-warm droplets of rain hammer suddenly from the sky. But I have not previously experienced anything quite like the 42-degree temperatures that are waiting for us near Nigeria's northern border. From the moment I step from the plane of an internal flight from Abuja, the country's capital, on to the runway of Sokoto's tiny domestic airport, I constantly have the dripping appearance of a man who has just taken a shower in all his clothes.

This is the Sahel, the semi-arid region of the continent where the same desert climate subsumes cities and towns irrespective of national borders. And it feels like the stifling, inhospitable conditions reflect the intensified nature of this section of my trip; the shift from Lagos's comparatively mild 30-degree bustle to a flat, parched and unexpectedly unpeopled landscape where young men at the roadside tap at iPhones while on camelback. To leave the relative comfort of the only Nigerian city I have ever visited is to sit with just how much I have probably underestimated about these four days with the charity.

The period after setting off from Lagos (just two days after I landed from London) comes back as a whirl of new experiences and emotional hazards. In Abuja, I meet Eden – a coolly unfazed fellow Londoner from the charity with big, expressive eyes – and eat a perfunctory burger and fries at a vaguely bougie pool bar where armed security guards check our taxi's boot for contraband or lurking would-be robbers. At the charity's offices, I sit in a long briefing, feeling my throat tighten as recent abductions, incidents of banditry or stray outbreaks of violence in the region are pointed out on a map of the broad area that we will be visiting. In Sokoto, after seeing hordes of scrabbling bodies clambering into a partially destroyed building to claim valuable pieces of scrap metal, we visit one of the charity's outpatient treatment centres for malnutrition; a dilapidated, courtyard hospital given over to scuttling lizards and a huge, bedraggled crowd of mothers and squalling, malnourished babies, all of them sheltering from the sun in the shade of trees, administering the peanut-based nutrient-rich paste that is freely distributed here, and so inured to the buzzing presence of flies that they don't even swat them away.

I have seen scenes like this in charity telethons, of course – the tearful presenter not quite able to keep it together in the midst of an unfolding humanitarian crisis. The to-camera plea to please give what you can. Yet it is something else to see it all first hand; something else to bear witness to such profound, harrowing scarcity when my only experience of food in Nigeria has been coloured by abundance, cultural symbolism and boundless joy. I have to briefly walk myself away from the slumped families either being assessed by tireless non-profit medical professionals or receiving treat-ment, to a quiet spot near a newly built outdoor latrine and some clucking chickens. Sadness and guilt (at the fact we are only briefly there to hear about these people's plight before hopping back in our air-conditioned cars) cling to me even as we head back to the hotel.

There is heat and then there is heat. I have sat in the car with my eldest brother as a Crayford panda car's sirens have blared and he has been told to pull over; I have had a Las Vegas police officer upbraid me for drunken jaywalking, in the manner of a particularly disappointed schoolteacher. But I have not, until I am in Sokoto State, waited at a law enforcement barricade in a region where fake, seemingly official checkpoints are apparently a time-honoured abduction method. On the way back from the outpatient treatment centre, the car I am in – filled with various members of the charity's media team and Lucas, the security officer – approaches a manned barricade across the road, formed from a couple of thick, fallen trees. There had, I remember, been a lot of discussion and cautiousness around who would be in which cars; about which roads were safest and hadn't recently suffered any incidences of the kidnapping operations that are a constant lurking threat in parts of the north. For a heart-thudding moment, it is not immediately obvious whether we have chosen the wrong route after all.

An officer in a sweat-dampened shirt approaches the passenger side and glowers through the glass at everyone in the vehicle. Peter, an Abuja native with a brisk demeanour and a neatly trimmed demi-fro, lowers the window and speaks to him in Hausa: one of the dominant languages (and ethnic groups) of Nigeria's north, and a cross-regional lingua franca that I do not understand even the tiniest bit of. Sentences come rapidly and the tone is friendly and explanatory as Peter gestures back to the rest of us in the car. The officer looks at me and says something; Peter laughs and says something back. And then, just as I begin to brace for some sort of direct interrogation, the officer is waving us on and the car is chicaning through the barricade and off down the pockmarked open road. Peter senses that the question is coming before I even have to utter it.

'He was looking at your hair and asking if you're a musician,' says Peter, with a chuckle, in his faintly Transatlantic sing-song voice. 'Or maybe a footballer.' I laugh too, as we drive on past hunched earthen huts and corrugated-metal roofs flashing in the sunlight. I am perfectly happy for him to not translate the extent to which the officer was taking the mick.

Obviously, this checkpoint stop is memorable as a tension-breaking moment amid the long drives and pummelling heat of those field visits. But sitting amid other Nigerians, and not really having a clue what is going on, also crystallises another revelation of my trip up to Sokoto and Abuja. Specifically: to be away from the majority Christian, heavily Yoruba bubble in Lagos is to awaken to how layered my outsider status is. When I navigate the sprawl of Lagos, family and strangers alike all regard me – with my stammering London politeness and scrupulous articulacy – as laughably British. But in the north, through interactions with Hausa and Fulani people in majority Muslim regions, one of my main points of distinction and difference is that I am very obviously a Yoruba southerner. It's like nesting dolls of identity.

Hausa conversations happen as I look on dumbly or ask translators to decipher some joke I've missed; the morning call to prayer rings out beyond the walls of my hotel room in a moderately grand Sokoto hotel (that my door number is scrawled on to a tacked-on piece of paper provides a daily reminder that this is Nigeria after all). Before venturing to Sokoto, we were reminded that in accordance with shariah law, and despite the heat, women are expected to not expose their legs and men should avoid vests or tank tops that don't conceal their upper arms. At a meeting with some of the state's civic representatives, Eden approaches to shake a man's hand only for him to politely back away and bow, physical contact with women other than one's wife being haram. Here is the destabilising thrill of encountering forms of Nigerian culture that are alien and often inscrutable. And here too, on the other side of it, is a feeling of belonging and ownership related to the designation of Nigerianness that is my birthright but doesn't always feel like something I can confidently grasp.

Naturally, this especially applies to food. Back in Abuja, we make a trip to Mabushi Market: an anarchic, sprawled favela of trade where stalls of every description lurk beneath pitched sheet-metal roofs and diesel fumes and soldering smoke mingle with overripe produce. Crude generators rumble as vendors call out. I buy two bottles of groundnuts, roasted to a ravishing gold, from a very young girl in a head-scarf. Young men frantically perform their ablutions before evening prayers, beside a sign threatening a 5,000 naira fine to anyone caught 'uriniting'. And then, near the car park and a few idling, yellow *danfo* buses, there are a couple of very busy food stalls.

One is another young girl tending to various lidded Tupperware buckets on a wooden table and doing a particu-larly brisk trade in something called *danwake*: wrinkled little dumplings of cowpea flour that are strained out from a hold-ing brine and served with a carmine red palm-oil stew and a spoonful of rust-orange *yaji* made with the solidified ground-nut paste, *kelewele*, powdered ginger and a profusion of spices and chillies. Her diners squat nearby to eat from shal-low bowls, which are then returned to her to be washed and reused. *Danwake* is, I'm told, a very common dish in Nigeria's north; cheap, belly-filling starch and protein that jostles with other forms of pap or swallow, spaghetti and things like instant noodles as a reliable source of fuel. That *danwake* is also a dish I have never encountered speaks to both the narrowness of my understanding of Nigerian food and the Yoruba emphasis that tends to dominate in many contemporary restaurants, cookbooks and beyond.

That said, I am advised against rolling the dice at this particular stall (one of our retinue says that he would not necessarily get a bowl from here). And so I drift, as I often do in Nigeria, towards a suya stand, dominated by burning logs of wood beneath a vast grill. There is a butcher's just behind, unrefrigerated animal parts lurking on more wooden tables, and the usual pile of meat skewers, pulverised into a kind of thin carpaccio and weighed down by a dark, sandy rub (I note, also, that the garnish here is freshly sliced red onion and shredded cabbage, rather than chopped, soft tomatoes). There are street cats prowling around nearby and they are not shooed away – a feature that strikes me as strangely un-Nigerian until Peter points out that they are effectively employed by the various meat vendors to keep opportunist rodents away. Somehow, that little grace note doesn't put me off and I am all set to get myself a newspaper wrapped package of beef suya.

Until, that is, I am invited by the suya stall's owner to try something else. He lifts a crumpled bit of plastic sheeting to reveal darkly braised pieces of goat, guinea fowl, beef and other indeterminate hunks of animal protein, sitting in a wet puddle of stewing juices. This, apparently, is *balangu*: a form of open-fire cooking that is a particular delicacy in the north and prizes very, very gentle slow-cooking through paper and mild spice over suya's flash-grilled riot of heat and textures. The suya seller jabs a toothpick into a piece of meat, sprinkles on a plastic spoonful of *yaji*, and hands it to me. The whole scene, as the sun sets on the market, looks like the kind of thing to make a food safety officer have a heart attack. I imagine my mum on my shoulder, cautioning me against heedlessness when it comes to Nigeria's food sellers and the unglimpsed bacterial horrors that may lurk in even a tiny morsel of food. I think of a safety briefing before Sokoto where we were advised to avoid local fruits and vegetables – because of recent incidences of lead poisoning linked to fresh produce. Eating in Nigeria, as I am increasingly learning, is complex and fraught with all manner of dangers and power imbalances. I bite down on the *balangu* anyway. It is so gently cooked that it has a tender, collapsing softness, alongside its rushing, ephemeral hit of smoke, dissolved animal fat and faint, peanutty burn.

This supposedly defining trip to Nigeria will not pan out exactly as I hoped. The security imperatives of my time in Abuja and Sokoto will give everything a slight confinement and isolation. I will miss the presence of friends who could show me these unfamiliar parts of the country in a freer and less controlled way. A small walk around the block of my hotel in Sokoto, never straying from the safe green zone that I have been gravely told to stick to, is the height of my independent exploration and rebellion. By the time I arrive at Abuja airport to fly home – forced by a surly security guard, in accordance with an inconsistent no-glass-in-the-cabin policy, to decant those bottles of groundnuts into plastic

bags – I will feel a little wearied by Nigeria's brusque interactions, infrastructural challenges and social limitations. I
will realise, after the fact, that the kind of cultural links I
want to foster are not the sort of thing accomplished in one
trip; they will take time and meaningful engagement. I will
crave a return to London, my family, the ritual of fussy
barista coffee made with real milk rather than lumpy
Carnation powder. And that will be fine too.

But whatever frustrations and revelations are yet to come,
I will always have the bite of that *balangu*. I will always
remember that it was all the more thrilling because it felt
like the kind of thing I would have never previously counte-
nanced as a child or a younger adult. It is a small but significant shift; a tiny bite that feels, in its own way, like a gigantic
act of defiance and discovery.

There are sacrosanct rules in our family when it comes to air
travel. One is to always share flight details and an itinerary.
Another is to immediately message everyone to say that you
have landed safely – a group chat ping that will be Mum's
cue to give thanks to God for what Nigerians poetically refer
to as 'journey mercies'. And the third, and perhaps most
strictly observed, is that we will always, always pack at the
very last minute.

That proud Famurewa tradition was very much being
observed at the old Crayford house, on a weekday morning
in spring 2022. Mum was due to fly from Heathrow that

afternoon; her plane bound for Baltimore, rather than Lagos, as she raced to support my Uncle Gori through another concerning period of ill health. But as I arrived to say goodbye and offer any help she might need, she did not necessarily present as someone who was getting on a plane in less than four hours. Fractious, understandably agitated and still in her housecoat, she welcomed me in and told me all the things that still needed to be done.

Clothes, gifts for US-based relatives and zip-locked bags of basmati rice and teabags were arrayed around an open, partially filled suitcase in the living room, as daytime TV played on an unwatched screen. My brother Folarin was there to drive Mum to the airport. And when the two of them were not locked in the familiarly co-dependent rhythms of their pugilistic relationship ('*Mum, we need to go!*' '*You think I don't know we need to go?*'), he either tried to empty the fridge or slumped, defeatedly, on the sofa. Amid the chaos, of bins being frantically taken out and suitcase padlocks being found, I noticed that Mum's attention was distracted by something in the kitchen: a blipping pot of tomato stew and some fried eggs, popping and spattering in a pan.

'Mum,' I said, trying to strike a gentle, non-accusatory tone. 'Why are you *cooking?*' Sadly, the precise wording of her strident, doubtlessly Yoruba response eludes me. But I remember that the basic sentiment was, *what the hell else are we going to eat?* The suggestion that I could just grab a sandwich on my way home, and that she and Folarin could eat at an airport brimming with varied dining options, was dismissed as unthinkable madness. And so, with the clock ticking down and the pressure mounting, Mum set about finishing the moderately elaborate brunch she was determined to serve us. It was like looking on as a passenger on a sinking ocean liner made a very involved snack for the lifeboat.

Mum made her flight and got to Baltimore (with the only blot on her arrival being the fact that she wasn't allowed to bring her carefully wrapped packages of plantain and British sausages on to US soil – a development that seemed completely unsurprising to everyone except her). But I mention this moment because it is maybe the first time I fully appreciated the fact that Mum's instinct to feed was a kind of uncontrollable compulsion. That all those of us who had benefited from her commitment to conjuring complex, mystically delicious dishes in unlikely circumstances had benefited, in some ways, from a benevolent mania.

She was, when it came to food, someone who couldn't ever help herself. And, crucially, what she couldn't resist – beyond the sense of calm and control that cooking gave her – was the happiness that specific meals would engender. It was evident in the one-litre bottle of cooking oil that took up permanent residence in her car boot, ever ready to be fetched and deployed in case she felt everyone needed her to fry up an emergency batch of *puff-puff*. It was there in the steaming Tupperware of stewed beans she would emerge from her kitchen with, having remembered that a child or nephew expressed an idle hankering a few days ago. There in the lavishly sauced 'slippery pasta' made for grandchildren, the mountains of jollof rice that flowed from her house as if from a tap, the constant arguments with her sons over exactly how much food was needed for a family gathering (her eternal view: much, much more than our miserly, English estimates). It was a source of stress and both emotional and physical exertion; the thing that meant her little kitchen was never far from a bomb-site disarray that we greedy beneficiaries never even saw. But it was the source of profound connection too. A means, as our lives grew ever more separate and atomised, of sustaining traditions and bringing everyone together as we feasted on the same cherished flavours in different corners of that gigantic global compound. Even now, there are former attendees of family gatherings who will speak about my mum's chicken, jollof, stew, yam *pottage* or Scotch eggs with a hushed, wistful reverence.

The downside of Mum's skill in the kitchen, especially when it came to traditional Yoruba dishes, was that it felt unassailable. This was part of why the earliest dishes I cooked and sought to master tended to be classically British or broadly European in origin. Why even attempt to make jollof when I knew, right away, that what I produced would be a lesser version of what she could so masterfully conjure? Why mangle a culinary language that she was so fluent in when I could hopefully gain mastery of an entirely new one? The upshot of this, particularly as my childhood pickiness dwindled to the point that I enjoyed the hardcore stews and swallows in the Nigerian canon, was that I had a bone-deep emotional connection to dishes I couldn't prepare for myself.

It was the pandemic that brought all of this into sharp relief. You do not realise how much you need certain dishes, or points of cultural connection, until they are taken away. For a time in those lockdown months, I petitioned Mum to give me lessons over FaceTime; to send over step-by-step jollof instructions or show me the precise, dextrous way that a wet, tacky *puff-puff* batter is formed in a palm and plopped into fryer oil with a nimble thumb. Anyone who has attempted to get a first-generation immigrant parent to set down recipes and codify years of inherited generational knowledge will not be surprised to hear that results were . . . mixed, to say the least. Mum's jollof recipe was a fitfully standardised but lengthy epic, full of jokes and insight (*'Turn the stew high enough that it splatters out – you can clean your walls and cooker later!'*) It was also attuned to her particular experience and unerring skill level; Yoruba sustenance on hard mode.

A lot is made of the important oral tradition of certain culinary cultures. Equally, it is probably true to say that a good deal of secrecy and obfuscation around recipes – the grandmother who leaves several vital components out of the ingredients list for her oxtail stew or keema – is a by-product of cooks not wanting to cede too much power. But the bigger issue with my mum, I have realised, is that it just isn't the way she thinks about cooking. Quizzing her about her method for peppered, Nigerian-style eggs, she was a bit perplexed by my endless badgering about frying times, quantity and introduction of certain elements. 'You just give the onions as long as they need . . . you know all this.'

Cooking, to her, is feel, judgement, repetition and luck, rather than a schematic set of processes to be dutifully followed. That something would be exactly the same every time isn't a realistic goal or even the point. When my mum praises a particularly good batch of jollof she has made, it is an act of surprised gratitude rather than personal boastfulness; an acknowledgement of the fact that, on that particular day, the caprices of the rice gods were in her favour. The result, for me, has been that I have had to find my own way to recreating Nigerian dishes with the use of recipes that are a little easier to grasp. In this, my jollof rice approach – cribbed, in a detail that would especially annoy my elders, from the method in a vegan cookbook – is a representation of my wider approach when it comes to eating identity. You need to find your own path. Parents and elders form our culinary approach by giving us something to both emulate and defy.

In 2010, with the ghostly flame-trail of Mama-mi's funeral suya still haunting my mouth, I set off hunting for more. It was a few days later and we were staying at Uncle Layi and

Aunty Toyin's estate again: a purpose-built, 1980s-era neighbourhood that served as a gated new town for well-heeled Lagosians who wanted both the added security of a vaguely separatist community and convenient proximity to the megacity's traffic-snarled expressways. Lacking the outward glitz of traditionally fancy districts like Ikoyi and Lekki, this 'Government Reserved Area' had its own churches, schools and medical centres; there were restaurants, jumbled minimarts, medical centres and a calm flow of residents, juddering over steep concrete speed bumps in SUVs or walking along wide, runnelled private roads to their houses. It felt like a tolerable quantity of Lagos's chaos, corralled and contained by high fortified walls and a set of rigorously patrolled security checkpoints.

This was the broad scene that Madeleine and I stepped out into, a day or two before our flight home, during the indolent, recuperative phase that followed the emotional exertions of Mama-mi's funeral. Having spotted the pluming smoke of a grill around the corner from my Aunty Toyin and Uncle Layi's house – a vast, darkened warren of wood-accented bedrooms, offices and first-floor living rooms that was temporary home to both my mum and at least one other uncle and his family – we had made our pitch to head out for an unchaperoned suya run. After some debate (and my mother's nervy insistence that my Lagos-hardened cousin, Tenne, accompany us), we were permitted, the wider family's desire for peppery barbecue having apparently superseded their palpable worries about the personal safety of two highly muggable outsiders.

So off we went. And I can still almost feel the bright, suppressing heat of the afternoon. Still see the ramshackle apparatus, impatient queue and hand-painted signboard that heralded the suya spot. Still smell the low, steak-house gust of skewers hitting the hot grill; the thwack of a heavy cleaver, scrunch of wrapped newsprint, spooned heapings of *yaji*, and the rustling exchange of grubby bills of naira. All of it is so vivid and so potently connected to my return to Lagos, the evolving nature of my relationship with my Nigerian identity, and the haunting encounter with my dad. In fact, suya in general – its ritual and power; its connection to both joy and pain; its paradoxical simplicity and infinite, barrelling mysteries – has come to acquire a certain enigmatic significance. Part of this, I think, comes from the wild way that it entered my life.

Drawn from Nigeria's predominantly Muslim north (the name 'suya' comes from a Yoruba corruption of 'tsire', a Hausa term meaning 'skewered meat') and synonymous with a mode of late-night, beer-loosened dining especially popular among Nigerian uncles, suya seemed to spring from a completely different gastronomic universe. Or comprise a kind of secret handshake. It was not something that I recall ever really encountering or hearing about before the late 2000s – belonging, as it did, to the pantheon of roadside snacks that I sensed were a highly suspect, bacterially dicey forbidden fruit for aspirant middle-class Nigerians like us.

But then, after an enterprising relative had smuggled a portion from Lagos to London in their hold luggage (it involved a highly complicated programme of tactical freezing, phased defrosting and an odour-blocking metal container), this delicacy came ripping out into our world. There it was, as a mass of ochre strips behind murky glass at the edge of a Lagos market. There it was, hidden from view in the back of a Peckham bakery before being brought out in a tight-packed foil tray, primed with enough *yaji* to prompt a spluttering coughing fit. There it was, in the garden of an aunty's house in Thornton Heath, unfurled pink butcher's paper causing a grateful scrum of cousins, uncles and unfamiliar hangers-on, of toothpicks, hungrily jabbed into soft lobes of beef flank. Unfurling out from that first taste, suya became a cross-generational offering and a wordless piece of communication; the one thing our home-centred dining culture wouldn't really bother trying to recreate in a domestic kitchen; the rare dish that elders would grudgingly countenance paying money for. Its searing heat and exuberance feels especially Nigerian. Suya is life and death, crisp-edged and tightly entwined.

Beyond that, it wasn't just that the experience of eating suya – a tactile and physically absorbing project of chilli sweats, tart, puckering raw onions slicked in animal fat, and the mouth-flooding savour of roasted peanuts – had both a primal simplicity and novel, finely calibrated more-ishness. It was that the moment of discovering it opened up a portal to new modes of distinctly Nigerian novelty and exhilaration. For so much of my life I had been in conscious retreat from Nigeria and Nigerianness. Beyond what family introduced me to, I made no real effort to see virtue or value in other aspects of the culture. I felt it had nothing to teach me; nothing to offer. But now, here was something joyous and thrilling that had previously eluded me. The childish simplicity of the realisation was part of its beautiful purity. If something like suya – and for that matter *balangu* – had been kept from me, then who knew what other definably Nigerian pleasures I'd been missing out on? In the drifting days after that run to the suya spot, Madeleine and I had explored the vast, pungent labyrinth of Alade market (where stallholders and hawkers called out with particular vigour, having spotted a white person); we had accompanied my cousins to the strobed crush of a Victoria Island nightclub where, with memorable shame-lessness, the DJ played the same Skepta track at least four times over the course of the night. This feeling of discov-ery was the undertow of finally being back in Lagos. The trip may have been anchored by the sadness of Mama-mi's loss, activated by my dad's spectral reappearance, and coloured by Lagos's enervating daily challenges, but it gave me a taste and a look at the part of myself, the broad, ever-evolving cultural inheritance, that I had been shrinking from. It was like a door that had been kept ajar, pushed just a little further open.

This is the other aspect of suya's link to this particular phase of reckoning. That 2010 trip marks the broad moment that I first began to appreciate how much my wary attitude to Nigeria and Nigerianness was connected to my wariness of my father. Yoruba culture had become bound up, in my mind, with his abandonment. Heritage – or at least Dad's self-deluding interpretation of it – was what emboldened him to live a life almost entirely separate from his children and his wife; it was the protective scaffolding that meant many of the uncles and family friends I encountered would regard my ambivalent attitude towards him as a sort of bizarre, lamentably English petulance. Dad, in my eyes, stood accused and so the culture with which he so strongly identified was guilty by association. As well as absorbing some of the mixed messages around ancestry that I had grown up with – namely, that it was a source of fierce pride in the abstract and fear and head-shaking frustration in the daily, dysfunctional reality – I think I probably had my father to thank for a somewhat resentful and mistrustful attitude when it came to Nigerian life.

The visit in 2010 and my ever-growing interest in West African culture, through the emergent pathways of food and music, showed me the folly of that approach. Not to mention that it denies all the many West African patriarchs who are imperfect but present figures, trying their best every day. One person and their behaviour could not damn nor define an entire culture. Experiencing Nigeria as an actual physical environment, rather than a powerful, looming idea, showed me that it contained enlivening, confounding multitudes. My mother and father might have struck me as somewhat hostage to the ideas and expectations of their culture; to the idea that marriage was for life no matter what, that men were allowed to behave as they pleased, that it was the role of the Nigerian matriarch to indomitably withstand and endure all manner of assaults on her spirit and sanity. Yet they were also merely fallible and conflicted individuals, interpreting the messages they received and the ever-shifting trials of life as best they saw fit. Dad's culture was not an excuse for his absence from our lives. Neither was it a justified reason for me to run from a part of myself; to not commit fully to reclaiming my heritage and finding my own interpretation.

In the days after the conference call with Uncle Joseph in Mum's bedroom, my resolve did not waiver. I honestly saw no reason to attend Dad's funeral, other than for the benefit of other people or the observance of some code of filial duty and loyalty. Once it was decided that Ray would attend to provide emotional support to Mum, I felt a kind of stilled relief and peace. Part of this may well have been edged in the shameful guilt of my older brother having spared me from an obligation that I knew would be difficult and emotionally onerous. To think that I was not there for how it all played out – the clenched interactions with Uncle Joseph and Uncle Deji; the swirling politics of different family hierarchies; Mum, defiant and glamorous as a jilted mob wife, making a speech as she rained sod on to the casket – is to feel that I dodged a social bullet. But, mostly, I think it was the calm of knowing that I was making what felt like the right decision for me – not necessarily through anger or a desire to make some sort of retaliatory point to Dad's side of the family. It was just an even-tempered knowledge of my own moral compass and what it could reasonably countenance.

I'm not deluded enough to assume that this calm or grace is anything but a daily work in progress. Now and again, anger or a deep, profound sadness flares; for me, for my mum, and for my brothers, who had a longer period of quasi-nuclear, familial normality and so feel the lack of it in a more pronounced way. Yet the fact that my grief is more for the loss of an idea, rather than an actual person, is revealing. These days, any feelings of searching rage or recrimination have cooled into something more like pity and gratitude.

The pity part comes from the fact that my dad did not know me or feel any of the love or admiration you would expect to flow from a son to a father. Marriage is hard; parenthood even more so. To try to navigate all those things and think that separation, divorce or estrangement could never happen to you is, again, to deal in delusion. Yet my

father, like many immigrant parents I'd wager, underestimated the repercussions of sending his children off to grow
up in another country and culture; underestimated the
degree to which this was likely to inculcate very divergent
perspectives and value systems. Imprisoned by hyper-mascu-
line Yoruba expectations and entitlements, my dad ended
up unknown and unmourned. Andy Birchall – Madeleine's
late dad and my de facto father-in-law – is one of the greatest
and most inspiring men I've ever known. I constantly think
about the vivid specifics of his zeal for life and his humour;
about watching Test cricket together and his tendency to
always convince everyone at a restaurant table that pudding
was absolutely a good idea. In contrast, there are no photographs of my dad in my home. And any that are shared of
him, either at my mum's house or on family WhatsApp
groups, have to be asterisked or appended with some explanatory context: like a portrait of a despot or some problematic
plundered artefact in a museum. What sort of a legacy is
that to leave? It is, whichever way you slice it, an enormous
shame, but I don't even know if he would have registered it
as such.

That said, his absence from my life also speaks to the
gratitude. So much of the rhetoric around absent fathers
and young men (young black men, especially) focuses,
understandably, on what is lost. On the vacant space where
a positive male role model should be and the issues and
dysfunction that ripple out from this void. I'm sure my

brothers and I have been negatively affected by the particular formulation of our upbringing in ways that it's difficult to fully calculate.

But I have come to regard the fact that I did not grow up under a lone patriarchal enforcer, with prescriptive, fixed ideas about what constituted 'being a man', as something of a gift. Though I now wish my mum had found someone else, been less loyal and selfless in the matter of her own rights to companionship and happiness, I am equally thankful that I did not have one of the ill-tempered, chaotic or disciplinarian stepdads that I would sense swooping into the lives of school friends. This pronounced void and the 'it takes a village' spirit of communality at the heart of Yoruba families almost gave the sense of having many different proxy dads; of picking my favoured dishes from a sprawled buffet of paternal options. Sensitive, mouthy, impressionable, I needed nourishment in all its forms and, despite it all, I got it by the bucketload.

Now, when I think about the people who filled that role, I think of a gallery of invaluable stand-ins. I think of Mum with her savage wit, manic generosity and insistence that I always show up as a guest at someone's house with a sleeve of Digestives or some other form of edible offering; I think of Folarin's bequeathed hip-hop cassettes and well-intentioned but vaguely harrowing lessons in how to win a playground fight; I think of Ray, who stood at the sidelines, usually wreathed in sideways rain, at every one of my schoolboy football matches; I think too of my Uncle Jibola buying me my first proper suit and plying me with Orangina; my Uncle Layi cracking the whip during SATs revision; my Aunty Toyin, who always buttered the bread before toasting and made us pancakes with the unexpected but extraordinary addition of gently fried slivers of onion; and dozens of others I could name. Here was another reason not to damn Nigerian culture at large because of my father's actions. It was that same culture's collectivism, love and instinct to feed that made me who I am and caused me to only really feel any kind of paternal absence in the abstract.

All of this brings me back to the spilled matchbox. My dad's decision to teach me some sort of bullying lesson by taking a photo that day means that there is, of course, pictorial evidence of this vivid, defining moment. Even today it is quite strange and piercing to look at it. There is the water streaking down my cheeks; my reddened eyes and oddly exhausted, hangdog expression as I crouch to scoop up the matches, embarrassed into a calmer state. But look to the left of me and there is something else. Something I had forgotten about. There, stooped and sombre, is my brother, Ray, wordlessly helping me to gather up the matches; a proverbial guardian angel helping me, as he always would, in a time of need. Someone who actually knew me and understood that the situation required empathy rather than ridicule.

Fatherhood really is something earned rather than declared. Dad's absence denied me an idealised hypothetical, but it inadvertently yielded something far more precious, tangible and hard-won. No, I did not grow up with just one father. I was far, far luckier than that.

Flash forward to my 2024 trip to Nigeria and these questions were very much at the forefront of my mind. Parents. Emulation. Legacy and the maintaining of cultural traditions. 'Mum isn't going to be around forever.' That had, between armchair theories about the fact she's 'blatantly ADHD', become a favoured line from Ray. And though it seemed unthinkable – though she always seemed like a woman dogged and bloody-minded enough to make the Grim Reaper slip away, cowering and apologising for ever having bothered her – it was an undeniable reality that we would one day have to live. Even Mum seemed conscious of this. Not just in the fact that her stock response to her children not calling her enough would be to remind us of her mortality ('*Ah-ah, you don't check on me? I could be dead.*'). But in the Yoruba that she would consciously use to her perplexed grandchildren; the unspoken words being the tenuousness of our cultural links, and the need to remember who we were.

Elsewhere, before flying up to Abuja and Sokoto, I had gone back to Ebun to visit the members of my family who were still living there. There was, as I pushed through that familiar old yard, no pop-up slaughterhouse or doomed cow. But it was hard to shake the feeling that the layered memories and tragic losses of our family's recent history had yielded an atmosphere thick with ghosts. Grandmama and Uncle Jibola were gone; Uncle Gori, who finally passed away in early 2024 and had moved back to Ebun for a period after the pandemic, was gone; my cousin Femi, who had been with us that day at the beach, watching the sunset and devouring chicken suya, was gone, having died suddenly in 2022. Even as I savoured the familiar radiating warmth of those that were there – my Uncle Kalia beaming at the bottle of duty-free Jack Daniels; my Aunty Tayo making me a plate of eggs and crooked chicken sausages that she hoped 'would be good enough for a restaurant critic'; my Uncle Yomi, silver-bearded and quick-witted as ever – I couldn't help but feel those absences. This is the gift and curse of a sprawled, ageing family. Though every atom of me willed it to not come too soon, I knew the big hurt of my mum's passing would arrive one day. And I knew that I would feel it most acutely through food. I knew that pain and longing would wrap itself around the joy of plates of jollof or stew or roasted chicken, wreathed in onion scent, that would be perfectly nice, but never, ever quite as magical or soul-soothing as hers.

The challenge, then, is to try to absorb as much as I can. To loiter and observe in the kitchen, even when my prince-ling's instinct only wants to pinch some stew meat and slump on the sofa gripping the greasy old Sky remote. And it is also, in lieu of actual recipes, to take whatever knowledge I may be presented with. One day, Mum was in our kitchen, fussing behind me as I got ready to fry some plantain. Madeleine and our kids were elsewhere in the house; 6 Music trilled away on the stereo, the heady waft of roasted sausages tendrilled out of the oven and Mum had been furnished with the late-afternoon instant coffees (two sugars; milk briefly warmed in the microwave beforehand; nip of brandy or even gin, if we have it) that are her petrol. I had just chopped the plantain into diagonal slices on the board when she tutted loudly at me.

'*Jimi*,' she said, fondly accusatory as she nudged me out of the way. She picked up the heel end of the heftily bruised, thick peel, held it over the stove, and squeezed a little hidden nubbin of sweet, soft flesh into the pan of rippling oil. This was the secret plantain: the concealed, extra little scrap of pleasure that could be found on the chopping boards and in the food bins of lamentably wasteful home cooks all across the world. It was an unplanned lesson in the ritualised resourcefulness and thrift that was part of my cultural inheritance. And it means that, whatever dishes she does teach me and however different my interpretation of her specialities is, we will always have this. Every time I squeeze out that little nubbin of plantain, every time I rhythmically thwack the edge of a wooden spoon against a pan and say a private prayer to the jollof gods, she is there, bustling at my shoulder, and making me smile and rage.

That my versions of the dishes she made will be different, and that they will often be paired with things that she would find strange or actively unpleasant, is part of the point. Here is jollof rice with jerk chicken, sausages, and garlicky kale lifted with a squeeze of lime; here is a gooey portion of stewed beans, delectably splashed with Mexican hot sauce, and yam with corned-beef stew, given a cheffy grating of salt-cured egg yolk; here is a bag of Abuja groundnuts that are eventually enjoyed in south-east London with a hazy pale ale brewed in Bermondsey.

This was the slow-blooming lesson of that 2024 Nigeria trip and of my life of picky eating more generally. I am the cultural inheritance that I have been given but I am also what I have given myself. Childhood fearfulness around food can always turn, against the odds, into a spirit of discerning adventurousness in adulthood. If your eating identity feels contradictory or conflicted, then that is exactly how it should feel. We are, none of us, just one thing. And life, like that secret scrap of plantain, is all the sweeter for it.

Acknowledgements

My initial vision for *Picky* was that it would be the equivalent of a kind of bracing, mid-meal sorbet; a light, frivolous palate-cleanser that would act as an easy, lighthearted counterpoint to the research-intensive writing, knackering fieldwork and heavy, traumatic histories of my first book, *Settlers*.

It was probably about midway through a punishing, overly caffeinated writing schedule that I recognised the laughable folly of this. *Picky* was a challenging book to write in ways that I didn't anticipate; a self-constructed trap of sorts that forced me to exhume and process exposing, occasionally painful memories, often for the first time, to the ticking clock of a fast-approaching deadline. Of course, the flip side to tricking myself into such uncharacteristically honest disclosure is that to go back in time and relive these experiences was also joyful, revelatory and hugely rewarding – a deep, scalding bath of nostalgia that I occasionally struggled to get into but often didn't want to leave. I'm very grateful, then, to everyone who encouraged me at *Picky*'s tentative beginning and offered support and belief right through to its gasping, psychologically and emotionally draining conclusion.

Thank you to my literary agent Imogen Pelham for the early faith, the necessary nudging to accentuate *Picky's* appeal, and the immense skill and nervelessness when it came to finding it the best home. Thank you to my extraordinary editor Susannah Otter, and to Lucy Buxton, Mila Melia-Kapoor, Becca Mundy and the entire *Picky* team at Hodder. Whatever qualities this book contains were only possible because of their secret sauce of belief, enthusiasm and supreme diligence. Not to mention a willingness to embrace a breakneck editorial schedule that was in equal parts thrilling and terrifying. Cheers to Theia Nankivell, Anna Muir and my KBJ Management crew too, for their general bolstering and wise counsel in relation to this project and a more general moment of professional transition.

Thanks to The Regiment for the supportive WhatsApps and to Dan Warrilow and Pete Hathway for their help providing belly laughs and corroborative details about the Fun Time Boys era. A huge hug of gratitude to everyone at Action Against Hunger for facilitating the hugely significant trip to Nigeria that rounded out this book's trilogy of Lagos chapters. Thanks to Jamie Oliver for the generous early cheerleading and for the one-pan fry up recipe that lit a spark of culinary interest in my teenage mind.

Nothing will make you appreciate the impact of family members on your life like raking over forty years of personal history. I am therefore particularly grateful to my family in Lagos, London and beyond, who were unwittingly drawn into this whirling hurricane of public disclosure. Thank you to Uncle Layi, Aunty Toyin and all at Ebun for the boundless generosity, love and jokes; thank you to all my relatives in America for those endless summers; thank you to the Birchalls, Bosences and Sealeys for the steadying words and stress-busting, festive laughs; thank you to Folarin, of course; and to Ray, for the lifetime of fraternal support, the invaluable insight on those early chapters, and for spurring me on when I was particularly worried about this book's levels of distinctly un-Nigerian blabbing about our family's shared, complicated history.

Mum: every time I write about my life I am knocked over anew by how lucky I am to have been raised by someone who has always modelled such intelligence, courage, mischievous humour, determination and cultural pride. Thank you for the sacrifice and the endless fact-checking and the lifetime of jollof, plantain and yam with corned beef stew. This is my version of events. I hope that you recognise at least some of it, that you can pick out some meaning from my usual incomprehensible mass of big, *oyinbo* words, and that you know that I only ever want to do us proud.

Finally, but most importantly, I need to thank the people that I share a house with. Dylan and Remi: you are my favourite picky eaters, I'm so unbelievably proud to be your dad, and I promise I will stop it with these boring grown-up topics and write that children's book that you both want soon. Thank you to Madeleine for, once again, being extremely understanding about a work project that effectively robbed you of a husband and co-parent for the best part of a year. The writing cabin trips; the library weekends; the head-in-hands moments of navel-gazing, artistic crisis that must have been unbearable to listen to. I honestly couldn't have navigated any of it without your wisdom, geeing up, calmness, support, love and immense belief. I appreciate all of it and hope I've done the shared part of our story justice. Magic Roll forever. Promise to not have quite so much of a breakdown next time.